THE HARD FACTS OF

THE GRIMMS' FAIRY TALES

MARIA TATAR

The
Hard Facts of the
Grimms' Fairy
Tales

PRINCETON, NEW JERSEY

PRINCETON UNIVERSITY PRESS

1987

COPYRIGHT © 1987 BY PRINCETON UNIVERSITY PRESS
PUBLISHED BY PRINCETON UNIVERSITY PRESS, 41 WILLIAM STREET
PRINCETON, NEW JERSEY 08540
IN THE UNITED KINGDOM:
PRINCETON UNIVERSITY PRESS, GUILDFORD, SURREY

LIBRARY OF CONGRESS CATALOGING IN PUBLICATION DATA WILL
BE FOUND ON THE LAST PRINTED PAGE OF THIS BOOK

ISBN 0-691-06722-8

CLOTHBOUND EDITIONS OF
PRINCETON UNIVERSITY PRESS BOOKS
ARE PRINTED ON ACID-FREE PAPER, AND
BINDING MATERIALS ARE CHOSEN FOR
STRENGTH AND DURABILITY. PAPER-
BACKS, ALTHOUGH SATISFACTORY FOR
PERSONAL COLLECTIONS, ARE NOT
USUALLY SUITABLE FOR
LIBRARY REBINDING

PRINTED IN THE UNITED STATES OF
AMERICA BY PRINCETON UNIVERSITY PRESS
PRINCETON, NEW JERSEY

For Daniel & Lauren

CONTENTS

[vii]

LIST OF ILLUSTRATIONS

During the whole time consumed in the slow growth of this family tree, the house of Smallweed, always early to go out and late to marry, has strengthened itself in its practical character, has discarded all amusements, discountenanced all story-books, fairy tales, fictions, and fables, and banished all levities whatsoever. Hence the gratifying fact, that it has had no child born to it, and that the complete little men and women whom it has produced, have been observed to bear a likeness to old monkeys with something depressing on their minds.

—CHARLES DICKENS, *Bleak House*

PREFACE

ADVANCED MIDDLE AGE appears to be a popular time for admitting interest in fairy tales. At age fifty-five, George Bernard Shaw
declared that he still considered "Grimm" to be "the most entertaining of German authors." C. S. Lewis confessed to reading fairy tales
on the sly for years; only after turning fifty did he feel free to acknowledge his addiction to the genre. Compelling in their simplicity
and poignant in their emotional appeal, fairy tales have the power
to stir long-dormant childhood feelings and to quicken our sympathies for the downtrodden. They also offer wit and wisdom in the
trenchant formulations of the folk. There is something in them for
every age and generation. It is hardly surprising that the Grimms'
Nursery and Household Tales ranks, by virtue of the number of its German editions and translations, as the runaway best seller of all German books.[1]

In 1818, the *Quarterly Review* proclaimed with great fanfare that
"the most important addition to nursery literature has been effected
in Germany, by the diligence of John and William Grimm, two antiquarian brethren of the highest reputation." As familiar as the
tales in the Grimms' collection may be and as much as the Grimms'
name has since become a household word, the brothers who compiled the now classic texts in the *Nursery and Household Tales* remain
unfamiliar figures on the map of European cultural history. The
Quarterly Review was neither the first nor the last to get their Christian names wrong. Some folklorists and philologists even have trouble keeping the two brothers apart, this despite the radical differences between them in temperament, physical appearance, and
intellectual leanings. Shaw seems to have labored under the illusion
that "Grimm" was a single individual, rather than a team of fraternal scholars. As Thomas Mann pointed out in a tribute to the Irish
playwright, Shaw never realized that his favorite German author
consisted of two people: the brothers Jacob and Wilhelm Grimm.
With what has become characteristic reverence for the Grimms and
their accomplishments, Mann hailed the brothers as "romantically

inspired lovers of German antiquity who listened to their fairy tales from the lips of the people and collected them conscientiously."[2]

Neither one of the two brothers, who divided their energies between folklore and philology and whose labors on a voluminous dictionary of the German language bear witness to much perseverance (and perhaps a streak of pedantry as well), could have foreseen the stunning success awaiting their collection of tales. Their friend Achim von Arnim, on receiving a copy of the Grimms' "story-book" with a full-page dedication to his wife and son, congratulated the brothers on their efforts. The handsome volume, bound in green leather with gilt edges, was "an excellent book" in his estimation. In what has proven to be a classic understatement, he predicted "a long sale" for the *Nursery and Household Tales*.[3] Still, he worried that the absence of illustrations and the inclusion of scholarly annotations would prevent the volume from reaching what he considered its appropriate destination: the shelves of nurseries and the bookcases of households. He felt reasonably confident, though, that eventually some shrewd publisher would see the commercial wisdom of printing an abridged edition of the tales with illustrations designed to capture the imagination of children. With time such figures emerged the world over.

Folklorists are quick to point out that fairy tales were never really meant for children's ears alone. Originally told at fireside gatherings or in spinning circles by adults to adult audiences, fairy tales joined the canon of children's literature (which is itself of recent vintage) only in the last two to three centuries. Yet the hold these stories have on the imagination of children is so compelling that it becomes difficult to conceive of a childhood without them. Growing up without fairy tales implies spiritual impoverishment, as one writer after another has warned.[4]

The degree to which fairy tales stir the imagination of children, inspiring strong passions and loyalties in them, is best captured by Charles Dickens' confession of his weakness for one figure in particular. Little Red Riding Hood was "my first love," he avowed. "I felt that if I could have married Little Red Riding Hood, I should have known perfect bliss."[5] Even as an adult, Dickens was by no means immune to the spell cast by fairy tales. His recollections of the powerful attraction of fairy-tale figures confirm the now tired cliché that these stories incarnate our deepest hopes and most ardent desires. Yet along with the daydream and its fulfillment comes the nightmare. Wishes and fantasies may come to life in the fairy tale, but fears and phobias also become full-blooded presences.

In this context, it is perhaps worth repeating a latter-day fairy tale about fairy tales, one that stresses a child's need for fairy tales without for a moment attempting to gloss over the horrifying elements of the stories:

> There was once a young boy whose pedagogically solemn parents resolved to do everything in their power to prevent their child from developing superstitious fears. They banned fairy tales from the household and saw to it that witches, giants, and other cannibalistic fiends were never once mentioned in the child's presence. All went according to plan until one night the parents awoke to the shrill cries of their son. Startled, they rushed to his bed only to learn that he was afraid of sleeping in the dark. They were even more startled after they asked the boy why he was afraid of sleeping in the dark, for the child's answer, punctuated by sobs, was: "There's a complex hiding under my bed."[6]

The equation developed in this story between phantoms of the mind and the very real ogres of fairy tales is telling, for it reveals the extent to which fairy tales, for all their naturalistic details, concern themselves with inner realities. In our time, Bruno Bettelheim has emerged as the most eloquent spokesman for psychological readings of fairy tales. "In a fairy tale," he writes, "internal processes are externalized and become comprehensible as represented by the figures of the story and its events."[7] By meditating on the conflicts acted out in fairy tales, he emphasizes, children can find solutions to their own specific problems and thus stand to gain powerful therapeutic benefits from the stories.

That fairy tales translate (however roughly) psychic realities into concrete images, characters, and events has come to serve as one cornerstone of my own understanding of the texts in the Grimms' *Nursery and Household Tales*. In this respect, they resemble dreams; but rather than giving us personalized wishes and fears, they offer collective truths, realities that transcend individual experience and that have stood the test of time. When Hans Castorp, in the renowned "Snow" chapter of Thomas Mann's *The Magic Mountain*, has a vision that is at once "anonymous" and "collective," he has slipped from the realm of dreams into the province of folklore and mythology. What he sees incarnates not his own personal phobias and idiosyncratic fantasies, but the deepest fears and hopes of mankind.[8] This is not to say that folktales and folklore function as repositories of a sort of Jungian collective unconscious. Rather, they capture psychic realities so persistent and widespread that they have held the attention of a community over a long time. They may invite us to take the royal road to the unconscious, but they also lead us off that now beaten track into uncharted territories. In the course of this book, I will follow that road yet stray freely from it whenever it seems appropriate to explore a tale's social and cultural realities.

It was the joke about the boy who feared the complex hiding under his bed that first drove home to me the full psychological import of fairy-tale plots. It took another joke—in the form of a cartoon—to teach me something about the formal aspects of fairy tales and to remind me just how much folkloric invention differs from literary creation. For all their rich variety, fairy tales have a remarkably stable—and therefore predictable—structure. "A girl is in the wood," Roger Sale writes. "Give her a brother and one has 'Hansel and Gretel,' give her many brothers and sisters and one has 'Hop o' My Thumb,' send the girl to dwarves and one has 'Snow White,' to bears and one has 'Goldilocks,' to grandmother and one has 'Little Red Riding Hood.' "[9] It may not all be quite that simple, but any avid reader of fairy tales will recognize that Sale's observations ring true after a fashion. The cast of folkloric characters is remarkably limited when compared to that of literature, and the plots in which the characters of folktales move unfold in a relatively uniform manner. The cartoon to which I referred (figure 1) may exaggerate the extent to which the brothers Grimm were locked into using set patterns to write the tales in their collection, but it does tell us something about the process of folkloric composition, about the way in which storytellers rely on formulas and conventions to spin their

"*All right, Wilhelm, we have the child walking through the woods.*"

"*Woods are always good, Wilhelm. Now, who does the child meet?*"

"*We did that, Wilhelm.*"

"*Please, Jacob, don't you think we've been using the woods too much?*"

"*Perhaps a dwarf or two?*"

"*How about a wolf, Jacob?*"

FIGURE 1. *The Grimms at work on their collection. Drawing by Stevenson.*

narrative threads. In the course of working his way through old, familiar routines the teller also makes occasional pauses to pick up new themes or motifs. A tale's structure remains intact even as the specific order of episodes and the details of plot vary from telling to telling. It is easy to understand just why the phrase "That's not the way I heard it" should become the programmed response to an item of folklore, be it story, song, or nursery rhyme. Beneath all the variations in its verbal realization the basic form still shines through.

In our century, the Soviet folklorist Vladimir Propp pioneered the study of the building blocks used to construct folktales.[10] Propp's project, one of the most ambitious in the realm of folkloric analysis, sought to identify and define recurrent features in a fixed corpus of Russian *wondertales* (stories roughly analogous to the classic fairy tales in the Grimms' collection). Psychology, history, sociology, anthropology—these disciplines initially meant little to a scholar who trained his attention exclusively on surface structures, investigating with empirical rigor the plot sequences of folktales.[11] Propp's rage for order has forever marked folkloristic studies. His systematic analysis gives us the rules of the game as it has been played by various tellers and transmitters of tales over the centuries. Knowing those rules makes it significantly easier to sort out vital elements of plot from extraneous details and to distinguish "authentic" oral narratives from literary retellings or from quirky, personalized versions of a story.

Bettelheim and Propp have much to tell us about the substance and structure of folktales. One an expert in the art of interpreting fairy tales, the other a master of ordering and analyzing their elements of plot, the two resisted the temptation to combine psychological readings with formal analysis. Propp saw himself as the champion of a "crude, analytical, somewhat laborious" method, one that was further complicated by a preoccupation with abstract, formal problems.[12] But his "uninteresting" work (the term is his) would pave the way, he believed, for more engaging and compelling investigations of folkloristic narratives. His own work was later to take the direction of historical and cultural analysis. Bettelheim stood as a logical heir to Propp's labors, yet curiously he does not once mention the Russian folklorist in his *Uses of Enchantment.* That he had much to learn from Propp's *Morphology of the Folktale* becomes clear when we find him inflating the importance of certain extraneous details in a folktale and treating literary variants of a tale as if they represented a prototypical form. In my own study, I have tried to take full advantage of Propp's legacy, while drawing on the fund of Bettelheim's more interesting, more imaginative (in both the positive and negative senses of the term), and certainly more provocative readings.

One additional mentor deserves mention in this context. For Propp, folktales operate with machinelike precision according to a set of fixed and unvarying laws; for Bettelheim, they embody in their various national incarnations timeless psychological truths. Only recently have historians come forward to declare themselves as legitimate interpreters of folkloric documents, to remind us that some elements of every folktale are culturally determined. Blue-beard acquired distinctly new personality traits once he crossed the Rhine; Little Red Riding Hood became more prim when she entered the pages of the *Nursery and Household Tales*; and Snow White became progressively sweeter and tidier as her story was translated into print and made its way from Germany to the United States. Foremost among historians who have concerned themselves with folktales is Robert Darnton, whose pathbreaking essay on the meaning of Mother Goose warns us to avoid the hazards of treating folkloric texts "flattened out, like patients on a couch, in a timeless contemporaneity." Folktales are historical documents, he tells us, each colored by the mental life and culture of its epoch.[13] Interpreting a folktale without troubling oneself to learn about its genesis and historical context can spell disaster. While I am not convinced that folktales necessarily offer electrifying and informative revelations about various cultural communities in which they developed (they generally only confirm what we already know through other, more reliable sources), I have kept Darnton's caveat in mind when reading the tales in the Grimms' collection.

Like any literary critic who ventures into the realm of folkloric studies, I have discovered that close textual analysis is a skill that does not always pay off in interpreting folktales. The tools of literary study in general cannot be directly applied to folklore but must first be adapted for use in examining oral narration, a form of literature paradoxically without letters. That literature and folklore are, despite their mutual contamination, separate in their genesis, intentions, and structure is an insight—obvious as it may seem—that I owe to scholars in the area of folkloric analysis, who never tire of reminding their literary colleagues to observe carefully the line dividing the two. Linda Dégh and Alan Dundes deserve special mention in this context. But folklore, as I have also learned from these scholars, is a discipline without real boundaries. It requires the paleontologist's love of the archaic, the historian's appetite for facts, the psychologist's curiosity about causes, and the anthropologist's passion for understanding cultural differences. Only after my own study of the Grimms' tales was complete did I discover that it takes something of a polymath to produce a fully convincing analysis of that collection. This will simply have to stand as one of the lessons of my tale.

Since polymaths have always been scarce, folkloric studies have become a battlefield on which scholars from various disciplines meet to dispute theories and to contest interpretations. The resulting strife and dissension have proved surprisingly healthy and have fostered a spirit of vitality that otherwise might be absent. The real casualties in folkloric studies are those who have made a point of keeping their distance from the fray and of remaining neutral. The one-sided approach in folklore is precisely the approach that is most likely to go wrong and to yield questionable results. For that reason, I have tried to adopt a synthetic approach wherever appropriate, drawing on the methods promoted by folklorists, the insights developed by psychoanalytic critics, and the data provided by historians.

It would take a book far longer than this one to do justice to the 210 tales in the Grimms' *Nursery and Household Tales*.[14] The collection is more than an anthology of fairy tales: it comprises fables, tall tales, anecdotes, cautionary tales, and all manner of other narratives that struck the Grimms as folklore. This book focuses on a limited number of tales in the collection: the texts that now belong to the classic canon of fairy tales; but its range extends beyond "Cinderella" and "Snow White" to include such lesser-known fairy tales as "King Thrushbeard" and "Darling Roland." For contrastive purposes, it also draws on tales in the Grimms' collection that do not by any stretch of the imagination number as fairy tales.

"It was like a fairy tale." Our everyday language reflects the conventional wisdom that fairy tales signify wishes fulfilled and dreams come true. But no one can read through the Grimms' *Nursery and Household Tales* without pausing to reflect on the contrast between the happy endings of fairy tales and the hard facts of fairy-tale life. The melodramatic plot begins with an account of helplessness and victimization, rehearses the conflicts between hero and villain, and concludes with detailed descriptions of reprisals taken against the villain and a report on the hero's marriage or accession to power.

The Grimms' "Hans My Hedgehog" clearly illustrates the way in which fairy tales dwell on pain and suffering rather than on blissful happiness. Hans My Hedgehog is the son of parents who made the error of wanting a child so desperately that they declared themselves prepared to accept a hedgehog for a son. Hans spends the first eight years of his life lying behind the stove. "His father grew tired of him and thought: 'If only he'd die.' But he didn't die, he just lay there." The next station of Hans's career takes him to the woods, where he spends many a year tending swine and donkeys, but also makes pacts with two different kings that result in promises to give Hans their daughters in marriage. The first king betrays Hans, but Hans gets even by kidnapping his daughter, then punishing and abandoning her.

> When they had distanced themselves a bit from the city, Hans My Hedgehog took off her clothes and stuck her with his quills until she was bloody, and said: "That's your reward for being false. Go away, I don't want you." Then he made her go back home, and she was disgraced forever.

The second king's daughter keeps her father's promises, weds Hans, and thereby sets in motion the process that turns Hans from hedgehog into prince: "When the princess saw him she was overjoyed. The two arose happily, ate and drank, and they celebrated their wedding. And the aged king made his kingdom over to Hans My Hedgehog." In its double movement from helplessness and victimization to retaliation on the one hand and restitution on the other, "Hans My Hedgehog" demonstrates the extent to which wish fulfillment in fairy tales implies punishments for villains and rewards for heroes.

Looking at the hard facts of fairy tales in the Grimms' collection calls first for a long, hard look at the genesis and publishing history of the *Nursery and Household Tales*. The collection took on a special character as it moved from manuscript form to its various printed editions—seven in all during the Grimms' lifetimes. The first chap-

ter of this book charts the principal stages in the editorial history of
the *Nursery and Household Tales* and attempts to define the narrative
status of the tales. It shows how the Grimms, ever responsive to the
values of their time and increasingly sensitive to pedagogical demands, transformed adult folk materials into a hybrid form of folklore and literature for children. Chapters 2 and 3 take up methodological questions. How do we make interpretive judgments on the
basis of a single published version of what was once an unfixed oral
narrative existing in many versions? To what extent is the Grimms'
variant of a tale type such as "Cinderella" culture bound and to what
extent does it veer off into pure fantasy? What does one make of the
fairy tale's repetitive patterns and recurrent motifs? These are some
of the issues raised in the course of theoretical reflections on fairy
tales. Chapters 4 and 5 focus on fairy-tale protagonists, male and female, and chapters 6 and 7 are about fairy-tale villains, male and female. I close with thoughts on the art of getting even as it is practiced in fairy tales.

   Until recently, it was impossible to read the Grimms' *Nursery and
Household Tales* in a reliable English version. Happily, this situation
changed when Ralph Manheim published his masterly translation
of the collection under the title *Grimms' Tales for Young and Old: The
Complete Stories*. A word of caution, however, is in order. Manheim
assumed that the edition on which he based his translation was the
second edition of the *Nursery and Household Tales*. This is not the
case. He worked from the seventh and final edition, published in
1857, which included the preface of the second edition, published
in 1819. Since the seventh edition is the least faithful to the spirit of
the folk originals collected by the Grimms, it is ironic that Manheim
wrote that he intended above all to be "faithful to the Grimm brothers' faithfulness."[15] Since I quote from various versions of the *Nursery and Household Tales*, it seemed sensible to rely in all cases on my
own words for rendering the German originals into English. My
translations may not be as elegant as Manheim's, but generally they
are more faithful to the letter of the original. Since Manheim's
translation is readily available, I have made a practice of using his
titles. For those who wish to consult the German originals, I include

in appendix C an alphabetical list of titles with their tale number and corresponding German title. My decision to use *Nursery and House-hold Tales* as the title for the entire collection was made largely on pragmatic grounds. As we will see, the German title (*Kinder- und Hausmärchen*) does not necessarily imply that the tales were for the nursery. But, for better or worse, this is the title by which the collection has come to be known in the English-speaking world, and its widespread currency does much to recommend it. To refer to the collection as *Grimm's Fairy Tales* (a not uncommon practice) perpetuates the misconception that the tales have a single author and furthers the mistaken notion that all 210 tales traffic in magic and enchantment.

Of the many scholars who have turned their attention to the *Nursery and Household Tales*, none has done so much to correct, refine, and expand our knowledge of the Grimms' achievement as Heinz Rölleke. His high editorial standards and rigorous methodological principles have given us authoritative texts for study and comparison. Without his efforts in both editorial analysis and textual criticism, readers and interpreters of the Grimms' tales would remain in the dark about even the most basic facts and would continue to labor under false assumptions. My bibliographical note lists the most important editions produced by Rölleke. All citations, unless otherwise noted, are from those volumes. In cases where I do not refer to a specific edition in my text, I quote from the seventh and final edition of the *Nursery and Household Tales*.

Portions of chapters 3, 4, and 6 were published separately in *Children's Literature Quarterly*, in the *Yearbook of Psychoanalysis and Literature*, and in the volume *Fairy Tales as Ways of Knowing*. I am grateful to Yale University Press, The Johns Hopkins University Press, and to the publishing house of Peter Lang for permission to reprint parts of those essays.

This book was completed during a sabbatical year at the University of Munich financed by the Alexander von Humboldt Foundation. I am indebted to the foundation for sponsoring my project at a crucial stage in its development. The staff of the archival resources in the Brüder Grimm-Museum in Kassel created the ideal environment for pursuing investigative research in the city where the brothers put together their collection. To Dieter Hennig, director of the Museum, and to Ursula Lange-Lieberknecht I owe special thanks. The rich resources of the Kinder- und Jugendbibliothek at Schloß Blutenburg in Munich also proved vital as I progressed in my work. As always, the staff of Widener Library at Harvard University stood ready to honor even the most arcane and complicated requests.

A number of colleagues have taken a special interest in my work and have helped to steer it in the proper direction. I am grateful to Klaus Kanzog, Ruth B. Bottigheimer, and Margaret Higonnet for reading parts of the manuscript and to Eric Blackall, Dorrit Cohn, Walter Sokel, and Theodore Ziolkowski for supporting this project in its early stages. Detlev Koepke greatly enriched the content of the volume by keeping me supplied with reading matter. I am also indebted to Annemarie Bestor, whose assistance during the final stages of my work proved invaluable. Without the help of Coruco-Monica Hernandez Sesma and Anke Vogel, who ran the nursery and household while I read the tales, this book would have required many more years to write. To Stephen Schuker, whose editorial skills did much to improve my prose and whose enthusiasm for this project kept me on course, I offer a special word of appreciation.

JANUARY 1987

I

CHILDREN'S LITERATURE?

1

SEX AND VIOLENCE
The Hard Core of
Fairy Tales

> These stories are suffused with the same purity that
> makes children appear so marvelous and blessed.
>
> —WILHELM GRIMM,
> preface to the *Nursery and Household Tales*

FOR MANY ADULTS, reading through an unexpurgated edition of
the Grimms' collection of tales can be an eye-opening experience.
Even those who know that Snow White's stepmother arranges the
murder of her stepdaughter, that doves peck out the eyes of Cinderella's stepsisters, that Briar Rose's suitors bleed to death on the
hedge surrounding her castle, or that a mad rage drives Rumpelstiltskin to tear himself in two will find themselves hardly prepared
for the graphic descriptions of murder, mutilation, cannibalism, infanticide, and incest that fill the pages of these bedtime stories for
children.[1] In "The Juniper Tree," one of the most widely admired
of the tales, a woman decapitates her stepson, chops his corpse into
small pieces, and cooks him in a stew that her husband devours with
obvious gusto. "Fledgling" recounts a cook's attempt to carry out a
similar plan, though she is ultimately outwitted by the boy and his
sister. Frau Trude, in the story of that title, turns a girl into a block
of wood and throws her into a fire. "Darling Roland" features a
witch who takes axe in hand to murder her stepdaughter but ends
by butchering her own daughter. Another stepmother dresses her
stepdaughter in a paper chemise, turns her out into the woods on a
frigid winter day, and forbids her to return home until she has har-
vested a basket of strawberries.

[3]

FIGURE 2. *A Moritz von Schwind illustration of one of the many gruesome episodes in "The Juniper Tree."*

Lest this litany of atrocities leads to the mistaken view that women are the sole agents of evil in German fairy tales, let us look at examples of paternal and fraternal cruelty. Who can forget the miller who makes life miserable for his daughter by boasting that she can spin straw to gold? Or the king of the same tale who is prepared to execute the girl if her father's declarations prove false? In another tale a man becomes so irritated by his son's naiveté that he first disowns him, then orders him murdered by his servants. The singing bone, in the tale of that title, is whittled from the remains of a fratricide victim; when the bone reveals the secret of the scandalous murder to the world, the surviving brother is sewn up in a sack and drowned. The father of the fairy-tale heroine known as Thousand-furs is so bent on marrying his own daughter that she is obliged to flee from her home into the woods. Another father is so firm a believer in female ultimogeniture that he prepares twelve coffins for his twelve sons in the event that his thirteenth child turns out to be a girl. One monarch after another punishes wicked females by forcing them to disrobe and to roll down hills in kegs studded with nails.

In fairy tales, nearly every character—from the most hardened criminal to the Virgin Mary—is capable of cruel behavior. In "The Robber Bridegroom," a young woman watches in horror as her betrothed and his accomplices drag a girl into their headquarters, tear off her clothes, place her on a table, hack her body to pieces, and sprinkle them with salt. Her horror deepens when one of the thieves, spotting a golden ring on the murdered girl's finger, takes an axe, chops off the finger, and sends it flying through the air into her lap. Such behavior may not be wholly out of character for brigands and highwaymen, but even the Virgin Mary appears to be more of an ogre than a saint in the Grimms' collection. When the girl known as Mary's Child disobeys an injunction against opening one of thirteen doors to the kingdom of heaven and tries to conceal her transgression, the Virgin sends her back to earth as punishment. There the girl marries a king and bears three children, each of whom is whisked off to heaven by the Virgin, who is annoyed by the young queen's persistent refusal to acknowledge her guilt. The mysterious disappearance of the children naturally arouses the suspicions of the king's councilors, who bring the queen to trial and condemn her to death for cannibalism. Only when the queen confesses her sin (just as flames leap up around the stake to which she is bound) does Mary liberate her and restore the three children to her. Compassion clearly does not number among the virtues of the Virgin Mary as she appears in fairy tales.

The Grimms only occasionally took advantage of opportunities to tone down descriptions of brutal punishments visited on villains or to eliminate pain and suffering from their tales.[2] When they did, it was often at the behest of a friend or colleague rather than of their own volition. More often, the Grimms made a point of adding or intensifying violent episodes. Cinderella's stepsisters are spared their vision in the first version of the story. Only in the second edition of the *Nursery and Household Tales* did Wilhelm Grimm embellish the story with a vivid account of the doves' revenge and with a somewhat fatuous justification for the bloody tableau at the tale's end: "So both sisters were punished with blindness to the end of their days for being so wicked and false." Rumpelstiltskin beats a hasty retreat on a flying spoon at the end of some versions of his tale, but the Grimms seem to have favored violence over whimsy. Their Rumpelstiltskin becomes ever more infuriated by the queen's discovery of his name; in the second edition of the *Nursery and Household Tales*, he is so beside himself with rage that he tears himself in two. Briar Rose sleeps for a hundred years while a hedge peacefully grows around the castle in the first recorded version of the story. In successive editions of the Grimms' collection, we not only read about the young prince who succeeds in penetrating the thorny barrier, but also learn the grisly particulars about Briar Rose's unsuccessful suitors. They fail because "the briar bushes clung together as though they had hands so that the young princes were caught in them and died a pitiful death."

The changes made from the first to the second edition in "The Magic Table, the Gold Donkey, and the Cudgel in the Sack" show just how keen the Grimms must have been to give added prominence to violent episodes. In the first edition of the *Nursery and Household Tales*, we read about the encounter between the story's hero and an innkeeper who confiscates the property of the hero's brothers.

> The turner placed the sack under his pillow. When the innkeeper came and pulled at it, he said: "Cudgel, come out of the sack!" The cudgel jumped out of the sack and attacked the innkeeper, danced with him, and beat him so mercilessly that he was glad to promise to return the magic table and the gold donkey.[3]

The second edition not only fills in the details on the crime and its punishment, but also puts the innkeeper's humiliation on clearer display.

> At bedtime [the turner] stretched out on the bench and used his sack as a pillow for his head. When the innkeeper thought his guest was fast asleep and that no one else was in the room, he went over and

began to tug and pull very carefully at the sack, hoping to get it away and to put another in its place. But the turner had been waiting for him to do exactly that. Just as the innkeeper was about to give a good hard tug, he cried out: "Cudgel, come out of the sack!" In a flash the little cudgel jumped out, went at the innkeeper, and gave him a good sound thrashing. The innkeeper began screaming pitifully, but the louder he screamed the harder the cudgel beat time on his back, until at last he fell down on the ground. Then the turner said: "Now give me the magic table and the gold donkey, or the dance will start all over again." "Oh no!" said the innkeeper. "I'll be glad to give you everything, if only you'll make that little devil crawl back into his sack." The journeyman answered: "This time I will, but watch out for further injuries." Then he said: "Cudgel, back in the sack" and left him in peace.

What the brothers found harder to tolerate than violence and what they did their best to eliminate from the collection through vigilant editing were references to what they coyly called "certain conditions and relationships." Foremost among those conditions seems to have been pregnancy. The story of Hans Dumm, who has the power (and uses it) of impregnating women simply by wishing them to be with child, was included in the first edition but failed to pass muster for the second edition of the *Nursery and Household Tales*. "The Master Hunter," as told by Dorothea Viehmann, the Grimms' favorite exhibit when it came to discoursing on the excellence of folk narrators, must have struck the Grimms as unsatisfactory. Viehmann's version, which was relegated to the notes on the tales, relates that the story's hero enters a tower, discovers a naked princess asleep on her bed, and lies down next to her. After his departure, the princess discovers to her deep distress and to her father's outrage that she is pregnant. The version that actually appeared in the *Nursery and Household Tales* made do instead with a fully clothed princess and a young man who stands as a model of restraint and decorum.[4]

Pregnancy, whether the result of a frivolous wish (as in "Hans Dumm") or of an illicit sexual relationship (as in "The Master Hunter"), was a subject that made the Grimms uncomfortable. In fact, any hints of premarital sexual activity must have made Wilhelm Grimm in particular blush with embarrassment. A quick look at the "Frog King or Iron Heinrich" (the first tale in the collection and therefore the most visible) reveals the tactics he used to cover up the folkloric facts of the story. When the princess in that celebrated tale dashes the hapless frog against the wall, he "falls down into her bed and lies there as a handsome young prince, and the king's daughter lies down next to him." No printed edition of the *Nursery and Household Tales* contains this wording. Only a copy of the original drafts for the collection, sent to the Grimms' friend Clemens Brentano in 1810 and recovered many years later in a Trappist monastery, is explicit about where the frog lands and about the princess's alacrity in joining him there. In the first edition, the frog still falls on the bed. After his transformation, he becomes the "dear companion" of the princess. "She cherished him as she had promised," we are told, and *immediately* thereafter the two fall "peacefully asleep." For the second edition, Wilhelm Grimm deprived the frog king of his soft landing spot and simply observed that the transformation from frog to prince took place as soon as the frog hit the wall. In this version, the happy couple does not retire for the evening until wedding vows are exchanged, and these are exchanged only with the explicit approval of the princess's father. The Grimms' transformation of a tale replete with sexual innuendo into a prim and proper nursery story with a dutiful daughter is almost as striking as the folkloric metamorphosis of frog into prince.[5]

Another of the "conditions and relationships" that the Grimms seem to have found repugnant, or at least inappropriate as a theme in their collection, was incest and incestuous desire. In some cases, incest constituted so essential a part of a tale's logic that even Wilhelm Grimm thought twice before suppressing it; instead he resorted to weaving judgmental observations on the subject into the text. The father of Thousandfurs may persist in pressing marriage proposals on his daughter throughout all editions of the *Nursery and Household Tales*, but by the second edition he receives a stern reprimand from his court councilors. "A father cannot marry his daughter," they protest. "God forbids it. No good can come of such a sin." In later editions, we learn that the entire kingdom would be "dragged down to perdition" with the sinful king. But in other cases, where there was no more than the hint of an incestuous tie between father and daughter, say in "Johannes-Wassersprung and Caspar-Wassersprung" (a tale that was ultimately eliminated from the collection), the Grimms were quick to add details pointing the finger of blame away from the father-king.

When a tale was available in several versions, the Grimms invariably preferred one that camouflaged incestuous desires and Oedipal entanglements. The textual history of the tale known as "The Girl without Hands" illustrates the Grimms' touchy anxiety when it came to stories about fathers with designs on their daughters. That story first came to the Grimms' attention in the following form: A miller falls on hard times and strikes a bargain with the devil, promising him whatever is standing behind his mill in exchange for untold wealth. To his dismay, he returns home to learn that his daughter happened to be behind the mill at the moment the pact was sealed. She must surrender herself to the devil in three years. But the miller's pious daughter succeeds in warding off the devil, if at the price of bodily mutilation: the devil forces the father, who has not kept his end of the bargain, to chop off his daughter's hands. For no apparent reason, the girl packs her severed hands on her back and decides to seek her fortune in the world, despite her father's protestations and his promises to secure her all possible creature comforts at home. The remainder of the story recounts her further trials and tribulations after she marries a king. This is the tale as it appeared in the first edition of the Grimms' collection.

The brothers subsequently came upon a number of versions of that story, one of which they declared far superior to all the others. So impressed were they by its integrity that they could not resist substituting it for the version printed in the first edition of the *Nursery and Household Tales*. Still, the opening paragraph of the new, "superior" version did not quite suit their taste, even though it provided a clear, logical motive for the daughter's departure from home. Instead of leaving home of her own accord and for no particular reason, the girl flees a father who first demands her hand in marriage, and then has her hands and breasts chopped off for refusing him.

There is no mention of devils in this version; the girl's father is the sole satanic figure. The Grimms found it easy, however, to reintroduce the devil by mutilating the folkloric text whose authenticity they so admired. The original introduction detailing the father's offenses was deleted from the tale and replaced by the less sensational account of a pact with the devil.[6]

Even without reading Freud on the devil as a substitute for the father, it is easy to see how the devil became mixed up in this tale. Just as God, Saint Peter, and Christ came to stand in for various benefactors in folktales, so Satan in his various guises was available for the role of villain and could incarnate forbidden desire. "The Poor Man and the Rich Man," "The Devil and His Grandmother," and "The Carnation" are among the many other texts in the *Nursery and Household Tales* that mobilize divinities and devils as agents of good and evil. The Grimms seemed, in general, to have favored tales with a Christian cast of characters over their "pagan" counterparts, although there was no compelling folkloristic reason for them to do so. For "The Girl without Hands," they chose to graft the introduction from what they considered an inferior version of the tale (but one that had the advantage of demonizing Satan instead of a father) onto a "superior (and complete)" variant. Clearly the Grimms were not particularly enamored with the idea of including plots concerned with incestuous desire in a collection of tales with the title *Nursery and Household Tales*. Incest was just not one of those perfectly natural matters extolled in their preface to the tales.

Sex and violence: these are the major thematic concerns of tales in the Grimms' collection, at least in their unedited form. But more important, sex and violence in that body of stories frequently take the perverse form of incest and child abuse, for the nuclear family furnishes the fairy tale's main cast of characters just as the family constitutes its most common subject. When it came to passages colored by sexual details or to plots based on Oedipal conflicts, Wilhelm Grimm exhibited extraordinary editorial zeal. Over the years, he systematically purged the collection of references to sexuality and masked depictions of incestuous desire. But lurid portrayals of child abuse, starvation, and exposure, like fastidious descriptions of cruel punishments, on the whole escaped censorship. The facts of life seemed to have been more disturbing to the Grimms than the harsh realities of everyday life.

How is one to explain these odd editorial practices? The Grimms' enterprise, we must recall, began as a scholarly venture and a patriotic project. As early as 1811, the brothers proclaimed that their efforts as collectors were guided by scholarly principles, and they therefore implied that they were writing largely for academic colleagues. Theirs was an idealistic effort to capture German folk traditions in print before they died out and to make a modest contribution to the history of German poetry. As Jacob Grimm pointed out during his search for a publisher, the main purpose of the proposed volume was not so much to earn royalties as to salvage what was left of the priceless national resources still in the hands of the German folk. The Grimms therefore were willing to forgo royalties for the benefit of appearing in print. Still, the brothers expressed the hope that the volume in the offing would find friends everywhere—and that it would entertain them as well.[7]

Weighed down by a ponderous introduction and by extensive annotations, the first edition of the *Nursery and Household Tales* had the look of a scholarly tome, rather than of a book for a wide audience. Sales, however, were surprisingly brisk, perhaps in part because of the book's title. Several of the Grimms' contemporaries had already registered respectable commercial successes with collections of stories for children, and the appearance of the *Nursery and Household Tales* coincided to some extent with a developing market for collections of fairy tales. By 1815 nearly all 900 copies of the first volume had been sold, and Wilhelm Grimm began talking about a second edition in light of the "heavy demand" for the collection. The Grimms had every reason to be pleased, particularly when one calculates that thirty years later (when literacy was more widespread and the demand for children's literature greater) a book such as the popular *Struwwelpeter* had a first printing of only 1,500. With their reputation for "revering trivia" and their endless struggles to get things published, they must also have been growing hungry for a measure of commercial success or at least for some indication of strong interest and support for their literary efforts. Before preparations were even set in motion for publication of the second edition of the *Nursery and Household Tales*, Wilhelm Grimm had already calculated exactly what the appropriate royalties would be for the first and second editions.[8]

The projected royalties for the collection were by no means inconsequential. These were lean years for the Grimms, and their letters to each other are sprinkled with references to financial pressures and to indignities visited on them owing to their impecunious circumstances. From Vienna, Jacob grumbled that he was short of cash and that his clothes were shabby and his shoes worn out. In 1815, Wilhelm Grimm complained that there was not a chair in the house that could be used without imperiling the physical welfare of its occupant. Books were often borrowed and copied out by hand because they were too dear an item in a household where the number of daily meals was limited to two. Thus the 500 talers that Savigny and Wilhelm Grimm had established as appropriate royalties for the first edition of the *Nursery and Household Tales* certainly must have been a welcome prospect. And the 400 talers that Wilhelm Grimm expected to receive for the second edition would have been a substantial addition to the household budget, particularly if we bear in mind that in 1816 Jacob Grimm drew an annual salary of 600 talers as librarian in Kassel, while Wilhelm received an annual salary of 300 talers. It is thus not surprising that the royalties for the *Nursery and Household Tales* would go a long way toward paying their many debts.[9]

That even Jacob, the less worldly of the fraternal team, was keen on strong sales is revealed by a letter of 1815 to his brother. It did not take long for him to begin thinking of the tales as a source of income as well as part of a noble scholarly and patriotic mission. "We will have to confer extensively about the new edition of the first part of the children's tales," he wrote to Wilhelm. "I do not think we can print it as it was; there is much to be improved and added—something that will also prove favorable for sales, since many who own the first edition will also purchase the second edition."[10]

Unfortunately for the Grimms, reasonably robust sales did not translate into generous royalty payments. Delighted to have found a way to get their collection in print, they made only the most casual contractual arrangements with Georg Andreas Reimer, their publisher in Berlin. Neither of the brothers had the experience, confidence, or foresight to ask Reimer to spell out specific terms. Wilhelm simply assented to Reimer's proposal that royalties would be paid after a certain (unspecified) number of copies were sold. Reimer's assurances that he would never lose sight of the Grimms' interests as authors and of his own obligations as editor were enough to satisfy the brothers. They felt it unnecessary to draft a written contract. When it began to dawn on them that Reimer constantly had to be prodded for information, action, and payment, they tried to pin him down on a precise financial agreement. But in 1817, nearly five years after the first volume of the *Nursery and Household Tales* had appeared, Reimer was evidently less prepared than ever to clarify the terms of publication. Although he visited Kassel at the end of that year, he found himself too busy to drop in on the Grimms to settle accounts.

With time the Grimms began to lose patience with Reimer. Again and again it fell on them to put a burr under his saddle about the *Nursery and Household Tales*. Royalty payments, when they came, were nearly always late. Worse yet, Reimer did not appear ready to make good on his promise to publish a second edition, even though the first edition was not to be had in most bookstores. Convinced that further delays in bringing out a second edition would work to the advantage of inferior competitors (in 1808 a volume entitled *Kindermährchen* had been published by an A. L. Grimm), Wilhelm Grimm threatened to take the *Nursery and Household Tales* to a rival firm unless Reimer proved willing to meet his terms for a second edition. At that point, Reimer showed his claws. He reminded Wilhelm that no written contract existed between them and that he was therefore under no obligation to pay anything more than half the promised royalties. Furthermore, sales of the *Nursery and Household Tales* were "no longer particularly strong," and he was left holding 350 worthless copies of the second volume. Nonetheless, he declared his readiness to move ahead with the second edition, and this time he set acceptable, though again not fully explicit, terms for royalties. Once again the Grimms made the mistake of working on the basis of a gentleman's agreement.

It was not until 1833 that the Grimms sat down, did some simple arithmetic, and began to realize the extent to which Reimer was taking advantage of their good will. The 50 louis d'ors that the brothers had received as royalties for the second edition were trivial compared with the 2,500 talers that Jacob Grimm calculated as Reimer's profit on the three volumes. The exchange between Reimer and the Grimms became more and more unpleasant in the following months, with much sarcasm let loose on each side. Reimer started by charging that the Grimms knew nothing about the realities of the book trade and ended by reminding them of the many "sacrifices" he had made for their brother Ferdinand, who had been working for Reimer since 1815 at the not exactly princely salary of 20 talers per month. Under the circumstances, the Grimms remained remarkably even-tempered in their responses. They reassured Reimer of their warm feelings for him but became ever more firm about demanding their due. In the end, the two parties failed to find a common ground—Wilhelm threw up his hands in despair and declared that there was no point in continuing to correspond with a man who was "impossible." The Grimms published the third edition of their fairy tales with Diederich in Göttingen, and Ferdinand Grimm lost his post after twenty years of service.[11]

The Grimms may never have made or even hoped to make a financial killing on the *Nursery and Household Tales*, but the profit motive was certainly not wholly absent from their calculations and to some extent must have guided their revisions of the first edition. Still, the potential financial benefits to be reaped from strong sales of the collection counted merely as a secondary gain. What really mattered, particularly in the years immediately following publication of the first edition, were the views of the larger literary world. Both brothers monitored reviews with special interest, and here one disappointment followed another. Jacob, on the road much of the time from 1813 to 1815 in diplomatic service, repeatedly asked his brother for news about the collection's reception. But none of the people who counted seemed to take much interest in reviewing the book, and those who actually did review it rarely had anything good to say. While the Grimms waited in vain for reviews from such luminaries as Goethe, minor talents like Johann Gustav Büsching—whose own collection of tales had been assailed by Jacob Grimm—and Friedrich Rühs—whose book on the *Edda* had been attacked by Wilhelm Grimm—seized the chance to get even. Büsching's anonymous review of 1813 in the *Wiener Literatur-Zeitung* compared the first volume of the *Nursery and Household Tales* unfavorably with another collection of tales, which happened to be Büsching's own *Folktales, Fairy Tales, and Legends (Volks-Sagen, Märchen und Legenden)*. "Once again," Büsching railed, "the Grimms see in themselves the sole source of salvation." Instead of acknowledging the efforts of their fellow toilers in the field of folkloric studies, wrote Büsching, the Grimms had taken the opportunity in their preface to the *Nursery and Household Tales* to belittle Musäus, Naubert, Otmar, and Büsching himself. Furthermore, the Grimms had remained blind to the fact that their collection was heavily tainted by Italian and French sources and therefore not really German. Wilhelm Grimm was so annoyed by this "silly" essay and by the lack of favorable reviews that, in desperation, he asked Achim von Arnim to publish a review, a move that was singularly inappropriate since the book was dedicated to Arnim's wife and son. Jacob Grimm described Büsching as the most miserable reviewer he had ever encountered.

Friedrich Rühs was somewhat more restrained than Büsching in his 1815 review of both volumes of the *Nursery and Household Tales*. That Rühs was no friend of the Grimms and of their collection was obvious from an 1812 essay in *Die Musen*, where he stated that the *Nursery and Household Tales* would deserve praise if the few good things that were in it had not been completely overshadowed by large quantities of "the most pathetic and tasteless material imaginable." But his review of 1815 recommended the collection with only a few minor reservations. This was not a book to put into the hands of children, Rühs emphasized. The stories in it may be short and simple, but some are likely to disturb children and lead to "uncomfortable feelings." Parents must therefore exercise good judgment in selecting appropriate stories for their children. The Grimms had no reason to be particularly distressed by this review, but by then they were also hoping for some panegyrics to redress the balance.[12]

The brothers' bitter feelings about the bad press given to their fairy tales is evident as late as 1820 in a letter from Jacob Grimm to Karl Lachmann: "Reviewers, who have a habit of praising idiotic things, ought to stop making such foolish statements about our collection of legends and fairy tales. Instead of stifling what there is of the public's interest in them, they ought to keep completely quiet about them." That the book was ignored by literary worthies continued to irritate Jacob long after its publication. "Those who do not object to our purpose and substance are so refined that they hold their tongues," he complained.[13]

For many observers, the *Nursery and Household Tales* fell wide of the mark and missed its potential market because the brothers had let their scholarly ambitions undermine the production of a book for children. The Grimms' seemingly slavish fidelity to oral folk traditions—in particular to the crude language of the folk—came under especially heavy fire. August Wilhelm Schlegel and Clemens Brentano felt that a bit of artifice would have gone a long way toward improving the art of the folk and toward making the tales more appealing. "If you want to display children's clothing, you can do that quite well without bringing out an outfit that has buttons torn off it, dirt smeared on it, and the shirt hanging out of the pants," Brentano wrote to Arnim. Arnim candidly told the Grimms that they would be wise to add, in the form of a subtitle, a consumer warning to the collection. Future editions ought to state that the book was "for parents, who can select stories for retelling." Other readers were less tactful. Heinrich Voß described the collection (with the exception of a few tales) as "real junk."[14]

More serious were the remarks of Albert Ludwig Grimm, no relation to the brothers but also a collector of fairy tales. When that Grimm used the preface to his *Lina's Book of Fairy Tales* (1816) to get back at the Grimms for having criticized him in *their* preface, Wilhelm took the trouble of placing a handwritten copy of the charges in his personal copy of the *Nursery and Household Tales*. Albert Ludwig Grimm found the style and tone of the Grimms' collection deplorable. Instead of searching high and low for an ideal folk narrator, the Grimms, he charged, had simply settled for the first nursemaid who happened to turn up. For him, nearly all the tales in the collection were flawed by the unrefined tenor of the narrative voice. Furthermore, in trying to serve two masters (scholars and children), the Grimms had failed to satisfy either. "It's impossible to think of that collection as a book that can be put in the hands of children," he grumbled. *Lina's Book of Fairy Tales*, by contrast, was conceived from the start as a book for children, and no one would find anything in it the least bit offensive.[15]

Albert Ludwig Grimm had indeed worked hard to avoid the "sketchy" style and the "distorted" plot lines of the *Nursery and Household Tales*. For "The Fairy Tale of Brunnenhold and Brunnenstark" (his version of "Thousandfurs"), he took fifteen pages to tell what the Grimms had summarized in one paragraph. In the Grimms' "Thousandfurs," the widowed father of the heroine (as noted earlier) tries to persuade his daughter to marry him. A. L. Grimm gave the episode a special twist that retained the motivation for the heroine's flight, but exonerated the father-monarch from blame, thus making the story in his eyes suitable reading matter for children. The father of his Armina never proposes marriage to his daughter; it is his court councilors who do everything in their power to arrange the marriage. The morally unimpeachable king refuses and uses the opportunity to pontificate on the rights of monarchs: "He explained to them that such a thing would be a sin in the eyes of man and God, for it had never before happened that a father wanted to take his daughter for a wife, and even as a king he could not allow himself what no man had ever done."[16]

Wilhelm Grimm lost little time in following the advice of his competitor, from whom he and his brother had so explicitly dissociated themselves in the preface to the first edition of the *Nursery and Household Tales*. In successive editions of the collection, he fleshed out the texts to the point where they were often double their original length, and he so polished the prose that no one could complain of its rough-hewn qualities. He also worked hard to clean up the content of the stories. Both A. L. Grimm and Friedrich Rühs singled out "Rapunzel" as a tale particularly inappropriate to include in a collection of tales that children could get their hands on. "What proper mother or nanny could tell the fairy tale about Rapunzel to an innocent daughter without blushing?" Rühs gasped. Wilhelm Grimm saw to it that the story was rewritten along lines that would meet with both critics' approval. Jacob Grimm may have responded to criticism by asserting that the collection had never been intended for young audiences, but his brother was prepared to delete or revise tales deemed unsuitable for children. He was encouraged in such efforts by his brother Ferdinand, who was all for eliminating anything that might offend the sensibilities (*Feingefühl*) of the reading public.[17]

Wilhelm Grimm proved to be as adept a bowdlerizer as Albert Ludwig Grimm. Consider the following passage from the first edition of the *Nursery and Household Tales* (Rapunzel's daily romps up in the tower with the prince, we learn, have weighty consequences).

> At first Rapunzel was frightened, but soon she came to like the young king so much that she agreed to let him visit every day and to pull him up. The two lived joyfully for a time, and the fairy did not catch on at all until Rapunzel told her one day: "Tell me, Godmother, why my clothes are so tight and why they don't fit me any longer." "Wicked child!" cried the fairy.[18]

In the second edition of the *Nursery and Household Tales*, Wilhelm Grimm made the passage less "lewd"—and in the bargain a good deal less colorful. Here, Rapunzel's "wickedness" has a very different cause.

> At first Rapunzel was frightened, but soon she came to like the young king so much that she agreed to let him visit every day and to pull him up. The two lived joyfully for a time and loved each other dearly, like man and wife. The enchantress did not catch on at all until Rapunzel told her one day: "Tell me, Godmother, why is it that you are much harder to pull up than the young prince?" "Wicked child," cried the enchantress.

It is easy to leap to the conclusion that Teutonic prudishness or the Grimms' delicate sense of propriety motivated the kinds of changes made in "Rapunzel." That may well be the case. But it is far more logical to assume that Wilhelm Grimm took to heart the criticisms leveled against his volume and, eager to find a wider audience, set to work making the appropriate changes. His nervous sensitivity about moral objections to the tales in the collection reflects a growing desire to write for children rather than to collect for scholars.

In the years that intervened between the first two editions of the *Nursery and Household Tales*, Wilhelm Grimm charted a new course for the collection. His son was later to claim that children had taken possession of a book that was not theirs to begin with, but Wilhelm clearly helped that process along. He had evidently already done some editing behind Jacob's back but apparently not enough to satisfy his critics. The preface to the second edition emphasized the value of the tales for children, noting—almost as an afterthought—that adults could also enjoy them and even learn something from them. The brothers no longer insisted on literal fidelity to oral traditions but openly admitted that they had taken pains to delete "every phrase unsuitable for children." Furthermore, they expressed the hope that their collection could serve as a "manual of manners" (*Erziehungsbuch*). Although it is true that Wilhelm Grimm was responsible for the lion's share of the revisions in successive editions of the *Nursery and Household Tales*, Jacob Grimm, who had once declared that the collection was not targeted for children, could not have offered vigorous opposition. After his brother's death, he made the curiously contradictory claim that he had invested as much time in the first editions of the collection as Wilhelm, yet he had also resisted the temptation to rewrite and embellish the source material. Had he done both, the *Nursery and Household Tales* would no doubt have developed in a very different direction.[19]

Sales of the second edition were not so brisk that the Grimms could afford to rest on their oars. It took another eighteen years for a third edition to appear in print. The collection did not meet with full-scale popular success until after 1825, the year that marked the publication of an abridged edition (the so-called *Kleine Ausgabe*). For this single, low-priced volume modeled on Edgar Taylor's financially successful British translation of selected tales from the *Nursery and Household Tales*, Wilhelm Grimm put together fifty of the best-known stories—more or less what became the classic canon of texts. The first printing of 1,500 copies sold well, and the brothers witnessed nine additional printings of this edition in their lifetimes. To be sure, the market for children's literature was gradually opening in those years—the frontispieces to collections of fairy tales begin, at about this time, to show nursemaids and grandmothers reading to children from books instead of narrating freely. But Wilhelm Grimm also had the right instincts about how to strengthen sales. For the abridged edition, he even went beyond Achim von Arnim's advice on how to turn the *Nursery and Household Tales* into a book for children. The preface and the notes were eliminated; illustrations were added (by the Grimms' brother Ludwig Emil); and the texts were based on the revised version of 1819. As Wilhelm wrote his publisher, anything that smacked of scholarship had no place in the volume.[20]

Eliminating references to unwanted pregnancies, introducing marriage before displaying the marriage bed, and explicitly condemning deviant behavior must have gone a long way toward silencing critics and appeasing parental objections to the first edition of the *Nursery and Household Tales*. It clearly made good commercial sense to move along those lines. But why intensify violence or take pains to portray the punishment of evildoers if one is aiming to reach an audience of children? For one thing, the Grimms were careful to eliminate violence whenever it appeared in too realistic a setting. "The Starving Children," for example, is less a fairy tale than a quasi-journalistic account; therefore it never appeared between the covers of the second edition. When it came to fairy tales, however, the Grimms adopted a different strategy. There they had no reservations about including detailed descriptions of children abused and of abusers punished; nor did they rush to excise passages that showed heads rolling or fingers flying through the air.

Professional raconteurs report that children are rarely squeamish when they hear about decapitation or other forms of mutilation. Grisly episodes often strike them as amusing rather than horrifying. Vilma Mönckeberg, a notable teller of fairy tales, recalls that her young audiences found episodes in "The Juniper Tree" to be "hi-

larious." The cannibalistic tableau in that tale did not elicit disgust
and outrage as she had feared. Another storyteller reports that children "howled with delight" when hearing about the agony of the
Jew in the brambles in the tale of that title.[21] And this for reasons
that probably had little to do with anti-Semitism. Obviously this kind
of laughter is more a release for pent-up anxieties than an expression of delight, but it also indicates that the depiction of physical violence in fairy tales has a special appeal for children, and not only in
connection with the punishment of villains. When it comes to descriptions of a hero's trials and tribulations, however, we are dealing
with a somewhat different matter. There, children, who invariably
count themselves among the downtrodden and underprivileged,
identify and empathize with the protagonist. The more Hansel,
Gretel, Cinderella, and Snow White are victimized by the powers of
evil, the more sympathy they elicit and the more captivating they are
for children. Wilhelm Grimm's editing procedures here again succeeded in making the *Nursery and Household Tales* more rather than
less attractive to young audiences.

All this is not to say that the Grimms were rank opportunists.
Rather they were part of a tendency that had become a trend by the
early nineteenth century. The stories collected by the two young
students of folklore and philology (Jacob was twenty-seven and Wilhelm twenty-six when the first volume of the *Nursery and Household
Tales* was published) could still be considered a source of entertainment for all age groups. They appeared in print just when folktales
were moving out of barns and spinning rooms and into the nursery.
The process by which adult entertainment was translated into children's literature was a slow one with a long transitional period when
the line between the two was by no means clear.

In many ways, the Grimms' collection (at least in its original form)
straddled the line between adult entertainment and children's literature. By giving their collection the title *Kinder- und Hausmärchen*,
the Grimms seemed from the start to imply that their tales were intended primarily for children and that their province was henceforth the domestic sphere. But as C. S. Lewis has said of fairy tales,
"Many children don't like them and many adults do." No age group

has ever had an uncontested monopoly on fairy tales. The Grimms' own gloss of 1819 on the title for their collection reveals that their first edition might have been produced for scholars but that the actual audience for those stories comprised both adults and children: "Children's tales [*Kindermärchen*] are told so that the thoughts and feelings of the heart can awaken and develop in their pure, mild light; but because their simple poetry can delight everyone and impart to them their truth and because they stay in the home and are passed on from one generation to the next, they are also called household tales [*Hausmärchen*]." Jacob Grimm himself stressed that the distinction made in the title of the collection between children's tales and household tales was more apparent than real. In his view, children and adults had equal claims on the folkloristic legacy of their ancestors. Thus a recent translation of the brothers' *Kinder- und Hausmärchen* as *Grimms' Tales for Young and Old* probably best captures the full spirit of the original, German title.[22]

Collections of fairy tales predating the Grimms' volume had already been designed to provide diversion for both young and old. A single tale could offer a sobering lesson for children even as it served as a source of light-hearted entertainment for adults. The double lesson appended to Perrault's "Bluebeard" reveals in telling fashion that there are two implied audiences for this grisly tale. The first moral (aimed at children—and most likely at women too) spells out the perils of curiosity: "In spite of its great charms, curiosity / Often brings with it serious regrets. . . . / For once satisfied, curiosity offers nothing, / And ever does it cost more dearly."[23] This is the lesson to be derived from the story of Bluebeard's last wife, a lesson that does not quite square with the tale's events, for the "curious" wife lives happily ever after with a "very worthy man" and forgets all about the evil days she passed with her brutish husband. A second moral emphasizes that "Bluebeard" is not to be taken all too seriously.

> If you take a sensible point of view
> And study this grim story,
> You will recognize that this tale
> Is one of days long past.

No longer are husbands so terrifying,
Demanding the impossible,
Being both dissatisfied and jealous;
In the presence of wives they're now gracious enough,
And no matter what color their beards may be
One does not have to guess who is master![24]

As J.R.R. Tolkien perceived it, fairy tales were retired to the nursery when they became unfashionable, just as "shabby or old-fashioned furniture is relegated to the play-room."[25] Exactly when the function of folktales shifted from amusement for adults to the edification and diversion of young children is not clear. From Noël du Fail's account of the *veillée*, where men and women listened to tales while discharging household chores, we know that folktales were still very much adult fare in sixteenth-century France. In certain parts of Germany, the art of composing and narrating folktales persisted as a widespread custom among adults up to the time of the Franco-Prussian War in 1870. But as industrialization gradually curtailed the need for the kinds of collective household chores and harvesting activities that had created a forum for oral narration, folktales as a form of public entertainment for adults died out. There may still exist many pockets of culture—both rural and urban—in which oral performance of tales and songs thrives, but on the whole it is safe to say that the nineteenth century witnessed a steady decline in the once intense preoccupation of adults with folktales.[26]

Since traditionally folktales were related at adult gatherings after the children had been put to bed for the night, peasant raconteurs could take certain liberties with their diction and give free play to their penchant for sexual innuendo or off-color allusions. In eighteenth-century French versions of "Little Red Riding Hood," the heroine unwittingly eats the flesh and drinks the blood of her grandmother, is called a slut by her grandmother's cat, and performs a slow striptease for the wolf. An Italian version has the wolf kill the mother, make a latch cord of her tendons, a meat pie of her flesh, and wine from her blood. The heroine pulls the latch, eats the meat pie, and drinks the blood.[27] Even this folktale, which in its latter-day version appears to be the most explicitly didactic of all, evidently started out as a bawdy tale for adults hardly suitable for children. As much as some readers may be shocked by the cruelty and violence of the Grimms' tales, they would find many of the stories tame by comparison with their corresponding peasant versions.

Walt Disney was by no means the first to disguise or eliminate sex, violence, and family conflict from the surface of the tales.[28] Long before Disney transformed Snow White's stepmother into an evil queen, the Grimms had seen to it that Snow White's treacherous biological mother was replaced by a stepmother. Although the brothers insisted that they may have tinkered with the letter but had never tampered with the spirit of the tales, just as they repeatedly asserted that the essential contours of each folktale plot remained intact, comparisons of successive editions of the *Nursery and Household Tales* suggest that the Grimms were either disingenuous, dishonest, or engaging in self-deception when they made such declarations.[29] Publicly and privately they observed that revisions had been made only in the interest of producing complete and authentic tales. In fact, Wilhelm Grimm rewrote the tales so extensively and went so far in the direction of eliminating off-color episodes that he can be credited with sanitizing folktales and thereby paving the way for the process that made them acceptable children's literature in all cultures.

As much and as often as the Grimms sought to advertise their tales as products of the "folk," recent scholarship has shown that they actually relied on sources at least at one remove from peasant culture. Since the Grimms began the process of compiling tales just when the stories were ceasing to play a vital role in the day-to-day activities of adult life, they received from their informants versions of the tales that already had been dramatically revised. The basic content may not have deviated sharply from what was told at harvesting time or in the spinning room, but off-color details along with crude language had no doubt been toned down or eliminated. The Grimms' informants were rarely unlettered peasants who spoke the inimitable language of the "folk," but literate men and women from various social classes.[30] They may have ranged greatly in age, but their educational and class backgrounds were not so different as to make any one of the principal contributors stand out from the crowd. Also, the Grimms were by no means opposed to resorting to literary sources for their "folkloric" texts. For their first volume in particular they raided one printed collection after another for tales to include in their own. Not until preparations were under way for the second volume did they begin to rely extensively on oral narratives.

Even when the Grimms had the opportunity to witness an "authentic" folkloric performance, they still were not able to capture that performance in all its "purity," as they had claimed. Like any auditors of folkloric performances, they played a role in shaping the plots of the tales they heard. Every storyteller has a unique repertory of tales, one developed in collaboration with an audience. Much as the tellers of the tales may appear to exercise unilateral control over their material, their powers of invention are to some extent held in check by their audiences. The successful retelling of a tale requires the narrator to take the measure of his listeners, anticipate their wishes, and veer away from what might offend their ears. Even in the heat of narration, the teller may allow his story to take new twists and turns as he trains his powers of observation on the audience, watches their reactions, and becomes attuned to their likes and dislikes. Thus the teller of tales works in concert with his audience to create popular tales. Or, to put matters differently, the folkloric community operates as a kind of censor, endlessly revising the content of a tale until it meets with full approval. Thus it is not surprising to find radically different versions of the same tale as one moves from one cultural context to another. Each community or culture participates in its own unique oral narrative traditions, imbuing them with their particular mores and values.[31]

For the Grimms, the process of recasting folktales unfolded in three stages. First, as audience or addressees, they influenced the telling of a tale simply by their physical presence. Their social standing, age, sexual identity, and body language worked in concert on their informants. Dorothea Viehmann, Jeanette Hassenpflug, and Dorothea Wild no doubt adopted a different manner and subtly changed the matter of their tales when reciting them for two young bachelors. Much as the brothers claimed that Dorothea Viehmann had an infallible memory for detail and corrected herself if for a moment she deviated from the standard phrasing for a story, it is hard to believe that her narrative tone and style remained exactly the same whether she was rehearsing her repertory for the Grimms or telling a tale to her grandchildren. No matter how precisely the Grimms recorded the oral renditions of those tales, they were still the receivers of texts shaped by their presence. They were, further- more, never able to capture anything other than the verbal dimen- sion of a performance. Intonation, gesture, facial expression, along with all the other vital components of a live performance, escaped their recording efforts.[32]

In a second, even more fundamental fashion, the Grimms altered the texture of the tales narrated to them. Like the early collectors of folktales, particularly those working before the age of the portable tape recorder, they could not resist the temptation to improve on what they heard, to render readable what might be pleasing to the ear alone. Take, for example, the Grimms' recasting of "Fledgling." A passage from the original, manuscript version reveals the extent to which the two brothers initially attempted to retain the flavor and tone of the oral account—at the expense of readability.

> Early the next morning the forester goes hunting at two o'clock, once he is gone Lehnchen says to Karl if you don't leave me all alone I won't leave you, and Karl says never, then Lehnchen says I just want to tell you that our cook carried a lot of water into the house yesterday so I asked her why she was bringing so much water into the house and she told me if I wouldn't tell anyone else, then she would tell me and so I told her I wouldn't tell a soul, and she told me after my father had gone hunting early the next morning she planned to boil a cauldron of hot water and to throw you into it and cook you.[33]

This passage makes it eminently clear that pedantic fidelity to a folkloric source is not necessarily a virtue. "Nursery tales told in the nurse's tone should spread through oral transmission," the German writer Wieland once warned, "but they should not be put into print." The oral version of a tale can easily fall flat when transferred to paper, just as the written version can fail to electrify an audience.

It is therefore not hard to understand what moved the Grimms to translate the verbal utterances of their informants into what purists have described as a stilted and artificial literary language.[34]

Still, the Grimms outdid themselves on occasion. While they may not have gone quite as far as Madame de Villeneuve, who so puffed up the story "Beauty and the Beast" that her version took up more than three hundred pages, they occasionally succumbed to the temptation to embellish a tale by expanding it. Here are a few lines from their original draft of "Briar Rose":

> [Briar Rose] pricked her finger with the spindle and immediately fell into a deep sleep. The king and his retinue had just returned and they too, along with the flies on the wall and everything else in the castle, fell asleep. All around the castle grew a hedge of thorns, concealing everything from sight.[35]

As Max Lüthi and others have enjoyed pointing out, that passage grew and expanded almost as quickly as the hedge surrounding the castle.[36] By the time the final edition came out, it looked like this:

> [Briar Rose] took hold of the spindle and tried to spin. But no sooner had she touched the spindle than the magic spell took effect, and she pricked her finger with it.
>
> The very moment that she felt the prick she sank down into the bed that was right there and fell into a deep sleep. And that sleep spread throughout the entire palace. The king and the queen, who had just come home and entered the great hall, fell asleep, and the whole court with them. The horses fell asleep in the stables, the dogs in the courtyard, the pigeons on the roof, and the flies on the wall. Even the fire that had been flaming on the hearth stopped and went to sleep, and the roast stopped crackling, and the cook, who was about to pull the kitchen boy's hair because he had done something wrong, let him go and fell asleep. And the wind died down, and not a single little leaf stirred on the trees by the castle.
>
> All around the castle a briar hedge began to grow. Each year it grew higher, and finally it surrounded the entire castle and grew so thickly beyond it that not a trace of the castle was to be seen, not even the flag on the roof.

The Grimms often went beyond mere stylistic expansion and embellishment. The opening passages of "Mother Holle" in the first and seventh editions, for example, offer an interesting study in contrasts. The 1812 version is direct and vivid in its simplicity.

> A widow had two daughters, one of whom was beautiful and hardworking, while the other was ugly and lazy. She preferred the ugly and lazy one, and so the other one had to do all the work and was the Cinderella of the household. Once the girl went off to fetch water and when she bent over to pull the bucket out of the well, she bent over too far and fell in.[37]

The 1857 version not only adds exegesis to exposition, but also makes a point of dilating on the physical hardships and mental torment that the heroine must endure.

> A widow had two daughters, one of whom was beautiful and hardworking, while the other was ugly and lazy. She preferred the ugly and lazy one, who was her own daughter, and so the other one had to do all the work and be the Cinderella of the household. The poor girl had to sit every day by a well on the main road and spin until her fingers began to bleed. Once it happened that the spindle was covered with blood and she bent over the well to wash it off. But the spindle dropped out of her hands and fell down into the well. She started crying, ran to her stepmother, and told her about her bad luck. The stepmother scolded her sharply and was so unsympathetic that she said: "If you let the spindle fall into the well, you'll just have to bring it back up again." The girl went back to the well and didn't know what she should do. Scared to death, she jumped into the well to get her spindle back.

Even if the Grimms are forgiven the sin of tampering with the language of the tales, there still remain countless other charges that can be leveled against the folkloristic authenticity of their collection. Critics have accused Wilhelm Grimm not only of creating a homogenous, stylized language for the tales, but also of introducing messages, motivations, judgments, morals, and other often pedantic touches. A prisoner of his passion for order, logic, and instrumentality, Wilhelm Grimm unfailingly smoothed the rough edges of the tales he heard and read, even as he imbued them with the values and pedagogical demands of his time. Just what these values were is not always easy to determine, but the following song chanted by schoolchildren in Ravensburg in the Grimms' day and age has been considered representative.

> Hard work and obedience:
> Those are the qualities to which
> All good citizens must aspire.
> . . . .
> Modesty and gentility,
> Skill, hard work, and love of labor
> Crown a girl and her achievements,
> Building the foundations of a woman's dignity.[38]

> *Fleiß und Gehorsam sind die Pflichten,*
> *Welche redlich zu entrichten*
> *Gute Bürger sich bestreben.*
> . . . .
> *Sittsamkeit und sanfte Triebe,*
> *Kenntnis, Fleiß und Arbeitsliebe*
> *Sind der Mädchen schönste Zierde,*
> *Gründen fest des Weibes Würde.*

This hymn to dutiful diligence does not, however, appear to harmonize perfectly with the ethical tone of fairy-tale worlds, where luck and chance often count for more than hard work and obedience. But this dissonance can easily be muted, in some cases eliminated altogether. Take the example of the editorial changes made in "Snow White." When Snow White meets the dwarves for the first time in the Grimms' earliest version of the tale, the dwarves ask nothing more of her than that she cook their meals in exchange for shelter. But by the first printed edition of the *Nursery and Household Tales*, the dwarves have already escalated their demands and propose different terms for the contract, terms that no doubt reflect the Grimms' notions on contractual relations between men and women: "If you will keep house for us, do the cooking, make the beds, wash, sew, knit, and keep everything neat and clean, you can stay with us and you won't want for anything."[39] We have already seen how "Mother Holle" was expanded in order to dwell on the details of the long-suffering heroine's painful, but ultimately rewarding, discharging of household duties. Although fairy-tale heroines the world over are often required to labor for their salvation while their male counterparts rely on magic or helpers to carry out chores, in the *Nursery and Household Tales* they work harder than in most other collections of tales. The Grimms seized nearly every available opportunity to emphasize the virtue of hard work and made a point of correlating diligence with beauty and desirability wherever possible.

Where a tale's heroine was not required to labor for her salvation, she was given attributes that conformed to those celebrated in the song of the Ravensburg schoolchildren. Briar Rose becomes both beautiful and dutiful (*sittsam*) in the second edition of the tales; the heroine of "Twelve Brothers" acquires a "tender heart" by the seventh edition; and the "girl without hands" becomes progressively more God-fearing from one edition to the next. In a tale such as "King Thrushbeard," the heroine's arrogant behavior comes under increasingly heavy fire with each new edition, just as the heroine becomes ever more contrite in the end. The changes made in "The White Snake" are also characteristic of Wilhelm's editorial practices. He could rarely resist the temptation to attach attributes to each and every figure in a story. In the first version of that tale there is a king plain and simple, a servant, and a princess. By the time the third version of the *Nursery and Household Tales* appeared, the monarch had become "renowned throughout the land for his wisdom," the servant had become "compassionate," "merciful," and "good," and the princess had become "beautiful" but "arrogant" and had a "proud heart." Rather than allowing the various figures of the tale to reveal their traits through their actions (this is one of the hallmarks of a folktale), Wilhelm Grimm felt obliged to stamp the tale's actors with his own character judgments and thus shaped his readers' views of them. That we are forever coming across wise monarchs, compassionate heroes, toiling beauties, and proud princesses has something to do with folkloric plot patterns, but it also has a great deal to do with Wilhelm Grimm's preconceived notions about sex, class, and character.

The Grimms actively and deliberately altered the folkloric material they claimed to have tried so hard to preserve in its pristine state. At times, those changes seem oddly arbitrary, almost more accidental than intentional. Who can tell why the hero of "Hans My

Hedgehog" looks after pigs in the first edition of the *Nursery and Household Tales* and finds himself tending both donkeys and swine in the second edition? At other times, the changes are cryptic and not easy to explain. A comparison of the opening passages of "Twelve Brothers" in the first and second editions of the *Nursery and Household Tales* raises some interesting questions about Wilhelm Grimm's intentions. The first edition shows us a king whose horror at the idea of having a daughter takes an extreme form.

> There was once a king who had twelve children—all were boys. He did not want to have a daughter and told the queen: "If the thirteenth child that you bear is a girl, I'll have the twelve others killed. But if it's a boy, they can all stay alive and live together." The queen wanted to talk him out of it. But the king would hear nothing more of it: "If it is as I have said, then they must die. I would rather cut off all their heads than have a girl among them."[40]

The second edition reverses this situation and gives us a king who is so set on the idea of a daughter that he is prepared to sacrifice his sons for her financial welfare.

> There were once a king and queen who lived together in peace with their twelve children, who were all boys. One day the king said to his wife: "If the thirteenth child you are about to bear is a girl, the twelve boys must die, so that her wealth may be great and that she alone may inherit the kingdom." He had twelve coffins made and had them filled with wood shavings. In each of them there was a little pillow. He had them taken to a locked room, gave the queen a key to it, and told her not to tell anyone about the matter.

In this particular case, it would take some effort to understand exactly what motivated Wilhelm Grimm to make this radical change.

In most cases, however, it is easy to account for changes made from one edition to the next. In addition to wanting to produce a volume appropriate for children and attractive to parents, the Grimms wanted to give the public a document of German folk culture in its most admirable form. To make it appear all the more German, every fairy (*Fee*), prince (*Prinz*), and princess (*Prinzessin*) was transformed into a more Teutonic-sounding enchantress (*Zauberin*) or wise woman (*weise Frau*), king's son (*Königssohn*), and king's daughter (*Königstochter*). Proverbs were added to give the collection a more folksy texture, and the proper moral sentiments were woven into the text, for this collection was to be in many ways a showcase for German folk culture. Thus a king condemns his wife to be burned at the stake in the first edition, but he does so only with the greatest regrets in the second edition: he stands at a window and watches her with tears in his eyes, "because he still loved her so much."[41]

It is clear that the stories in the Grimms' collection do not by any stretch of the imagination come close to capturing the folkloric narratives that the Grimms originally intended to preserve between the covers of the *Nursery and Household Tales*. Successive editions of the tales, instead of moving closer to those narratives, widened the gulf between oral source (when it existed) and printed text. There were, of course, occasions on which Wilhelm Grimm inadvertently eliminated contamination by literary influences from a tale. For their version of "Rapunzel," the Grimms relied on a written account by Friedrich Schulz. When they rewrote his text, they also—as noted—deleted Rapunzel's naive question about the tightness of her clothes, a touch that must have come from Schulz's pen, for it is not found in his sources. But this sort of restoration to folkloric authenticity proved to be the exception rather than the rule.[42]

It is an error to see in the Grimms' collection printed transcriptions of oral folktales. The tales are simply too far removed from oral source material to deserve that title. But what name do they then merit? Clearly one cannot call them literary fairy tales, for, notwithstanding Wilhelm Grimm's unending editorial interventions, they are a far cry from the kind of narratives penned by E.T.A. Hoffmann, Hans Christian Andersen, or Oscar Wilde. The texts in the *Nursery and Household Tales* seem to lead an uneasy double life as folklore and literature. As Stith Thompson reminds us, there is no distinct line dividing oral and written traditions.[43] Skilled raconteurs might find themselves appropriating material from printed sources to flesh out their stories; resourceful writers might draw on recollections of oral tales to thicken their plots. On the narrative spectrum that leads from folklore to literature, the Grimms' collection is located somewhere near the midpoint. While some texts gravitate toward one end of the spectrum and others to the other, most occupy the middle ground.

Even if the issue of the narrative status of the Grimms' tales is settled, or at least clarified, the terminological dilemma remains.[44] Folklorists, who stress the roots of those tales in oral traditions, tend to refer to the Grimms' collection as folktales. Others, foremost among them literary critics, designate the stories as fairy tales, if only because that is the term conventionally used to translate the German word *Märchen*. Still others prefer the German *Buchmärchen*, a word that points to the blend of literary and folkloric elements in the tales. Then there are critics who shrewdly avoid all terminological controversy by coining new terms such as *chimerat* or by simply using the phrase *Gattung Grimm* (the Grimm genre).

Before resorting to awkward neologisms or to even more cumbersome foreign designations, it is perhaps worth exploring the advantages and limitations of applying the terms *folktale* and *fairy tale* to the texts in the Grimms' collection. It would be easy to use *folktale* for tales that lie to the left of the narrative spectrum that moves from folklore to literature and *literary text* for tales that lie to the right:

folklore	Grimms'	literature
(oral folktales)	*Nursery and Household Tales*	(printed literary texts)

The Grimms' collection, representing a class of hybrid texts, might be called literary folktales. But the term *folktale* traditionally has been used in two senses. On the one hand, *folktale* refers to oral narratives that circulate among the folk; on the other it designates a specific set of tales, namely oral narratives that take place among the folk, that is, in a realistic setting with naturalistic details. I will henceforth distinguish the one from the other by calling the entire class of traditional oral narratives *folktales* and by calling its naturalistic subset *folk tales*.

The term *fairy tale*, by contrast, has been associated with both oral and literary traditions but is above all reserved for narratives set in a fictional world where preternatural events and supernatural intervention are taken wholly for granted. A fairy tale can thus belong to the category of folktales, but it stands in contrast to the folk tale, which is sharply biased in favor of earthy realism. On the spectrum that takes us from naturalistic settings to supernatural ones (in practice, often from the farm to the enchanted forest), folk tales occupy the left side, fairy tales the right.

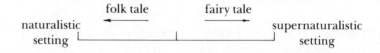

Some of the stories in the *Nursery and Household Tales* are, to be sure, not easy to place on this spectrum. Fables and tall tales, for example, are by no means realistic, but they also have little in common with classic fairy tales. While most fables in the Grimms' collection fulfill the didactic purpose of that particular genre, the tall tales give us slapstick and comic exaggeration. The allegorical mode of the fable admits the possibility of the impossible, just as the absurd elements of the tall tale stretch the limits of plausibility. Still, since these tales lack the magical and marvelous elements found in fairy tales and tend to the naturalistic in their overt or covert concern with human behavior, they are in many ways more at home among the class of folk tales.

If we map out the contrasting pairs folklore / literature and folk tale / fairy tale in graphic terms, the following configuration emerges:

The circle formed by the broken line encompasses the types of texts found in the *Nursery and Household Tales*.

Identifying specific examples from the Grimms' collection of the four types of tales housed in the four quadrants is not difficult. "Snow White" stands as a classic example of an oral fairy tale—the Grimms give us a version of the plot that has enjoyed widespread circulation. "Snow White and Rose Red," on the other hand, gives us a literary fairy tale, one based on a story by Caroline Stahl and rewritten for the *Nursery and Household Tales*.[45] "The Peasant's Clever Daughter," with its village setting and down-to-earth characters, stands as a clear example of an oral folk tale—its narrative armature can be detected in stories told the world over. And finally, "Sharing Joys and Sorrows," borrowed from Jörg Wickram, appears to be a compact form of the literary folk tale.

The Grimms' *Nursery and Household Tales* can be said to embrace both folk tales and fairy tales and to run the gamut from folklore to literature. Since the fairy tale, rather than the folk tale, constitutes the main concern of this study, I shall define that term with greater precision in chapter 3. For now, the rough division between folk tales and fairy tales will have to suffice as a terminological indicator.

From the time that the Grimms first began assembling folk tales and fairy tales until the final edition of the *Nursery and Household Tales*, Wilhelm Grimm acted as a tireless and relentless editor, attempting again and again to improve on the original source material. Some scholars would argue that he made changes so fundamental to the spirit of the *Nursery and Household Tales* that the values and tastes embodied in individual tales represent nothing more than a reflection of his own personal ethos. In short, they tell us nothing at all about the German national character. And since they are not authentic creations of the folk, they also tell us little or nothing about the collective unconscious that ordinarily speaks through the voice of folkloric performances. Yet closer inspection of the changes introduced by the Grimms into the tales shows that the brothers did not distort beyond recognition the substance of the tales. And even if they did, we still are fortunate to have the original drafts of many of the tales along with variant forms from Germany and the rest of Europe. The task of reconstructing a tale's basic form is by no means impossible.[46]

The marked predictability in the Grimms' editing procedures also makes it possible to separate the essential and authentic from what is mere editorial embellishment or authorial affectation. Take the case of what is perhaps the best-known tale in the Grimms' collection: "Hansel and Gretel." The Grimms, one scholar has argued, turned what was originally a powerful tale of parental malice and family conflict into a relatively tame story utterly lacking the emotional intensity to touch upon or stir childhood anxieties. In successive editions of the *Nursery and Household Tales*, he claims, they exonerated the father from blame in abandoning his children, just as they wholly exculpated the biological mother by placing the stepmother in her role.[47] Thus a frightening story of child abuse and abandonment became a tale about a stepmother so wicked that no child would ever contemplate identifying her with his mother. A quick glance at the Grimms' manuscript version of "Hansel and Gretel" (the version that, in all likelihood, is most faithful to the authentic oral folk narrative) tells us that the father of the two children could hardly be accused of collaborating with his wife in a plot to desert his offspring. Only after a good deal of nagging does he finally cave in and agree to lead the two children into the forest.[48] The mother alone stands as villain—even in versions untouched by the Grimms. It is true that she becomes more explicitly bad-tempered in subsequent versions of the *Nursery and Household Tales* while her husband becomes more long suffering in his role as harassed husband. Still, there is no fundamental change of character in the two figures as they evolved in various versions recorded by the Grimms, only a deepening of their already established character traits.

Wilhelm Grimm's habit of intensifying maternal malice ultimately led him to make at least one significant substantive change in a number of tales. Again, it is easy to identify that change and instructive to study the motive for it. In "Hansel and Gretel," the biological mother of the children becomes, in the fourth edition of the collection, a stepmother. The mother of "Snow White" undergoes the same metamorphosis in the second edition of the tales, as does the biological mother of the heroine in "Mother Holle." As successive editions of the *Nursery and Household Tales* rolled from the presses, Wilhelm Grimm must have become acutely aware of the collection's role as a repository of bedtime stories for children rather than as a source of entertainment for adults. What might have been perfectly acceptable as adult entertainment required considerable modification for children. Thus the heartless mother who leaves her children to starve so that she and her husband might live and thrive becomes a wicked stepmother, and the evil queen driven by sexual rivalry to do away with her daughter slips easily into the role of the jealous stepmother who plots the murder of her beautiful stepdaughter. In each case, Wilhelm Grimm recognized that most children (along with those who read to them) find the idea of wicked stepmothers easier to tolerate than that of cruel mothers.

Countless other examples of editing procedures can be noted, but the point should be obvious. The Grimms' censorship tended to operate in a uniform and consistent fashion that focused on precisely those facts of fairy-tale life that were the most difficult to tolerate. "Faced with monstrously cruel mothers and with fathers driven by incestuous desires, they sought their salvation in the editing of texts," one critic concludes.[49] Thanks to the existence of the original manuscripts and of the first edition of the *Nursery and Household Tales*, many of the Grimms' changes can be identified, and a survey of those changes can often be as telling as an encounter with the unvarnished truth of the original tales.[50] Those are precisely the changes that tell us something about the Grimms' mentality and about what they found unacceptable in the thinking of the folk so revered by them.

The stories collected by the Grimms passed through three separate phases before reaching the definitive, printed form of the final edition. The first phase did not involve active intervention by the brothers but resulted in substantial changes in the tales they heard. The Grimms' physical presence alone, with eyes alert and pens poised, could not but affect the utterances of the tales' tellers. The second involved vigorous editing, the translating of a spoken idiom into readable, literary language. Only the third phase witnessed the kind of wholesale rewriting that altered the shape and substance of the tales' plots. As the stories moved from oral performance to written text, they became more readable but less transparent. What was stated directly in oral versions became veiled by the time the tale found its place between the covers of the *Nursery and Household Tales*. What appeared too crude or offensive for children's ears was eliminated. Coarse, inelegant phrasing was polished and refined. What seemed unmotivated was given a cause. If folk wisdom along with the preoccupations of peasants and workers remained very much on the surface of tales in their oral form, they became ever more deeply buried as the Grimms pursued their editorial activities.

To search for the hidden meaning of the Grimms' fairy tales is therefore not so fatuous an exercise as some would have us believe. That these tales have entered the realm of "children's literature" does not necessarily mean that they are "innocent" stories devoid of psychological depth. Ever since oral folk narratives were translated into stable written texts intended to entertain children, their original meaning has become masked, or at least obscured. Yet it is not impossible to recover that meaning and its implications. The folk may never have required the assistance of folklorists and psychologists to decode the tales told while spinning wool or husking ears of corn, for they prided themselves on boldness of language and baldness of narrative exposition. Censorship was as unwelcome as it was unnecessary in the company of adults, and the hard core of the plots could remain intact. The modern, written counterparts to these narratives can, by contrast, appear both cryptic and abstruse, in part because original text and context are forever lost to us. For that reason, they invite, indeed demand, interpretation.

2

FACT AND FANTASY
The Art of Reading
Fairy Tales

The fairy tales of my childhood have a meaning deeper
than the truths taught by life. —SCHILLER, *Wallenstein*

WHEN it comes to fairy tales, nearly everyone has something to say,
and they all have something different to say. Folklorists, cultural
anthropologists, historians, sociologists, educators, literary critics,
psychologists—even criminologists—have all laid claim to occupying
privileged positions as judges and interpreters of those tales.
Take the case of "Little Red Riding Hood," a story that has probably
suffered more interpretive trials and tribulations than any other
fairy tale. Charles Perrault had no trouble explaining this tale to his
readers.

> From this story one learns that children,
> Especially young lasses,
> Pretty, courteous, and well-bred,
> Are wrong to listen to any sort of man.[1]

Since then, generations of parents have taken advantage of Perrault's "Le Petit Chaperon Rouge" and the Grimms' "Rotkäppchen"
as cautionary tales to read to their children. Few have taken the
story literally, as does one folklorist, who claims that the tale is based
on actual accounts of werewolves attacking and devouring children.
For a time, British mythologists preached the view that Little Red
Riding Hood represents the burning sun which, in the course of a
day, sets out on a westward journey until it is engulfed by the dark-

3. *Gustave Doré.*

4. *Moritz von Schwind.*

FIGURES 3–5. *Gustave Doré, Moritz von Schwind, and Arpad Schmid-hammer had quite different ways of portraying the bedroom scene in "Little Red Riding Hood."*

5. *Arpad Schmidhammer.*

ness of the night. Nonsense! was the response of psychoanalytically
oriented critics, who had their own ways of reading this tale. For one
of them, the wolf displays pregnancy envy by attempting to put living beings into his belly. In the end he is killed by stones, symbols of
sterility that "mock his usurpation of the pregnant woman's role."
Another contends that the story speaks of "human passions, oral
greediness, aggression, and pubertal desire," with the wolf as nothing more than a projection of Red Riding Hood's "badness." Ideol-
ogists of the Third Reich, who hailed the Grimms' *Nursery and
Household Tales* as a "sacred book," saw Red Riding Hood as a symbol
of the German people, terrorized and victimized, but finally liberated from the clutches of a Jewish wolf. A recent American reading
of the tale discovers in the story "a parable of rape" that teaches
young women about the "frightening male figures abroad in the
woods" and implies that "females are helpless before them."[2]

Each of these interpretations tells us as much about the ideological orientation and professional bias of its author as about the tale itself. There is clearly something about the story that lends itself to pluralistic interpretations, and we shall later see just what it is. But with such an embarrassment of interpretive riches, we might do well for the moment to turn a deaf ear to Red Riding Hood's critics and to trust her tale alone. But which tale should we trust? Perrault's seventeenth-century story that ends with Red Riding Hood's death? The Grimms' nineteenth-century tale of rescue and reconciliation? Various oral versions that have been recorded over the centuries by folklorists and anthropologists? Do we look only at tales featuring girls with red caps, or do we focus on all tales that turn on an encounter between predatory beast and innocent child?

One of the chief sources of irritation for the interpreter of fairy tales is the nature of folkloric sources. For nearly every tale, there are at least a dozen versions, in some cases hundreds of extant variants. In other words, rather than a single, stable literary text in which even the finest points of detail may function as bearers of significance, we have an infinite number of corrupt "texts," spoken and written, each representing one version of a single tale type, and an imperfect version at that. No matter how gifted the transcriber of a tale is, he cannot fully succeed in capturing and recreating the spirit of an oral performance. Much as fairy tales invite interpretation, the facts of their origin and diffusion imply the impossibility of textually grounded interpretation. Even the anthropologist who can go straight to the source, observe the teller, study the community in which a tale flourishes, and record that tale still has nothing more than a single version, one no more and no less authoritative than other oral variants.

The critic who undertakes the task of interpreting a tale without first studying the relation of a folkloric text to its variant forms may find himself drawing generalizations based on false premises. The Prairie Band Potawatomi may be able to state with impunity that the folktale hero P'teejah is a full-blooded American Indian boy, but the folklorist who fails to recognize that P'teejah is the French folk hero Petit Jean masquerading as an Indian will find himself drawing embarrassing conclusions about Amerindian culture. When Bruno

Bettelheim and Ernest Jones analyze the symbolic significance of a prince's transformation into a frog by telling us that the "clammy sensations" aroused by frogs link those creatures to the male sexual organ, they both willfully ignore the fact that an entire set of stories features frogs that turn out to be enchanted princesses. And when Erich Fromm insists that the bottle carried by Little Red Riding Hood on the way to her grandmother's house stands as a symbol of virginity (hence the warning not to break it) and proceeds to build an entire interpretation of the story based on this and a few other details, he seems to have failed to take into account the many versions with neither bottle nor admonition.[3]

Any attempt to unearth the hidden meaning of fairy tales is bound to fail unless it is preceded by a rigorous, if not exhaustive, analysis of a tale type and its variants. That analysis enables the interpreter to distinguish essential features from random embellishments and to identify culturally determined elements that vary from one regional version of a tale to the next. Folklorists can count themselves lucky that a model for assembling and classifying folktales from around the world was designed in the early part of this century by Kaarle Krohn and his fellow Finn Antti Aarne, a man who became known as the Linnaeus of folkloric studies. Since then, the so-called historic-geographic method has come to be practiced on an international scale, although exponents of that method are still known as students of the Finnish School. The system proposed by Aarne in his *Types of the Folktale* (*Verzeichnis der Märchentypen*, 1910), which the American folklorist Stith Thompson subsequently expanded and refined, still provides the authoritative classification scheme for folktales.[4]

Once Aarne had surveyed and identified the various tale types (his monograph listed nearly two thousand), it remained for his disciples to focus on individual tale types or cycles of tales. The most renowned publications in this vein include Kurt Ranke's analysis of tales concerned with two brothers, Archer Taylor's meditations on the "black ox" theme, and Warren Roberts' reflections on tales featuring "kind and unkind girls."[5] These scholars begin by singling out one tale type and recording its textual variants as they appear in literary sources, in archival collections, or in notes from fieldwork. They then attempt to reconstruct the parent tale from which various versions of the tale evolved. Accurate dating of textual variants and careful tracing of a tale's paths of dissemination figure as key components in the process of arriving at the archetypal form. The task of collecting all variants of one tale type, after all, defies completion. And even with all variants assembled, it may not always be possible to locate and define the point of origin from which a tale spreads more or less "like ripples in a pond"; nor is it necessarily always clear which tale most closely approximates the original ideal type.[6] As serious as these problems may appear, they have rarely deterred converts to the historic-geographic method from drawing up elaborate charts and from marshaling pages upon pages of statistical evidence and textual variations to document the faces and fortunes of particular tale types.

Exponents of the Finnish School are, for the most part, the drones of the folkloric industry. To them has fallen not only the arduous labor of locating, assembling, and recording folkloric material, but also the vexing task of building systems for classifying that vast treasury. They may be unlikely to win awards for imaginative readings and fresh, new insights into oral narratives, but without their efforts, folkloric studies would surely be more an art than a science. Interpreting a folkloric item without being able to perceive its basic structure and to identify those features subject to wide variation is a risky enterprise. There are no definitive versions of fairy tales. In fact, it is not even clear that there ever was a *single* parent text from which variant forms descended. What we have instead is an almost unlimited number of variations on a tale, each with its own idiosyncratic features.

What the Finnish School has succeeded in demonstrating is that the basic structure of specific tales is everywhere roughly the same. The architectural fulfillment, by contrast, varies as we move from, say, Russia through Germany to France. If the structure of a specific tale type has not yet been precisely defined, it is all the more important for the interpreter of a folkloric text to proceed comparatively in order to identify regional peculiarities, narratorial eccentricities, religiously motivated substitutions, modernizing tendencies, and other deviations from the norm. Comparative analysis of the tales compiled by the Grimms is greatly facilitated by three massive volumes that summarize plots from the world over of variant forms of each tale in the *Nursery and Household Tales*.[7] Produced by Johannes Bolte and Georg Polívka, the multivolume study stands as an indispensable, if somewhat dated, reference tool for those seeking to sharpen their knowledge of what makes a story from the Grimms' collection stand out from other national and international variants.

We have already seen how Wilhelm Grimm took pains to ensure that no hint of bawdiness appeared in "Rapunzel." The heroine of his edited version still gives birth to twins during her exile, but there is no indication that conception took place in the tower or, for that matter, that it took place at all. Wilhelm Grimm may have eliminated any hint of a causal relationship between the prince's visits and Rapunzel's pregnancy, but his counterparts in other countries were less inclined to do so. Mlle de la Force, who claimed to have invented the story "Persinette," treats the discovery of pregnancy in the following way:

> The prince was happy, Persinette also grew to love him; they saw each other every day, and soon thereafter she found that she was pregnant. That unfamiliar state worried her seriously, the prince knew of it and did not want to explain what had happened for fear of making her unhappy.[8]

Here the facts of life are treated in a matter-of-fact tone, and Rapunzel remains an innocent despite carnal knowledge.

The Pentamerone by Giambattista Basile handles the episode in a different fashion. Petrosinella and the prince have been meeting secretly in the tower. Every day the heroine pulls the prince up into her room, where he "feasts with that sprig of parsley at the banquet of love." An old gossip in the neighborhood soon warns the ogress of the tower to be on her guard, "for Petrosinella and a youth were in love with one another and she feared, from the buzzing of that big fly as he went in and out, that things had gone pretty far; also she thought those two wouldn't be waiting till May before they were flitting, carrying off with them all there was in the house."[9] Basile

clearly was writing with a different audience in mind. His uninhib-
ited, ribald account deviates sharply from Wilhelm Grimm's solemn
treatment of the episode. And his Petrosinella seems to display a
healthy carnality not much different from that of the prince.

These kinds of national variations in tone, moral outlook, and detail are the rule in both oral narratives and in their printed counterparts. Behind the Piedmontese figure of Silver Nose, it is not hard
to recognize the French Bluebeard and the German wizard of "Fowler's Fowl." The sisters of the Italian heroine scorch the rose they
wear in their hair when they open the door forbidden to them; the
sisters of the French heroine drop a key in a pool of blood; the sisters of the German heroine drop an egg in their fright at the spectacle behind the locked door. Clearly, it is risky to read too much
symbolic significance into the rose, the key, and the egg. The function of the objects in each of these cases remains the same: the
singed rose, the bloody key, and the bloody egg stand as indelible
markers of disobedience. Only the object changes from region to region. In many cases, geography and climate can also leave their imprint on a tale. Versions of "Snow White" told in temperate regions
have the heroine's mother wishing for a child with skin as white as
marble or milk. In Russia, it is Grandfather Frost who often gives
folkloric heroines a hard time. The juniper tree, in the celebrated
German tale of that title, turns into a rose tree when the British tell
the story and into a birch tree when Russians recount it. And a Roman Jack Strong ("Slayer of Five Hundred") proves his strength to
a giant by squeezing water from a rock that is really a hunk of ricotta.

Italo Calvino has observed that every tale, no matter what its origin, "tends to absorb something of the place where it is narrated—a
landscape, a custom, a moral outlook, or else merely a very faint ac-
cent or flavor of the locality."[10] Sometimes that something can be
trivial (ricotta substituted for plain cheese), but often it takes on a
representative significance, telling us something about the ethos
and assumptions of the culture in which a given tale took hold and
developed in new directions. Comparative studies of folkloristic materials tell us that the hero of German tales often distinguishes him-

self from other folk heroes by his industriousness and by the alacrity
with which he undertakes even the most arduous task. Heroines of
French fairy tales have been found to be more sophisticated and
worldly than their German counterparts, but they are also less frequently of royal blood. Magic is less likely to set events in motion in
German than in Russian fairy tales, and its role is even less pronounced in French stories.[11]

When we read and interpret a fairy tale, it is important to bring to
it some knowledge of national and international variants of the tale.
Once we realize that German female Cinderellas did not outnumber
male Cinderellas until the eighteenth century, we look at the
Grimms' version of the story with different eyes. The discovery of
male Cinderellas and Snow Whites in modern Turkish folklore invites further meditations and investigations. That Russian folklore
has a male Sleeping Beauty reminds us that we must show caution
in drawing generalizations about female developmental patterns on
the basis of that plot. And we are obliged to think twice about male
hero patterns when we come across a collection of tales depicting
heroines who carry out tasks normally put to male heroes alone or
who denounce fathers too weak to protect them from evil-minded
stepmothers.

Even with the assistance of an archetypal form, it is not always
easy to determine which aspects of a fairy tale are culture bound and
which elements function as part of its timeless, universal structure.
It is even more difficult to establish the precise cultural epoch that
influenced the moral climate of an entire folkloric text or that gave
rise to changes in particular narrative details. Take the case of the
Grimms' collection. To what extent do those stories embody the
Grimms' values and moral outlook? To what degree did the narrators of the tales place the stamp of their own personalities on the
tales? Who were the informants of those narrators, and what was
their precise contribution to the texture of the stories they passed
on? Many of the Grimms' sources may have been middle class, but
they could have heard the tales from persons of lower social standing. Are the stories reflectors of early nineteenth-century Hessian
life, of the milieu in which the brothers heard and collected the

tales? Or, since many of the Grimms' informants came from solid Huguenot stock and told tales heavily colored by Perrault's influence, do they bear the trademark of eighteenth-century French mores and manners? Even the famous "alte Marie" (old Marie), long heralded as possessing impeccable credentials as a rugged elderly German narrator and therefore a star witness for the "Germanness" of the Grimms' collection, turned out to have been Marie Hassenpflug (a middle-class woman of Huguenot ancestry) and not Marie Müller (an elderly servant in the house in which Wilhelm Grimm's wife grew up). Then again, as some critics have suggested, the tales may tell us something about the mentality and outlook of central-European peasants. Can we perhaps take them as mirrors of late-medieval customs and values, especially since the social structures of the tales resemble the hierarchies of that era?[12]

With so much lack of clarity about the social, national, and temporal origins of the texts in the Grimms' collection, it becomes difficult to make considered judgments about the extent to which they reveal something about the German folk and about the Grimms. The notoriously conservative character of folklore makes matters all the more difficult; folktales tend to change far more slowly than the world in which they are told. The Grimms' rewriting of texts is, in this respect, particularly felicitous, for it gives us concrete evidence of the changes the Grimms made to satisfy themselves and the tastes of the German audience for which they were preparing the collection. Those changes generally had more to do with cultural codes and rules of conduct than with social and economic realities. While the behavior of various characters in the Grimms' tales often squares with our own conceptions of early-nineteenth-century life, the setting in which those characters move is distinctly medieval. On the most basic level, the fairy tale's cast of characters— kings, queens, princes, princesses, soldiers, craftsmen, and peasants—reflects the social stratification of a feudal society. That life at the court often resembles the daily routine on the farm, that a king may display peasant cunning rather than regal wisdom, or that a queen does not find it beneath her dignity to louse a bear are facts that need not detain us here. What counts is that the fairy tale's institutions generally mirror those of feudal times. The inheritance customs set down in tales featuring a man and his three sons remind us that we are in a premodern world where favoring the eldest son is essential to preserving the patrimony. "Hans in Luck" and other stories of foolish exchanges that turn hard-earned gains into worthless pebbles reflect the preoccupations of a society in which much of the economic activity was based on bartering. The degree to which spinning stands as a woman's destiny (unless she is rescued from household drudgery by a prince or clever enough to convince her husband that spinning will deform her) points once again to the early origins of these tales. It takes no special degree of historical sophistication to recognize that the social structures, institutions, and economic networks of many fairy tales are based on medieval or, at least, premodern models. To be sure, the origins of these tales may well go back even further, though to date them from the Ice Age, as one critic does, seems to be stretching a point.[13]

No one has succeeded in establishing the exact (or even approximate) time during which the story "Hansel and Gretel" took place, yet historians seem to have focused on it as an especially rich source of cultural data. One historian argues that the tale is wholly realistic, reflecting premodern social conditions in which "wicked stepmothers were not a subject of fantasy any more than castout children." According to the Grimms, the situations in their particular collection were so commonplace that most readers would have no trouble recognizing them as true to life. For an example of the many "basic situations" depicted in the tales, they referred their readers to the case of impoverished parents who drive their children from hearth and home, leaving them to starve in the woods. Another was the case of the hard-hearted stepmother who is an expert in child abuse, making life unbearable for her husband's children.[14]

Even as late as 1806, the year in which the Grimms first began collecting tales, child abandonment—along with infanticide—was not so uncommon a practice among the poor as to make its fictional portrayal appear more sensationalistic than realistic. And given the high mortality rate for women during their childbearing years, a stepmother in the household (and a hostile one at that) came perilously close to counting as the rule rather than as the exception. Situations that stand as exceptional in our own day and age were not necessarily unheard of in another era. As shocking as the deeds of Hansel and Gretel's parents may seem to us (especially if we momentarily divorce them from their fairy-tale context), they may have tallied with the cruel social realities faced by readers and listeners of earlier generations. For the Grimms, in any case, the basic facts of fairy-tale family life often squared with the facts of everyday life.

Eugen Weber has correctly argued that fairy tales can tell us much about "real conditions in the world of those who told and those who heard the tales." But to suggest, as he does, that those tales may be about "real people" strains credibility. Hans Traxler's witty volume on the "truth" about Hansel and Gretel amply demonstrates the folly of taking too literal a view of fairy tales. The amateur archaeologist who figures as the hero of Traxler's chronicle decides to do what no one before him has ever contemplated doing: he reads the tale of Hansel and Gretel "as if it were a factual account." And after a few years of spade work, he succeeds in identifying the precise location of the two protagonists' family home (directly adjacent to the Autobahn connecting Frankfurt to Würzburg), in discovering the foundations of the witch's hut (in the darkest reaches of the forest), and in unearthing various artifacts (ossified remnants of *Lebkuchen* and other sweets). All those archaeological "finds" document and verify the historic encounter between children and witch.[15]

It is an error to see in folktales nothing more than historical documents that can enrich our understanding of previous epochs. Even the most seemingly realistic tales (stories of discharged soldiers, tricksters, apprentices, or thieves) tend to the absurd and rarely chronicle the exploits of actual individuals. Still, there is much in every folktale that requires awareness of social realities, just as there is much that defies historical explanation. The prelude to the principal action in "Hansel and Gretel," for example, is largely realistic, if also melodramatic. Parental abandonment of children is no routine, everyday event, but it remains within the confines of plausibility. Not so with the incidents that follow hard upon the desertion of the children. Here, fairy tales and facts part company. Once Hansel and Gretel enter the forest, they find themselves in a world that not only admits the supernatural, but also takes it completely for granted. Here houses can be made of bread, roofs of cake, and windows of sugar; witches with red eyes lie eagerly in wait for young innocents; and ducks routinely offer children ferry service. Supernatural events, by their very nature, invite interpretation. The stepmother in "Hansel and Gretel" may be nothing more than a stepmother and may therefore act in psychologically predictable terms, but the witch in that same tale is clearly a figure invested with symbolic significance pointing beyond the historical realities of witchcraft. Who would be so literal minded as to try to explain Hansel and Gretel's encounter with her in realistic terms?

Those who train their interpretive powers on Hansel and Gretel's conquest of the witch must therefore move from literal to symbolic readings of the plot. There are, of course, many ways to interpret the struggle that takes place between children and witch. That struggle may be symbolic rather than realistic, but symbolic of what? Reduced to its essential components, it represents a situation in which x threatens y, and y (the weaker of the two) turns the tables on x. The tale may pit adult against child, but it may also (and has been said to) dramatize a conflict between aristocracy and peasantry, master and slave, or between two hostile nations. Reduced to its essential components, it mounts a struggle between any two entities with competing interests. The simplicity of fairy-tale plots invites multiple readings and allows interpretive pluralism to reign supreme. "Little Red Riding Hood," to return to our initial example, lends itself to the sort of reductive operations performed on "Hansel and Gretel." There again, strength confronts weakness and any predatory power can be substituted for the wolf, with any innocent standing in for the heroine. There is inevitably a certain arbitrariness in determining exactly what kind of symbolic struggle is enacted in fairy-tale episodes that depart from everyday reality.

Just as fairy tales veer off from reality into fantasy, so fairy-tale interpretations can easily leave the firm ground of textual realities to drift off into airy regions of ideological fancy. It is easy to shut out the realistic opening paragraph of a fairy tale and to focus solely on the skeletal outlines of the larger, surrealistic content. But the facts of family life that so often set the stage for a hero's adventures form an integral part of each tale; to ignore them is to do violence to the entire text. For that reason, interpretations that neglect to take the hero's full history into account often fail to ring true. Since fairy tales concern themselves with family conflict and since conflicts at home so often anticipate the struggles that lie ahead, it makes eminent sense to look at the psychological dynamics of the initial conflict as a source of interpretive clues and cues for the body of the text. Most fairy tales consist of two parts seamlessly joined: focusing on one alone can lead to a kind of interpretive arbitrariness that allows fairy tales to serve as the scaffolding for anything ranging from a personal philosophy to a political ideology.

That arbitrariness is revealed in its most pronounced form in the interpretive fashions of British folklorists writing during the Victorian era. For those scholars, myths, heroic legends, and folktales alike had nothing to do with the facts of human life; instead they dramatized cosmological battles between the sun and the night. A dragon-slaying hero was enshrined as the solar hero conquering the dark forces of the night, the gleaming rays of the sun represented by his sword, spear, or arrows. The entire pantheon of Greek heroes, from Achilles to Odysseus, became exemplars of solar heroes who undertake long westward journeys filled with arduous labors culminating in death and rebirth. Fairy tales were no exception to the rule that human drama is a metaphor for expressing cosmic processes. One of the more renowned exponents of comparative mythology saw solar deities in both Cinderella and the Frog-King, but also in nearly every other fairy-tale hero. For him Hansel and Gretel were nothing but dawn children; the gold that is their reward at the end of the tale represents the radiance of the sun. The sweet voice of reason ultimately reasserted itself in folkloric studies when Andrew Lang counseled against hurrying to explain every incident in a fairy tale as a "reference to the natural phenomena of Dawn, Sunset, Wind, Storm, and the like." Our own day and age has witnessed (to borrow a phrase from Richard Dorson) the total eclipse of solar mythology, which has become an obscure science of little more than antiquarian interest.[16]

The errors of solar mythology sound a warning to proceed with caution when it comes to decoding the symbolic action of fairy tales. But by translating fairy tales about human conflicts into plots about the movement of celestial bodies, the comparative mythologists of the nineteenth century stood to gain in at least one respect: they were able to protect themselves from facing the entire array of disturbing events portrayed in folktales and myths. Max Müller, one of the founding fathers of comparative mythology, was not in the least embarrassed to admit that his interpretive methods were particularly helpful in divesting classical myths of their more revolting features.[17] For him as for his colleagues, a cannibalistic father was not a monstrously unnatural parent, but a cipher for the heavens which periodically devour and release the clouds. Children abandoned by their parents in the woods were nothing more than stars sent out to brighten the night. In short, myths and fairy tales tell us almost nothing about human nature; instead they are testimony to primitive man's obsession with the activities of nature.

If comparative mythologists reduced fairy tales to allegories about the natural processes that surround us, psychoanalytically oriented critics have moved to the other extreme by viewing fairy tales as symbolic transcriptions of psychic processes. Within one year of Freud's publication of *The Interpretation of Dreams*, Friedrich von der Leyen set forth the thesis that fairy tales were nothing but narrated dreams—dreams passed down from one generation to another until their source became obscured. More recently, Géza Róheim has argued for applying the tools of dream analysis to folktales and myths, which in his view began as narrated dreams and ended as communal property after having enjoyed wide circulation and general popularity. From introspection, however, most of us know that dreams rarely possess the surface logic and integrity of folktales and myths. And from personal experience, we also know that dreams recounted to us by others may be amusing but rarely have the compelling qualities of folkloric performances. To state flatly that dreams are the ultimate source of folktales is to reduce

fairy tales and folk tales to whimsical fantasies that, for want of information about those who dreamed them, defy interpretation. Few
psychoanalysts would be prepared to analyze a dream knowing
nothing about the dreamer.[18]

Still more wrong-headed than the attempt to reduce fairy tales to
narrated dreams is the art of finding sexual symbolism in every con-
cave or convex shape that appears in the path of fairy-tale heroes.
Ernest Jones's essay on psychoanalysis and folklore exemplifies the
extent to which the efforts of critics can be misguided by excessive
emphasis on sexual symbolism. Taking off a bride's shoe, Jones asserts, has "the same defloration significance as to tear through the
bridal wreath or to loosen [a] girdle." "Symbols with the same meaning," he adds, ". . . are the cowry shell, the crescent moon, innumer-
able cups, goblets, cauldrons, and caskets, and almost any object
with an opening, from door portals and snake-stones to hollow trees
or even the opening under a leaning ladder."[19] One can scarcely
help wonder how Jones would have interpreted the tale of Thousandfurs, who flees her father's castle with a golden ring, a spinning
wheel, and a bobbin, and then hides in the hollow of a tree, conceals
her clothing in a nutshell, and prepares a tureen of soup with a ring
at its bottom for the king who marries her in the end. The possibilities become too dizzying to contemplate.

That psychoanalytic critics rarely agree on the symbolic meaning
of an object or a figure in a tale is also not designed to inspire confidence in their methods. When one critic tells us that the dwarves
in "Snow White" should be viewed as siblings of the heroine, another asserts that they represent the unconscious, and a third declares them to be symbols for creative activity, is it any wonder that
the layman raises an eyebrow in bewilderment? And when we are
further offered the option of looking at those figures as symbolic
representations of the heroine's genitals or as a knot of homosex-
uals, it becomes difficult to stifle a protest.[20] Such variations in interpretive judgments are, of course, not characteristic of the psychoanalytic school alone, but the broad range of critics attracted to
that school (many from neighboring disciplines) produces more
than the usual diversity. There are the Jungians with their emphasis

on initiation rites and mother-daughter relationships, the Freudians with their Oedipus and Electra complexes, and the legion of disciples who have carried the precepts of the masters in novel, often unorthodox, directions.

Some psychoanalytically oriented critics are more sophisticated in their interpretations, if not necessarily more convincing. Karl Abraham's reading of "The Magic Table, the Gold Donkey, and the Cudgel in the Sack" is almost perversely ingenious in its tidiness and comprehensiveness. The tale he analyzes recounts the fortunes of three sons driven from home by their father. Each learns a trade and is rewarded by his master at the end of a long apprenticeship. The first son receives a table that responds to the command "Set yourself!" by making an entire meal appear out of nowhere. The second son receives a donkey that answers to the word "Bricklebrit" by expelling gold pieces "both from the front and the behind." The third son receives a stick that reacts to the order "Cudgel, come out of the sack!" by jumping out of its receptacle and giving its owner's enemies a sound thrashing. This folktale, according to Abraham, represents "a triple wish fulfillment related to the three erogenous zones." The first son receives full gratification of oral desires; the second son succeeds in satisfying anal hoarding impulses; the third son, who triumphs in the end and wins the approval of his father, has reached the genital stage, characterized by potency, command, and control (along with a good measure of sadistic aggression, though Abraham neglects to mention this). In seizing on the parallels between a plot pattern and a psychoanalytic doctrine, Abraham ends by telling us more about the Freudian doctrine than about the tale. In effect, he replaces one myth with another. Those who make it their business to study fairy tales must see to it that they tell us more about the tales than about their particular school of thought.[21]

For all its excesses, psychoanalytic criticism has scored numerous successes in its encounters with fairy tales. When we review some of the preferred themes of fairy tales (incest, fratricide, child abandonment, cannibalism, and so on), it becomes clear that in this arena even the most restrained Freudian interpreter can have a field day. Fairy tales take us into a world where taboos may still be in force but where transgression is the motor of the plot. The notorious flatness of fairy-tale characters may discourage critics from trying to read their minds and analyze their motivations, but the boldness of their deeds invites careful scrutiny. Those deeds may be rooted in realistic situations, but they are often so far removed from reality that they demand symbolic readings. Psychological realism and social realism do not stand as special strengths of the fairy tale.

Lenin was right (as Soviet folklorists never tire of declaring) to state that "there are elements of reality in every folktale." But it would be naive to believe (and Lenin evidently understood this) that folktales mirror the social conditions of an earlier age. Even when the cast of characters in a folktale consists of peasants, soldiers, noblemen, and knaves (rather than talking animals, enchanted princes, or demons in the wood), those figures engage in acts so preposterous or outrageous as to defy credibility. "Who has ever seen fools deceiving everyone and never bested?" Vladimir Propp quite rightly inquires. "Do there exist clever thieves who steal eggs from under a duck or the sheet from under a landowner and his wife? . . . In the Russian folktale there is *not a single* credible plot." The same holds true for the Grimms' collection, which recounts the fortunes of a Master Thief (who steals sheets from under a count and abducts a priest and sexton), of Bearskin (who vows not to comb his hair, cut his nails, or say a prayer for seven years), and of Liza-Kate (who dries a wet cellar floor by sprinkling flour on it and repairs gouges in the road by pouring butter into them). Here too, the episodes hardly aim at achieving verisimilitude, and the characters are generally unlike any encountered in everyday life. As W. H. Auden wrote: "No fairy story ever claimed to be a description of the external world and no sane child ever believed that it was." The assumption that folktales faithfully record reality simply does not hold up under close scrutiny of the tales. In certain fine points of detail we can find traces of the epoch in which a tale was told, just as new twists and turns given to the development of plot and character may reveal something about the cultural climate in which a tale developed.[22]

In sum, there are always bits and pieces of historical and cultural realities in folktales, but they are often embedded in a text that tends toward the surreal. Fairy-tale heroes may begin their folkloric careers at home in a commonplace setting and they may end them in a castle in a naturalistic milieu, but the world that lies in-between is less natural than supernatural, less ordinary than extraordinary, and less real than surreal. The magic and enchantment of that world have some bearing on everyday reality, but it is generally pointless to turn the historian's beacon on that particular world in search of signs of the times. Once a fairy-tale hero leaves the realistically portrayed world designated as home to enter a realm that admits the supernatural, he moves into an arena that lends itself more readily to literary and psychological analysis than to historical inquiry. The magical spells cast by witches, ogres, and fairies have a habit of transforming not just a single character, but an entire universe. An enchanted prince lives in a charmed world; a talking animal inhabits a marvelous realm; and a princess who cannot laugh lives in a quaintly exotic kingdom. These spheres are more likely to harbor inner than outer realities, to incarnate psychic truths rather than social facts, and to represent figurative expressions rather than literal meanings. The first step toward understanding some of the timeless ideas embedded in fairy tales requires identifying the recurrent themes, stock characters, and repetitive patterns that constitute folkloric texts. For this we will have to look to the tales and then move from the folklore of fairy tales to the folklore of the human mind.

3

VICTIMS AND SEEKERS
The Family Romance of Fairy Tales

> Truth is I would not give one tear shed over Little Red
> Ridinghood for all the benefit to be derived from a
> hundred histories of Tommy Goodchild.
>
> —SIR WALTER SCOTT

IN REAL LIFE, every unhappy family may be unhappy in its own
way, but in fairy tales unhappy families are all very much alike.
Nearly every sibling is a rival, and at least one parent is an ogre. The
protagonists of the Grimms' tales are less heroes doing battle with
dark forces than victims of hostile powers. Mary's Child is almost
burned at the stake; Cinderella suffers at the hands of her stepmother and stepsisters; Thousandfurs leads a wretched life sweeping ashes in the kitchen; Little Brother is bewitched by his stepmother; young boys in "The Carnation" and in "Fledgling" are the
targets of murderous plots hatched by the cooks in their households; Snow White is left to die in the woods; and Rapunzel is exiled
to a tower because of her mother's strange cravings. As the fairy-tale
heroine known as Two-eyes tells the prince who rescues her from a
life of being bullied and tormented by her sisters, One-eye and
Three-eyes, "I've been suffering hunger and thirst, misery and
hardship from dawn to dusk. If you were to take me away with you
and save me from all that, I would be very happy." Hers is no over-
statement for most fairy-tale heroes.

Time and again we find that an accident of birth or an event following hard upon the birth of the hero accounts for the misfortunes
chronicled in the tale. Mothers die in childbirth; parents are so des-

perate to have a child that they declare themselves prepared to accept a hedgehog for a son; a slighted tutelary spirit makes a sinister prophecy at a christening; parents trade their newborn for a trifle; poverty or evil omens induce one or the other parent to abandon a child. Magic and plain old-fashioned bad luck often conspire to torment a fairy-tale hero, but ultimately the hero's parents—his progenitors and guardians—are directly implicated in the misfortunes

FIGURE 6. *Hansel and Gretel rank among the most renowned victims of parental abuse. Hermann Vogel's illustration for that story reminds us that fairy-tale heroes and heroines generally react to a crisis by sitting down and having a good cry.*

that besiege him. The errors of their ways, ranging from neglect to tyranny, fuel the conflicts that drive fairy-tale plots.[1]

It may well be that some of the fairy-tale episodes rehearsed above capture aspects of the harsh social climate of past eras. Child abandonment, as noted earlier, was by no means an uncommon practice in earlier centuries, particularly in times of war, famine, and other extreme situations. Yet even in cultures where child abandonment is supposedly rare or unknown, the theme of children deserted at birth figures prominently in folkloric traditions. Ruth Benedict discovered that among the Zuni, the largest Pueblo tribe in the Southwest of the United States, the theme loomed large in folktales, although the practice was wholly alien to the culture. This stark contrast between narrative convention and contemporary social custom could not, for Benedict, be adequately explained by the cultural conservatism of folklore, by its tendency to lag behind the times. The popularity of the theme of abandoned children seemed rather to stem from psychic sources, from childhood daydreams and fantasies about grudges and reprisals against parents. Since folktales described abandonment in elaborate detail and dwelt on the misery of the deserted victim, Benedict reasoned that they were "motivated by resentment" with the intent of maneuvering the daydreamer into the martyr's position. So deeply rooted were the feelings that gave rise to those plots that even adults appeared to have no trouble identifying with the child-hero, rather than with the parental figures.[2]

Fantasy, more than fact, seems to serve as the basis for that vast class of fairy tales in which the central figure is a victimized hero. Such tales can be found all over the world; they are by no means limited to the stories told by the Zuni or to the texts compiled by the Grimms. Although they constitute only a portion of all fairy tales, they exercise an enduring fascination on the popular imagination, numbering among the most compelling tales in the folkloric repertory. Tales of victimized heroes may be anchored in a realistic situation, but they are far more likely to veer off in the direction of the whimsical, bizarre, and supernatural than folk tales concerned with peasant lore or with barnyard wisdom. By virtue of their deep supernatural coloring, they belong to (and to a great extent comprise) the category of what folklorists call magic tales (*Zaubermärchen*) or wondertales.[3] Family conflicts, rather than the class conflicts of folk tales set on farms and in villages, lie at the heart of these stories. The family drama of fairy tales lines up hero against parent, then often puts the hero at a further disadvantage by allying siblings (usually of the same sex as the hero) with that parent. As the tale unfolds, the intrafamilial conflict escalates; parents and siblings become ever more vindictive, and the hero's sufferings multiply.

Magic tales concerned with family conflicts typically take place in a domain where the supernatural is accepted as part and parcel of everyday reality. The appearance of witches, gnomes, or seven-headed dragons may arouse fear, dread, or curiosity, but it never evokes the slightest degree of surprise or astonishment. Not a single fairy-tale character marvels at the marvelous. Even more than other literary fictions, magic tales demand the willing suspension of disbelief. Lacking the satirical strain found in folk tales about peasant life as well as the pronounced didacticism of animal fables, they stand as a breed apart. These are typically adventure stories, short on descriptive passages and psychological analysis, but packed with drama and melodrama. The characters are defined solely by their relationship to the protagonist, each belonging unambiguously to the camp of good or of evil. Fairy tales chart the rise of a single, central hero as he moves through a magical foreign realm from an oppressed condition in the drab world of everyday reality to a shining new reality. The hero of such tales is a "traveler between two worlds," a secular pilgrim on the road to wealth and marriage.[4] He is the outsider who becomes the insider, the rebel who turns conformist, the victim who triumphs over his oppressors. As he moves from humble origins to an elevated rank, he passes through an enchanted realm that becomes a stage for the deeds that constitute his history. Stories depicting the rising fortunes of a humble hero as he passes through a supernatural world have come to be known in popular discourse as fairy tales (the most comfortable English equivalent for the German term *Märchen*). As the true purveyors of magic and enchantment, they are clearly more entitled to that name than the many cautionary tales, legends, ghost stories, jests, and animal fables liberally sprinkled throughout the Grimms' collection. Even if they rarely contain actual fairies, they take place in a realm that readily admits the possibility that such creatures exist.

Vladimir Propp gives a useful preliminary definition of what I refer to as the oral fairy tale. (Propp's English translator uses the term *wondertale* to designate this class of folktales.) "A wondertale," Propp writes, "begins with some harm or villainy done to someone (for example, abduction or banishment) or with a desire to have something (a king sends his son in quest of the firebird), and develops through the hero's departure from home and encounters with a donor. . . . Further along, the tale includes combat with an adversary . . . a return, and a pursuit."[5] In morphological terms, an act of villainy and the presence of a need are functionally equivalent; that is, they can both stand as first links in the chain of events that constitutes the fairy tale's plot. But *villainy* and *lack* are curious as paired terms in that they stand in no evident relationship of analogy with or opposition to each other. To understand how they can operate as homologous terms in the narrative logic of fairy tales, we must turn to textual examples. The Grimms' Hansel and Gretel, we recall, begin their adventures as victims of parental villainy. Parental malice does not, however, drive the Russian Sister Alyonushka and Brother Ivanushka to go out into the world to seek their fortunes; a dark cloud whisks away their parents, leaving them orphaned. In a British version, both parents fall ill and die. An Italian variant has a child who loses her parents by straying too far into the woods in search of chicory. In all of these cases, either the presence of evil (villainy) or the absence of good (lack) is the prime mover of events. Villainy and lack ultimately have the same function, even if they appear under different narrative guises.

Just as villainy creates victims, a lack leads to a search. The hero of a fairy tale can be either victim or seeker, a meek martyr or a bold adventurer. As a passive victim of circumstances, adventures befall him; as an active seeker of worldly glory, he embarks on a search with a specific goal. These two contrasting characterizations of fairy-tale figures pertain as much to German as to Russian stories, though it is easy to show, on a statistical basis, that the Grimms' collection has a disproportionately large number of oppressed heroes, while Russian collections tend to favor dragon slayers. Still, in practice, it is not always easy to distinguish between victim-heroes and seeker-heroes.[6] Think of the many simpleton sons who are banished from home by belligerent fathers yet who are engaged in a quest of some kind. The line between victim and seeker becomes very hazy indeed in nearly all tales of that type. If victims can easily turn into seekers, seekers can readily slip into the role of victim. On the first leg of her journey to a distant kingdom, where she is to meet her betrothed, the Goose Girl is coerced into changing roles with her servant and lives in the most humble of circumstances as an assistant gooseherd. The search in this case is subverted by a villain who turns the protagonist into a victim. While many fairy tales cast their heroes in the double role of victim and seeker, others feature a victim and a seeker in the same tale, with a subordinate role assigned to one or the other. A tale may be narrated from the victim's point of view (as in "Cinderella"), but it will include a seeker (the young prince who marries Cinderella); or it may be told from the vantage point of the seeker (a dragon-slaying prince), who liberates a victim (an enchanted princess held captive by a beast). In sum, victims and seekers may peacefully coexist within a single role or alternatively collaborate as separate, unequal partners.

Propp's definition of the fairy tale is based on a rigorous analysis of one hundred tales from Alexander Afanas'ev's collection of Russian folktales (*Narodnye russkie skazki*), but it seems to know few national boundaries and fits certain Neapolitan tales as neatly as it does some Finnish tales. Although Propp's full model of the fairy tale's specific components tallies best with Eurasian narratives, it can be applied with some modification to African and North American folklore. Just as certain motifs occur with astonishing regularity (often with a unique twist) at every point on the folkloric map, certain fundamental patterns emerge as one studies the way in which those motifs are ordered in a specific narrative. Fairy tales have many marvelous features, but none perhaps so disarming as their persistent thematic and structural uniformity. Reading fairy tales from the world over, one is struck time and again by a feeling of *déjà lu* or *déjà entendu*.

Folklorists have advanced two different, although not entirely incompatible, theories to account for the remarkable congruity found among fairy tales of all cultures. The first, known as the theory of migration or borrowing, proceeds along the assumption that nothing new is ever discovered so long as it is possible to copy.[7] Or, as Sir Walter Scott put it after observing the striking resemblances among tales from widely varying cultures, "the poverty of human imagination" is greater than he would ever have surmised.[8] In its most extreme formulation, the theory of migration states that one specific locale (nineteenth-century German scholars fixed on India as the favored candidate) served as the generating matrix for all fairy tales. During the random process of transmission via oral and literary traditions, variant forms of the tales surfaced in other, often remote, regions. The original content and underlying structure of the tales, however, remained intact in all the essentials throughout the tale's travels. To many folklorists, this theory seems inadequate, for even where there are no discernible paths of diffusion linking two regions, it is still possible to detect striking similarities between the tales that thrive in each. More seriously, the theory of migration utterly fails to consider the vital question of where the tales came from in the first place. Still, this is the theory that has enjoyed wide appeal among folklorists of a historical bent, in particular among exponents of the Finnish School.

The view that one parent tale in one fixed location spawned numerous progeny the world over has come to be known as the theory of monogenesis and diffusion. The contrasting theory of polygenesis assumes that resemblances among tales can be attributed to independent invention in places unconnected by trade routes or travel. Vladimir Propp challenged the truth of monogenesis and diffusion when he asked: "How is one to explain the similarity of the tale about the frog queen in Russia, Germany, France, India, in America among the Indians, and in New Zealand, when the contact of peoples cannot be proven historically?"[9] Although Propp hedged on the answer, he seemed to favor a psychological explanation, a

theory that traced the resemblances among tales to the uniform disposition of the human psyche. While those who subscribe to the theory of monogenesis repeatedly draw attention to the birth and evo-
lution of tales (when, where, and how they arose and developed),
defenders of polygenesis endorse the notion of spontaneous generation and focus on the meaning of tales. For the latter, the human
psyche figures as the breeding ground for folkloristic plots; it needs
no contact with external sources to conceive the universal fantasies
embodied in fairy tales.

According to those who hold that similar tales arise all over the
world by a process of spontaneous generation, something about the
texture of life exercises a limiting force on the folkloric imagination.
To cast this view in its most banal terms: "The limitations of human
life and the similarity of its basic situations necessarily produce tales
. . . everywhere alike in all important structural aspects." Or as Wilhelm Grimm declared more than a century ago to explain the recurrent themes in the tales collected by him and his brother: "There
are certain situations so simple and natural that they can be found
everywhere." On a more sophisticated level, critics have argued that
fairy tales translate the eternal truths of mental life into concrete actions and images. They may incarnate the highest hopes and the
deepest fears of every childhood, or they may preserve the fantasies
and phobias of an earlier age, of the childhood of mankind. In the
savage practices and violent events depicted in fairy tales, those critics have found an expression of regressive modes of thought or of
primitive ways of life. Both these views—one emphasizing the uniformity of life in general, the other stressing continuities in the life
of the mind—suggest that fairy tales traffic in truths so fundamental
to life and so universal in their application that they are necessarily
alike everywhere.[10]

Although the theories of monogenesis and polygenesis are useful
in accounting for the prevalence of certain basic themes in fairy
tales, neither is especially compelling in its formulation. Literature
in general, after all, shows signs of foreign influences and concerns
itself with the fundamentals of human life yet fails to exhibit the curiously inbred qualities of fairy-tale plots. Roman Jakobson, how-

ever, has convincingly argued that the freedom of creative invention is far more severely curtailed in folkloric forms than in literature: "The socialized sections of mental culture," he writes, "as for instance language or folk tale, are subject to much stricter and more uniform laws than fields in which individual creation prevails." Folklore operates as a system oriented toward conventions sanctioned by a cultural community; literature, by contrast, permits a far broader range and variety of utterances that can conform to or violate the conventions of the system from which they derive. The strictures imposed on folkloric inventiveness, it should be added, stem to a great extent from the censorship exercised by the audiences for the tales. The work of an individual can flout convention, run counter to the expectations of its contemporary readers, and meet with nearly universal disapproval. Yet it may still eventually join the canon of classical works. A folktale, on the other hand, must win the consensus of a collective body before it becomes part of a standard repertory of tales.[11]

It is easy to make a case for contrasting folkloric convention with literary invention, but it becomes more difficult to identify the strict and uniform laws to which folkloric performances must adhere. As a "socialized section of mental culture," folklore may be the product of a collective activity and serve as a vehicle for expressing collective psychic processes, but its actual laws remain elusive. To identify and define those laws, we must begin by turning to Propp's study of the Russian fairy tale, a work that appeared only one year before Jakobson's analysis.

Propp's declaration that "all fairy tales are of one type in regard to their structure" is startling in its simplicity. In Afanas'ev's collection of Russian folktales, Propp isolated two sets of recurrent features: one concerning the functions of the characters, the other the distribution of their roles. Function is understood by Propp as "an act of character, defined from the point of view of its significance for the course of the action."[12] The thirty-one functions identified by Propp range from absentation and interdiction through various acts of villainy to the hero's final marriage and/or accession to the throne. Not all thirty-one functions are obligatory, but where they do occur, they must always stand in the sequence outlined by Propp. These functions are assigned to seven "spheres of action" designated by the following roles:

1. the villain
2. the donor (provider of magical agents)
3. the helper
4. the princess (or sought-for person) and her father
5. the dispatcher
6. the hero
7. the false hero

Propp recognized that there was no exact one-to-one correlation between his theoretical "spheres of action" and the actual roles of various characters in the tales. The number of characters in a tale can in fact be easily reduced or expanded. One character may take on multiple roles; a witch, for example, can figure at once as a villain, a hostile donor, or an involuntary helper. Think of the crones in "Hansel and Gretel" and "Snow White," or of Rumpelstiltskin, who begins his fairy-tale career as a helper and ends it as a villain. By the same token, several characters may be implicated in a single "sphere of action"; that is, the hero may encounter a number of villains or helpers in his path. Think of the various youngest of three sons who are assisted first by creatures of the air, then by creatures of the sea, and last by creatures of the land.

One of the first Russian reviewers of Propp's *Morphology of the Folktale* hailed its pathbreaking formulations and predicted a great future for the volume. But that future still lay some thirty years off. In the Soviet Union the book failed to provoke interest or to create much of a stir. Only with the appearance of the first English translation in 1958 did Propp's ideas begin to generate enthusiasm among folklorists and literary scholars on both sides of the Atlantic. But even as those ideas caught on, they also came under heavy fire. In the Soviet Union, Propp was vilified as an unpatriotic scoundrel who had "deprived the Russian fairy tale (so dear to us) of all national, ideological, and artistic peculiarities." By daring to suggest that Russian tales were really no different from those "of other European peoples, of the Australians, Polynesians, etc.," Professor

Propp had "bled white" the Russian tale and, worse yet, "robbed it of its soul."[13]

Criticism of Propp's ideas took a somewhat less chauvinistic turn in the West. Although Propp had habitually referred to the "structure" of tales in his morphological analysis, his work was branded hopelessly formalistic by structuralist scholars of the 1960s. (The work *was* formalistic, but not hopelessly so.) In focusing primarily on the linear sequence of events that comprises the narrative pattern of the folktale, Propp had concerned himself with the syntagmatic aspects of narration and neglected its vitally important paradigmatic dimension. He had limited his vision, in other words, to the shallowness of empirical observation and had consequently explored nothing more than the manifest content of folktales. ("I am an empiricist, indeed an incorruptible empiricist," Propp later declared in an attack on Lévi-Strauss, whom he derided as "a philosopher.") What Lévi-Strauss and others searched for in vain in the *Morphology* was an attempt to unearth the fundamental structures of meaning in folktales. It was simply not enough to list thirty-one functions and seven spheres of action. How did each of those thirty-one functions and seven spheres of action relate to each other? What fundamental patterns of meaning did they reveal? These were the paramount issues for Propp's audience in the West.[14]

Those of a structuralist persuasion found in A.-J. Greimas an impassioned champion for their critique of Propp's formalistic errors. With the hope of deepening Propp's syntagmatic analysis by assimilating it to Lévi-Strauss's model of paradigmatic analysis, Greimas appropriated Propp's seven spheres of action, reduced them to three pairs of actors, and placed them in binary opposition to each other. Those binary relations, Greimas observed, formed the basis of a model (*modèle actantiel*) that generates an infinite number of texts, the entire repertory of folkloric performances.[15] Greimas' scheme consists of six actors placed in a syntactic relation (indicated by arrows) to each other:

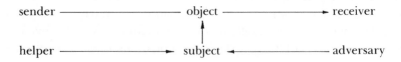

If Propp's roles are mapped onto this diagram, the following scheme emerges:

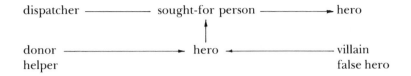

```
dispatcher ——————— sought-for person ——————→ hero
                            ↑
donor ———————————→ hero ←——————————— villain
helper                                false hero
```

The superimposition of Propp's spheres of action on Greimas' model results in a duplication of the hero's role—he is at once the central subject and the receiver in the tale. Greimas is therefore obliged to argue that the folktale, by unfolding a situation in which these two roles are fused, presents a special case in narrative. Yet the folktale, as one critic has noted, is by no means the sole narrative form in which a character desires something and then either receives it or fails to receive it.[16] Furthermore, Greimas' model, by placing the relationship sender-receiver on an equal footing with the relationship helper-adversary, deflects attention from the primacy of the helper-adversary opposition in folktales. Nearly every tale has clearly defined helpers and adversaries: the dwarves versus the wicked queen in "Snow White"; a white duck versus the evil witch in "Hansel and Gretel"; the faithful Falada versus a false maid in "The Goose Girl." Extending this list is nothing more than child's play. By contrast, the sender-receiver opposition is fuzzy and becomes problematic once applied to fairy tales. Who is the dispatcher in "Snow White"? Can the stepmother function as dispatcher in "Hansel and Gretel" even if there is no "sought-for person" in that story? The elderly queen in "The Goose Girl" dispatches her daughter to a king, but that king is not the tale's hero.

A far more satisfying arrangement of Propp's dramatis personae has been proposed by the Soviet folklorist Eleazar Meletinsky. For Meletinsky, the hero stands in contrast to all other characters, whose roles are defined solely from his point of view. His is the only "pure" role in the sense that it does not overlap with other roles or merge with its opposite. All other actors in the tale are not necessarily unalloyed villains, helpers, or donors. Rather, they must be situated at some point on a spectrum connecting one functional domain to another. As Propp had already noted, many characters in folktales play multiple roles or share functions with other characters. The witch in "Hansel and Gretel," we recall, figures both as villain and donor (if not motivated by altruism in the latter role). Meletinsky illustrates the continuity between the roles of villain and donor with the following diagram:

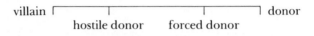

All the functional fields defined by Propp (with the exception of the dispatcher, whose role tends to be peripheral) can be paired and viewed as the initial and terminal points on a continuum. If mapped on a circle, one half-arc of that circle encompasses those who aid the hero in his quest by offering him gifts and counsel, and the other half-arc includes those who test or threaten the hero and thus function as his adversaries.[17]

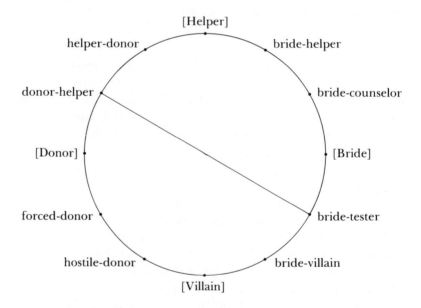

At the risk of engaging in radical reductionism, some folklorists have advanced the view that the fairy tale stages a conflict between

a hero and a villain, with all other characters playing nothing more than supporting roles as allies of one or the other.[18] The hero with his helpers is pitted against a villain and his henchmen. This dichotomy between hero and villain, or between helpers and adversaries, is as basic to the fairy tale as the other pervasive binary oppositions between good and evil, weak and strong, humble and royal, young and old, familiar and alien. Indeed, it seems to serve as the generating source for all those contraries.

In order to extend our understanding of the significance of the fairy tale's ruling tensions, it is useful to analyze the situations that induce the hero to leave home for the marvelous terrain of a foreign realm. The family (specifically, the nuclear family) furnishes the basic configuration of the tale's characters: mother, father, and child. Only rarely is a grandparent cast in a cameo role; uncles, aunts, cousins, and other more distant kin are, as a rule, absent from the repertoire of characters. The world of fairy tales is generally inhabited by two groups at opposite ends of the social and economic spectrum: humble folk and royal personages. Fairy tales habitually trace a trajectory from rags to riches, from feeble dependence to royal autonomy, from the dissolution of one nuclear family to the formation of a new one. The tale's hero is a wanderer, if not always in body at least in spirit. Exiled from home or, what amounts to the same, banished to the hearth, his path takes him from a lowly condition at home to a world of enchantment and finally back to a modified and elevated form of his original condition. Cast in the dual role of victim in one set of family circumstances and seeker in another, he can slip with ease from a state of abject self-pity to one of bold resourcefulness.

The hero's story typically takes place in the remote past, "a long time ago, when wishing was still of use," as the Grimms put it. Yet the wishes of the fairy tale's young heroes are rarely realized on the spot, as some observers have it. The main body of fairy-tale plots is instead devoted to hardships, struggles, and narrow brushes with death both at home and on the road. Those plots may have a happy ending (summed up in a single sentence at the end of the tale), but they also have a habit of translating phobias and fears into palpable physical presences rather than incarnating wishes and desires.[19]

The familiar formula—"once upon a time"—that launches most fairy tales and constitutes their most characteristic feature also introduces the specific family situation that drives the hero from home to the arena of the marvelous. Home, normally the locus of stability and security, becomes the abode of powers at once hostile and sinister.[20] Beginning with a stable situation—the nuclear family at home—the fairy tale quickly shifts to a state of disequilibrium. One member of the family disturbs the initial tranquillity and renders life at home intolerable. The motives for the hero's departure vary: he may be a financial burden to his impoverished parents—yet another mouth for them to feed; he may be a nuisance owing to his stupidity; he may be the target of maternal or paternal rage; or he may wish to avoid punishment for some transgression. In the following tales, the child-hero stands as a victim of parental malice; he has been neglected, chastised, or abandoned by one of his parents. Like every "persecuted" child, he dreams of running away. Escape from home becomes his sole hope and source of consolation. Yet his flight takes him not into a magical kingdom where every wish comes true, but rather into a world peopled by villains with powers far more formidable than those of the villains he left behind him.

The story of Hansel and Gretel admirably illustrates the way in which an evil parent is reflected and distorted in the mirror of the fairy-tale world. The stepmother who fails to nurture the children and who drives them from home reemerges in the woods as a false provider, as a cannibalistic fiend masquerading as a magnanimous mother. In other tales, say "Little Brother and Little Sister," the equation between the two figures is explicitly stated: the witch in the forest is indeed the stepmother stripped of her parental disguise. The evil forces at home habitually reappear, with all their flaws writ large, in the enchanted realm that constitutes the tale's principal setting. The performance of physical feats or the demonstration of mental prowess in the magical world prepares the way for return to a new home. Conquering the forces of evil there implies at once liberation from domestic oppression and elevation to a higher social rank.

The hero generally enters the fairy-tale world in order to escape conditions at home but is exposed to far more perilous situations in the terrain where he seeks refuge. Although he has no allies at home, he finds that enchanted forests and magical kingdoms house not only monstrous adversaries, but also humane helpers. More often than not, his adversaries—whether they take the shape of cunning witches, plotting stepmothers, or foxy chambermaids—retain eminently human features. His allies, on the other hand, are of a different species; diligent bees, bountiful trees, and patiently obliging foxes hasten to the hero's aid. When the Goose Girl leaves her mother to journey to the kingdom of her betrothed, she is accompanied by two attendants, a treacherous maid and a trusty mount. The maid usurps her mistress's place; the faithful Falada reinstates her to a royal position. Cinderella may be subjected to disgrace and humiliation by a stepmother and her daughters, but nature comes to her rescue. Birds discharge her household chores, and a tree planted on her mother's grave provides regal attire for the ball. Although the evil mother or stepmother is very much alive in the fairy tale, the good mother—protecting, loving, and nurturing—is always dead.[21] Yet she does not abandon her child completely, for she inevitably returns in the shape of benevolent natural powers.

The hero of the fairy tale is, in the double sense of both the English and the German terms, a natural child (*ein natürliches Kind*). He may be in danger at home, but he invariably finds shelter and sustenance in nature. At the same time, he is, as both the English and German terms imply, an illegitimate child, the offspring of a union that is, if not illicit, at least mysterious or problematical. It is not entirely by coincidence that so many fairy tales split the mother image to create two wholly separate entities: a superhuman and diabolical stepmother who is fiendishly spry and vigorous, and a benevolent biological mother who is simply no longer around. Nor is it entirely fortuitous that the hero of fairy tales is often portrayed as a stepchild, a child whose true father or mother is not clearly identified and characterized. Note also the number of tales in which one parent is conspicuously absent: only a mother *or* a father makes an appearance. To explore one possible source for the twin themes of "naturalness" and illegitimacy, we must turn from the folkloristic legacy of the Grimm brothers to the fictional fantasies of the human mind.

In a remarkable study entitled "Family Romances" ("Der Familienroman der Neurotiker"), Freud advanced the view that the psychic lives of a certain class of neurotic patients can yield insights into the workings of children's imaginative lives.[22] These patients, rather than abandoning their childhood daydreams, had—in the course of maturing, or rather, aging—preserved, strengthened, and magnified them. Although the so-called family romance of such patients could not be recalled on command, Freud found that parts of it came to light and could be pieced together through psychoanalysis. In his essay, he outlined the main features of the daydreams and fantasies of children as deduced from the fantasy life of certain neurotic patients.

According to Freud, the family romance first takes shape at a time when a child begins to liberate himself from parental authority. A growing sense of dissatisfaction with his parents, stemming from a sense of being slighted or neglected, leads the child to seek relief in the idea that he must be a stepchild or an adopted child. Even after puberty, the child's imagination may be preoccupied with the task of ridding himself of his own parents and replacing them with those of higher social rank. He fancies himself the child of a prominent statesman, a millionaire, an aristocratic landowner—of a person appointed with the very qualities in which his own parents seem most wanting. Such daydreams, Freud points out, serve as the "fulfillment of wishes" and as a "correction of actual life."[23] Freud further observed that although the new, exalted parents are equipped with the attributes of the actual, humble parents and that the child's family romance thus reflects nostalgia for the days when his own mother and father seemed the most noble persons on earth (and when he basked in the light of their glory), he identified an element of revenge and retaliation in the minds of these young romancers. Nostalgia and revolt, exaltation and debasement, reconciliation and revenge: these are the twin motors driving the family romance.

The glorification of one family at the expense of another also constitutes a hallmark of the fairy tale. The family romance spun by the childish imagination seems to replicate the principal thematic features of the family fairy tale created by the popular imagination.[24] Both are generated within the context of an ordinary family setting. The daydreamer of the family romance sees himself as a stepchild or an adopted child and creates a new social order in which he is elevated from humble birth to aristocratic origins. He rids himself of a socially unacceptable father, of a negligent mother, or of otherwise imperfect parents by fashioning a myth about the special circumstances of his birth. Fairy-tale plots differ, however, in one central respect from family romances: while the daydreamer of the family romance succeeds in ridding himself of his parents by rejecting them and fabricating new ones, fairy-tale heroes are rejected by their parents. Fathers are forever banishing their sons, and mothers in the guise of stepmothers habitually exclude their daughters from the family circle. While the protagonist of the family romance is little more than a victim of circumstances (confusion of identity, death of a biological parent, and so on), the hero of the fairy tale is a victim of overt parental malice.

Contrary to conventional wisdom, fairy-tale heroines have no monopoly on victimization. Male and female figures seem to suffer in equal parts, though the narrative duration of female suffering tends to be greater. And the tyrants that oppose and oppress the protagonists of fairy tales are just as likely to be a father as a mother, a king as a queen. Snow White has to dodge traps set by her mother (later turned into a stepmother by the Grimms), but Thousandfurs has to use her wits to elude her father. The hero of "The Three Languages" nearly falls victim to his father's murderous schemes, but the young boy in "The Juniper Tree" is assassinated by his stepmother.[25]

One set of fairy tales casts biological parents (or thinly disguised versions of them) in the role of oppressors but makes those parents so cruel or bloodthirsty that it becomes impossible to think of them as next of kin. The only way to account for their unnatural behavior is to assume that they are impostors who have somehow usurped the position of the real parents. The family established at the tale's end comes to constitute the hero's true family circle of kindred spirits. A second set of fairy tales creates a more complicated scenario with two sets of parents at the very start: the biological progenitors and the adoptive parents. Here the foundling-hero must find his way back from humble foster parents to a royal pair. At this point we must pause to look at a tale from the Grimms' collection to see exactly how fairy tales modify and transform the plot of the family romance even as they preserve its basic structure.

"The Devil with the Three Golden Hairs" recounts the story of an abandoned male child. A "poor woman" bears a son at whose birth a fortuneteller predicts that he will one day marry the king's daughter. Angered by the prophecy, the king of the land (a man who is "wicked at heart") gets his hands on the child, places him in a coffin-like box, and exposes him to the waters. The box miraculously floats down the river and is eventually intercepted by a miller and his wife, who agree to adopt the child. Years later, when the king meets up with the boy, he tries once again to have the lad murdered, but succeeds only in unwittingly engineering a marriage between him and his daughter. Still, the king places further obstacles in the path of his future son-in-law, among them a mission to descend into the underworld to fetch three golden hairs from the devil's head. Once that mission is accomplished, the boy lives happily ever after with his wife, while the king, as punishment for his sinful ways, is obliged to live out his days as a humble ferryman rowing travelers across a stream.

Unlike the classic family romance, this tale gives us three parent couples: a "poor woman" and her husband, a miller and his wife, a king and a queen. This fairy tale also seems to deviate from the plot of the family romance by presenting humble biological parents *and* humble adoptive parents. But these differences are easily reconciled. Note, for example, that the husband of the biological mother and the wife of the king are barely mentioned, thereby creating a situation that pairs the biological mother with the king as co-conspirators in abandoning the child-hero. The "poor woman" consents to give up the child; the king exposes the child to the waters. We are therefore left with two parent couples that roughly correspond to the real and imaginary parents of infantile fantasies: a humble miller with his wife and a royal progenitor with his consort.

Note here that the fairy tale turns the fiction of the family romance into fact. The lowly miller and his wife who raise the hero as their son turn out to be nothing more than foster parents, stand-ins for the royal progenitor and his consort. The malice of the biological parents performs a double function in the narrative economy of the fairy tale: it pins the blame on the parents for the hero's low social status and explains just why the hero was deprived of his birthright in the first place. To the hero falls the task of reaffiliating himself with his royal family, in this case through marriage to a figure who could, on one level, be seen as his half-sister. As noted, the hostility felt by young romancers toward their real parents is translated by fairy tales into victimization by hostile parents. A king who is both father and tyrant or a queen who is both mother and persecutor stands as the most frequent incarnation of parental malice.

When Otto Rank referred to the "paranoid structure" of certain fairy tales, he surely had such stories as "The Devil with the Three Golden Hairs" in mind.[26] Again and again these types of tales paint children as the victims of evil-minded or negligent parents. The hero of "The King of the Golden Mountain," for example, is sold down the river by his own father, who unthinkingly strikes a bargain with the devil. Years later the son returns home as the monarch of a foreign land only to find himself cast out once again for violating his merchant-father's dress codes. Like the royal father figure in "The Devil with the Three Golden Hairs," this paternal persecutor stands between the young, innocent hero and his beloved. But mothers and even aunts are perfectly capable of setting the machinery of the family romance in motion. The eponymous hero of "Fledgling" is orphaned owing to parental neglect: when his mother dozes off under a tree, a marauding eagle plucks him from her lap and deposits him in a treetop. A forester subsequently adopts and raises the foundling. In "The Three Little Birds," two brothers and their sister are thrown into a river by royal aunts but are rescued from a watery grave by a fisherman, who rears the three children with his wife. Evil is generally balanced by good; for every persecutor of royal blood or arrogant bearing, there is generally a meek, benevolent counterpart who subverts the crafty designs on the hero's life.

The family romance serves as the scaffolding for a number of classical fairy tales. But while the wishes and fantasies of young romancers may function as the foundation for those tales, they undergo considerable modification before entering the public sphere of folklore. A child's murderous hostility toward his parents (which manifests itself in the form of disavowal and repudiation of parents in childhood fantasies) shows up in folklore as parental hostility toward a child. To obviate the profound sense of guilt aroused by unacceptable thoughts, an aggressor can take advantage of a willfully clever stratagem. He turns himself into an innocent martyr and casts the victim of his guilt-tainted thoughts into the role of a nefarious villain. The psychological mechanism at work here, known as projection, was neatly illustrated by Freud in the syntactical conversion of the sentence "I hate him" into "He hates me." A bold inversion of actual conditions often takes place before private fantasies make their way into the public domain. The belligerent romancer slips imperceptibly into the role of the victim who fashions a fairy tale recounting his persecution. There is no doubt much truth in Otto Rank's view that adults invest the lives of folkloric heroes with the details of their own infantile history and that they thereby create the stuff of fairy tales by means of retrograde childhood fantasies.[27]

For some, drawing in this way on the lexicon of depth psychology can seem remarkably inappropriate for analyzing stories that are notorious for the shallowness of their character descriptions. Rapunzel may be "the loveliest child under the sun" and remains desperately lonely in her tower, but that is as much as we ever learn about her. Faithful Johannes (in the tale of that title) lives up to his name, but he possesses no other memorable character traits. The miller's daughter in "Rumpelstiltskin" is poor and beautiful, but otherwise wholly undistinguished and indeed indistinguishable from other fairy-tale heroines. King Thrushbeard is a man who can be differentiated from the garden-variety monarch only by the bizarre shape of his chin. If fairy tales offer minimal information when it comes to describing their heroes' attributes, they show even more restraint when it comes to making pronouncements about their mental states.[28] Feelings and emotions are habitually externalized. In "The Frog King," a servant's sorrow takes concrete form in the three iron rings constricting his body. Thirst (instinct unrestrained) transforms the male sibling of "Little Brother and Little Sister" into an animal. Excessive curiosity is depicted in "Mary's Child" as the desire to open a forbidden door. By rigorously avoiding psychological analysis, the plots of fairy tales become charged with symbolic meaning. The physical descriptions and outer events of the tale serve not only to further the plot, but also to fashion ciphers of psychological realities.

Psychoanalyzing a fairy-tale plot is tantamount to psychoanalyzing a fairy-tale character. As Tzvetan Todorov has noted, fairy tales radically compress the gap between a psychological trait and the action it provokes.[29] No sooner are we told that Snow White's mother is jealous of her daughter than we learn of her murderous designs on the girl. A character's physical and mental traits serve not only to define him, but also to elicit an action—they are at once descriptive and causal. Those traits, furthermore, nearly always have a single predictable consequence, rather than opening multiple possibilities for the course of the tale. In the narrative logic of the fairy tale, jealousy translates into murder. The unrivaled beauty of a heroine attracts a suitor and gives rise to marriage. The desire to travel leads to a voyage. Fear breeds ogres and sundry other monsters. Helplessness and despair magically produce assistants. Compassion brings a reward. Curiosity elicits a prohibition. Odd as it sounds, it appears that we must look to the plot in order to read the minds of fairy-tale characters.

The heroes of fairy tales are invariably introduced to us in dreary realistic settings utterly lacking the magical qualities associated with the genre. But once the hero sets out in search of a distant ideal or finds himself obliged to take to the road, events suddenly take on the coloring of the marvelous and function as physical projections and representations of psychic processes. The shift from the realistic milieu described in the tale's opening paragraph to the marvelous world of the tale proper is accompanied by a corresponding shift from the figurative meaning of words to the things that those words designate. As Wallace Stevens wrote: "Reality is a cliché from which we escape by metaphor." "It is only au pays de la métaphore qu'on est poète," he added.[30]

.In fairy tales, the hero escapes the tiresome clichés of reality by entering a world where the figurative or metaphorical dimension of language takes on literal meaning. Ideas become matter. The mother or stepmother who is like an ogress at the beginning of a tale becomes an actual witch. The scolding mother in the Grimms' original manuscript of "The Three Ravens" becomes a *Rabenmutter* (in German both an "unnatural mother" and a "mother of ravens"). As she denounces her three sons for their frivolous ways, they turn into black ravens and fly into the distance.[31] All of the "natural" children of fairy tales literally become children of nature, aided by nature and protected by it from the highly unnatural villains of their home life. Such literalizations of metaphors can at times translate into grotesque effects. One fairy-tale heroine becomes "the girl without hands" after her father brazenly demands her hand in marriage. When refused, he chops off both appendages. Countless princes lose their heads over proud princesses who test the mental or physical prowess of their suitors with insoluble riddles and impossible tasks. The list could easily be extended, but the point is clear. In taking the figurative literally, fairy tales once again display the degree to which they are situated in the mental universe of childhood. There, as in fairy tales, the literal dimension of language reigns supreme, and belief in the omnipotence of thought holds sway.

The symbolic codes woven into fairy tales are relatively easy to decipher, for they are often based on familiar allusions or on readily decodable verbal substitutions. As Freud observed, folklore in general takes advantage of symbols that have universal validity.[32] Kings and queens as a rule represent parents; a prince or a princess signifies the self. A deep, impenetrable forest symbolizes the dark, hidden depths of the soul. A body of water is often associated with the process of birth; think of the countless tales in which foundlings float down the river to a predictable rescue by humble folks. These and other equally timeless symbols are ordinarily quite transparent and yield readily to interpretive pressures.

Symbols generated by literalized metaphors and by visual puns are also relatively easy to decode. In his *Interpretation of Dreams*, Freud cited examples of each in the dreams of patients. One woman reported to him a dream in which she had been "left sitting," the literal sense of the German expression used to designate an unmarried state (*sitzen geblieben*). Another woman recounted walking through fields, cutting off ears of wheat and barley (*Ähren*) in a dream that was patently about the loss of honor (*Ehre*: a homonym for *Ähre*). In these cases, as in the verbal substitutions cited, the keys are generally well known and laid down by firmly established linguistic usage.

Unlike the private symbols found in literary works of a modernist turn, the symbols of folkloric art are highly accessible to the public imagination, in large part because they are shaped, if not created, by a collective body. Still, there remain numerous knotty problems for those who wish to crack the symbolic codes of fairy tales. A frog may be a "standard phallic symbol" in folklore, but it is not infallibly so.[33] Animals may generally function as helpers and thereby underscore the hero's closeness to nature, but occasionally they take on a predatory role. A stream can carry a hero to safety and shelter, but it can also transform him into an animal. Nonetheless, it comes as no great surprise that Jung, for one, turned to fairy tales as vehicles for understanding the workings of the human mind and that Freud sharpened his knowledge of dream symbols by consulting folktales. As Jung observed, the content of fairy tales is not subject to the whims and caprices of individual logic, but is determined by eternally valid processes of thought.[34] The symbolic language of fairy tales reflected, for him, the unchanging, ever stable structure of the human psyche.

The fundamental distinction between literature and folklore finds confirmation in the different symbolic codes used by each mode of narration—one private and arbitrary, the other public and set down by custom. Roman Jakobson is not far from the truth when he describes folklore as "a socialized section of mental culture." Although the theory of migration and borrowing may suffice to elucidate the prevalence of certain themes and motifs in tales, it fails to offer a satisfying explanation for the uniformity of the tales' shape and structure. Only careful analysis of the psychological dynamics of the tales can extend our understanding of their means of representation and recurrent patterns of thought.

In his study of "fairy stories," J.R.R. Tolkien argued that "to ask what is the origin of stories (however qualified) is to ask what is the origin of language and of the mind."[35] The search for the origins of fairy tales may not necessarily produce earthshaking insights about the genesis of language and of man's capacity for thought. But the study of fairy tales tells us something about the way in which the mind draws on the double movement of language between literal meaning and figurative expression to fashion stories that dramatize psychological realities. The family romance numbers among the most significant of those inner realities.

II

HEROES

4

BORN YESTERDAY
The Spear Side

"There comes an old man with his three sons—"
"I could match this beginning with an old tale."
—SHAKESPEARE, *As You Like It*

IDENTIFYING fairy-tale heroes by name is no mean feat. In the Grimms' collection, only one in every ten actually has a name. But it is also no secret that the most celebrated characters in fairy tales are female. Cinderella, Snow White, Little Red Riding Hood, and Sleeping Beauty: these are the names that have left so vivid an imprint on childhood memories. With the exception of Hansel, who shares top billing with his sister, male protagonists are exceptionally unmemorable in name, if not in deed. Lacking the colorful descriptive sobriquets that accord their female counterparts a distinctive identity, these figures are presented as types and defined by their parentage (the miller's son), by their station in life (the prince), by their relationship to siblings (the youngest brother), by their level of intelligence (the simpleton), or by physical deformities (Thumbling).[1]

Most people may be at a loss when it comes to naming fairy-tale heroes, but few have trouble characterizing them. "In song and story," writes Simone de Beauvoir, "the young man is seen departing adventurously in search of woman; he slays the dragon, he battles giants." And what are this young man's attributes? One commentator on the Grimms' collection describes him as "active, competitive, handsome, industrious, cunning, acquisitive." That list sums up the conventional wisdom on the dragon slayers and giant killers of fairy-tale lore.[2]

That conventional wisdom, however, proves to be a fairy tale so far as German folklore is concerned. A reading of the first edition of the *Nursery and Household Tales* reveals that there are exactly two dragon slayers and only one giant killer in the entire collection of some 150 tales.[3] One of those stories, "Johannes-Wassersprung and Caspar-Wassersprung," rehearses the classic story of the slaying of a seven-headed dragon and the liberation of a princess, but (for unknown reasons) the tale never made it to the second edition of the *Nursery and Household Tales*. The other dragon-slaying hero bears the distinctly unheroic name Stupid Hans (Dummhans), and the contest in which he dispatches three dragons, each with a different number of heads, is less than gripping. As for the giant killer, he succeeds in decapitating three giants, but only because the proper sword is placed directly in his path. If there is any attribute that these heroes share, it is naiveté. Like so many other heroes in the Grimms' collection, they are decidedly unworldly figures. "Innocent," "silly," "useless," "foolish," "simple," and "guileless": these are the adjectives applied repeatedly to fairy-tale heroes in the Grimms' collection.

Among folklorists, it is the fashion to divide heroes into two distinct classes. There are active heroes and passive heroes, "formal heroes" and "ideal heroes," dragon slayers and male Cinderellas, tricksters and simpletons.[4] According to theory, the oppositions active/passive, seeker/victim, brave/timid, and naive/cunning serve as useful guides for classifying fairy-tale heroes. In practice, though, it is not always easy to determine whether a hero relies on his own resources or depends on helpers. Does he have a zest for danger or does he simply weather the various adventures that befall him? Just what is his level of intelligence? What at first blush appear to be straightforward choices turn out to be fraught with complexities. The happy-go-lucky simpleton who appears to succeed without trying is not always as doltish as his name or reputation would lead us to believe, and the roguish trickster does not always live up to his reputation for shrewd reasoning.

There is a further complication. Despite their seeming artlessness, the *Nursery and Household Tales* are not without occasional

ironic touches that subvert surface meanings. In particular, the epithets and predicates reserved for their protagonists can highlight
utterly uncharacteristic traits. The eponymous heroine of "Clever
Else" ranks high on the list of dull-witted characters; "Hans in Luck"
charts a steady decline in its hero's fortunes; and the brave little tailor in the story of that title displays more bravado than bravery.[5] In
the world of fairy tales, a simpleton can easily slip into the role of a
cunning trickster; a humble miller's son can become a king; and a
cowardly fool can emerge as a stout-hearted hero. Character traits
display an astonishing lack of stability, shifting almost imperceptibly
into their opposites as the tale unfolds. Bearing this in mind, let us
take the measure of male protagonists in the Grimms' collection to
determine what character traits they share and to assess the extent
to which the plots of their adventures follow a predictable course.

If the female protagonists of fairy tales are often as good as they
are beautiful, their male counterparts generally appear to be as
young and naive as they are stupid. Snow White's stepmother may
be enraged by her stepdaughter's superior beauty, but the fathers
of male heroes are eternally exasperated by the unrivaled obtuseness of their sons. To the question, Who is the stupidest of them all?
most fairy-tale fathers would reply: my youngest son. Yet that son is
also the chosen son, the son who ultimately outdoes his older and
wiser siblings. In an almost perverse fashion, fairy tales featuring
male protagonists chart the success story of adolescents who lack
even the good sense to heed the instructions of the many helpers
and donors who rush to their aid in an attempt to avert catastrophes
and to ensure a happy ending. "You don't really deserve my help,"
declares one such intercessor in frustration after his sage advice has
been disregarded on no less than three occasions.[6]

In fairy tales all over the world, the one least likely to succeed paradoxically becomes the one most likely to succeed. Merit rarely
counts; luck seems to be everything. Aladdin, the prototype of the
undeserving hero who succeeds in living happily ever after, begins
his rise to wealth and power under less than auspicious circumstances. The introductory paragraphs of his tale give the lie to the
view that classical fairy tales reward virtue and punish evil. "Once

upon a time," begins the story "Aladdin and the Enchanted Lamp,"
"there lived in a certain city of China an impoverished tailor who
had a son called Aladdin. From his earliest years this Aladdin was a
headstrong and incorrigible good-for-nothing." When he grows
older, he refuses to learn a trade and persists in his idle ways until
his father, "grieving over the perverseness of his son," falls ill and
dies. Yet this same Aladdin, who becomes ever more wayward after
having dispatched his father to the grave, ultimately inherits a sul-
tan's throne. As one critic correctly points out, the story of Aladdin
and his enchanted lamp exalts and glorifies "one of the most undeserving characters imaginable." It is telling that Aladdin made his
way so easily from the pages of German translations of *The Thousand
and One Nights* to the oral narratives of one region of Germany.
Once his exotic name was changed to Dummhans, he was evidently
quickly assimilated into Pomeranian folklore, so much so that it was
difficult to distinguish him from native sons.[7]

   The heroes of the *Nursery and Household Tales* may, for the most
part, be unlikely to win prizes for intelligence and good behavior,
but they are even less likely to garner awards for courage. Their stories chronicle perilous adventures, but they often remain both cowardly and passive. When summoned to discharge the first in a series
of three tasks, the simpleton in "The Queen Bee" simply sits down
and has a good cry. In "The Three Feathers," the hero sits down and
"feels sad" instead of rising to the challenges posed by his father.
Fairy-tale heroines have never stood as models of an enterprising
spirit, but it is also not rare for fairy-tale heroes to suffer silently and
to endure hardships in a hopelessly passive fashion.

   For all their shortcomings, the simpletons in the Grimms' fairy
tales possess one character trait that sets them apart from their fraternal rivals: compassion. That compassion is typically reserved for
the natural allies and benefactors of fairy-tale heroes: the animals
that inhabit the earth, the waters, and the sky.[8] Even before the simpleton embarks on a journey to foreign kingdoms or undertakes di-
verse tasks to liberate a princess, he must prove himself worthy of
assistance from nature or from supernatural powers by displaying
compassion. Of the various tests, tasks, and trials imposed on a hero,

this first test figures as the most important, for it establishes his privileged status. Once he exhibits compassion—with its logical concomitant of humility—he can do no wrong, even when he violates interdictions, disregards warnings, and ignores instructions. This preliminary test of the hero's character comes to serve the dual function of singling out the hero from his brothers and of furnishing him with potential helpers for the tasks that lie ahead.

Two fairy tales from the Grimms' collection illustrate the extent to which compassion is rewarded. In "The Queen Bee," the youngest of three sons defends an anthill, a bevy of ducks, and a beehive from the assaults of his mischievous brothers. "Leave the animals alone," he admonishes his elders on three occasions. Compassion pays off in the end, for this youngest son is also the one to escape being turned to stone—a punishment that perfectly suits the crimes of his callous siblings. With the help of his newly won allies, the simpleton of the family discharges three "impossible" tasks written for him on a stone slab. He gathers a thousand pearls that lie strewn about the forest, fetches a bedroom key from the sea's depths, and succeeds in identifying the youngest of three "completely identical" sisters. To be more precise, the ants gather the pearls, the ducks fetch the key, and the bees identify the youngest sister. Yet the simpleton is credited with disenchanting the palace in which the trio of princesses resides; he thereby wins the hand of the youngest and earns the right to give the other two sisters in marriage to his brothers.

The hero of "The White Snake," like the simpleton of "The Queen Bee," hardly lifts a finger to win his bride. Once he displays compassion for wildlife by coming to the rescue of three fish, a colony of ants, and three ravens, he joins the ranks of the "chosen," who receive assistance from helpers as soon as they are charged with carrying out tasks. Although male fairy-tale figures have customarily been celebrated for their heroic feats, their greatest achievement actually rests on the passing of a character test. By enshrining compassion and humility, which—unlike intelligence and brute strength—are acquired characteristics rather than innate traits, the Grimms' tales make it clear to their implied audience (which gradually came to be adolescents) that even the least talented youth can rise to the top.⁹

Once the hero has proven himself in the preliminary character test, he is braced for the tasks that lie ahead. The grateful beneficiaries of his deeds are quick to even out the balance sheet. As soon as the hero finds himself faced with an impossible task—emptying a lake with a perforated spoon, building and furnishing a castle overnight, devouring a mountain of bread in twenty-four hours—help is at hand. For every task that requires wisdom, courage, endurance, strength, or simply an appetite and a thirst of gargantuan proportions, there is a helper—or a group of helpers—possessing the requisite attributes. And ultimately the achievements of the helper redound to the hero, for he is credited with having drained the lake, built the castle, and consumed the bread.

Passing the preliminary test and carrying out the basic tasks are sufficient to secure a princess and her kingdom. Nonetheless, a number of fairy tales mount a third act in keeping with the ternary principle governing their plots.¹⁰ The final trial the hero must endure is motivated by the reappearance of the fraternal rivals who vexed the hero in his earlier, preheroic days. The brothers seize the earliest opportunity to pilfer the hero's riches, alienate him from his beloved, malign his good name, or banish him from the land. Yet they are no match for the hero, who deftly outwits them and survives their assaults. Although the hero is rarely instrumental in carrying out the tasks imposed on him, in the end he acquires the attributes of his helpers and gains the strength, courage, and wit needed to prevail.

Just as the humble male protagonist matures and is elevated to a higher station in life, so his antagonists are demeaned and demoted in the final, optional segment of the tale. If the hero often distinguishes himself by showing mercy for animals, he remains singularly uncharitable when it comes to dealing with human rivals. "Off with everyone's head but my own," proclaims the hero of "The King of the Golden Mountain." And he makes good on that threat. Even brothers and brides are dispatched by fairy-tale heroes without a moment's hesitation once their deceit comes to light. The hero of

"The Knapsack, the Hat, and the Horn," for example, does away with his wife once he uncovers her duplicity. Treachery is punished as swiftly and as predictably as compassion is rewarded. This third phase of the hero's career endows his story with a symmetry and balance for which all tales strive. Like the first two acts, the final act stages a contest between a youth and his two older, but morally inferior brothers. Both dramatic conflicts culminate in the rewarding of good will and the punishment of treachery; the last act simply intensifies the reward (a princess and a kingdom) and the punishment (death). In doing so, it adds not only moral resonance, but also a measure of finality to the tale. The hero has not only attained the highest office in the land, but has also eliminated his every competitor. For that office, he was singled out in the tale's first episode, made singular in the tale's second part, and celebrated as the sole and single heir to the throne in the tale's coda.

The trajectory of the hero's path leads him to the goal shared by all fairy tales, whether they chart the fortunes of male or female protagonists. In keeping with the fundamental law requiring the reversal of all conditions prevailing in its introductory paragraphs, the

FIGURE 7. *Otto Ubbelohde's hero of "The King of the Golden Mountain" surveys the scene of carnage that stands as the final tableau in the story.*

fairy tale ends by enthroning the humble and enriching the impoverished. The male heroes of fairy tales are humble in at least one, and often in both, senses of the term. More often than not they are low on the totem pole in families of common origins. But whether born to the crown or raised on a farm, they are also frequently humble in character; without this special quality they would fail to qualify for the munificence of helpers and donors. Thus, humility seems to be the badge of the fairy-tale hero. And since humbleness, in one of its shades of meaning, can inhere in members of any social class, both princes and peasants are eligible for the role of hero in fairy tales.

Humility also comes to color the psychological makeup of fairy-tale heroines. Female protagonists are by nature just as humble as their male counterparts, but they display that virtue in a strikingly different fashion and at a different point in their fairy-tale careers. Fairy tales often highlight psychological characteristics by translating them into elements of plot; in the case of female heroines, this proves especially true. Daughters of millers and daughters of kings alike are not merely designated as humble; they are actually humbled in the course of their stories. In fact, *humbled* is perhaps too mild a term to use for the many humiliations to which female protagonists must submit.

Since most fairy tales end with marriage, it seems logical to assume that a single tale suffices to illustrate the contrasting fates of male and female protagonists. Yet though there is often a happy couple at the end of a fairy tale, the fate of only a single, central character is at stake as the tale unfolds. That pivotal figure stands so firmly rooted at the center of events that all other characters are defined solely by their relationship to him and consequently lack an autonomous sphere of action. In "Cinderella," for instance, even the bridegroom, for all the dashing chivalry attributed to him by Walt Disney and others, remains a colorless figure. The tale tells us nothing more about him than that he is the son of a king. Lacking a history, a story, and even a name, he is reduced to the function of prince-rescuer waiting in the wings for his cue. The brides in stories of male heroes fare little better. Relegated to subordinate roles, they too fail to engage our interest. Still, there are exceptions to every rule, and the Grimms' collection provides one noteworthy variation on the principle that only one character can occupy center stage in fairy tales. "The Goose Girl at the Spring" weaves together the fates of both partners in the marriage with which it concludes. To be sure, there are signs that the tale is not of one piece, that at some historical juncture it occurred to one teller of tales to splice two separate plots.[11] Nonetheless, the two plots conveniently dovetail to create a single narrative. The story of the humble count and the humbled princess who marries him offers an exemplary study in contrasts between the lot of males and that of females in fairy tales culminating in wedding ceremonies.

"The Goose Girl at the Spring" commences with an account of the heroine's future bridegroom. The young man is handsome, rich, and noble, yet he must—like the most lowly fairy-tale heroes— prove his mettle by displaying compassion and humility. Without these virtues, his otherwise impeccable credentials would prove utterly worthless. And indeed, we learn that the young count is not only able to "feel compassion," but that he is also, despite his noble station, not too proud to translate compassion into action. Once he demonstrates his humility by easing the burdens of a feeble old hag shunned by everyone else, he earns himself a passport to luck and success. Like his many artlessly benevolent folkloric kinsmen, the count becomes the recipient of a gift that accords him a privileged status among potential suitors of a princess. The emerald etui bestowed upon him by the old hag ultimately leads him to his bride— a princess masquerading as a shepherdess.

Neither the count nor his rustic bride can boast humble origins. The unsightly girl tending geese at the beginning of the tale is not at all what she seems. At the well, she peels off her rural costume along with her rough skin to reveal that she must be a princess. Despite her aristocratic origins, she too can ascend to a higher position, for her fairy-tale days are spent in the most modest of circumstances. Unlike her groom, however, she was pressed into assuming a humble position when her own father banished her from the household. Like countless folkloric heroines, she suffers a humili-

ating fall that reduces her from a princess to a peasant, from a privileged daughter to an impoverished menial. Fairy-tale heroes receive gifts and assistance once they actively prove their compassion
and humility; heroines, by contrast, become the beneficiaries of
helpers and rescuers only after they have been abased and forced to
learn humility.

There are many well-known tales of victimized female heroines
who rise to or return to the ranks of royalty once they have been
humbled and humiliated.[12] But no tales more explicitly display the
humiliation prerequisite to a happy ending than "King Thrushbeard," "The Mongoose," and "The Six Servants." King Thrushbeard's bride furnishes a classic example of the heroine who earns a
king and a crown after straitened circumstances break her arro-
gance and pride. It is not enough that she curses the false pride that
led to her downfall; her husband must also solemnly state: "All of
this was done to crush your pride and to punish you for the haughty
way in which you treated me." When King Thrushbeard generously
offers to reinstate her to a royal position, she feels so deeply morti-
fied that she declares herself unworthy to become his bride. The
princess in the tale known as "The Mongoose" also finds herself
humbled by her prospective husband. Nonetheless, she takes the
defeat in stride and observes to herself with more than a touch of
satisfaction: "He is cleverer than you!" The princess-heroine of
"The Six Servants" is also cheerfully repentant and resigned to her
fate by the end of the story. Reduced to tending swine with her husband (a prince who has duped her into believing that he is a peasant), she is prepared to accept her lot: "I've only got what I deserved
for being so haughty and proud." After revealing the true facts of
his life, her husband justifies the deception by declaring: "I suffered
so much for you, it was only right that you should suffer for me."

As the tale "The Six Servants" makes clear, young men "suffer"
by taking the credit for tasks carried out by animal helpers, human
servants, or supernatural assistants. Women suffer by being forced
into a lowly social position. In short, male heroes demonstrate from
the start a meekness and humility that qualify them for an ascent to
wealth, the exercise of power, and happiness crowned by wedded

bliss; their female counterparts undergo a process of humiliation and defeat that ends with a rapid rise in social status through marriage but that also signals a loss of pride and the abdication of power.

Before moving to another category of heroes, a quick review of our first class is in order. The naive hero in tales of three sons lacks the brains and brawn conventionally associated with heroic figures; he must rely on helpers with superhuman or supernatural powers to carry out every task demanded by a king in return for the hand of the princess. Instead of slaying dragons, he offers to louse them; instead of killing giants, he befriends them and makes himself at home in their dwellings. His demonstrations of compassion set the stage for the reversal of fortunes characteristic of fairy-tale plots. Only from a position of humility can he be elevated to the loftiest office in the land. Just as this hero works his way up the social ladder by climbing down it, so too he acquires intelligence and power by displaying obtuseness and vulnerability. Although it is never explicitly stated that he becomes smart and strong in the end, most fairy tales imply that their heroes have acquired the attributes of royalty right along with the office of king.

The youngest of three sons makes his way through magical kingdoms where an ant might plead for a favor, an enchanted princess could call on his services, or a dwarf might demand a crust of bread. But a second group of heroes in the Grimms' *Nursery and Household Tales* moves in what appears to be the more realistic setting of folk tales: villages and the roads connecting them. The cast of characters in tales with these heroes includes kings and princesses, yet the tales lack the supernatural dimension of fairy tales and tend to be more earthy in humor and down-to-earth in tone. The heroes are often far enough along in life to have a profession; many are apprentices, but some are tailors, foresters, tradesmen, or mercenaries. Many are men and not boys. (One is so old that he finds himself obliged to choose the eldest of twelve princesses when a king offers him one of his daughters in marriage.) Still, these heroes do not seem equipped with much more intelligence, strength, or valor than the young simpletons of fairy tales. They may not be village idiots, but in accordance with the general tendency of German folklore to avoid endowing male protagonists with heroic traits, their strengths are rarely described in much detail.

Naiveté also appears to be the principal hallmark of village boys and men. But what appears to be a character defect is in fact turned to good account once the protagonist determines to seek his fortunes in the world. Nietzsche once observed that fear is an index of intelligence, thus confirming the old saw that fools rush in where wise men fear to tread.[13] The more naive the hero, the more foolhardy and fearless he is, and the more likely he is to rise to the challenges devised to foil the suitors of a princess. Naiveté implies fearlessness, which in turn can take on the character of courage.

In much the same way that naiveté can shade into courage, it can translate into cunning. A hero's stupidity can take such extreme forms that it utterly disarms his antagonists. A young man who starts out handicapped by naiveté may in the end triumph over his adversaries by outwitting them. The protagonist unwise to the ways of the world can therefore be in the best possible position to exhibit heroic qualities by the close of the story.

Heroic feats performed by figures with clear character defects—lack of wisdom and wit—can end by producing comic effects. Blockhead, Numbskull, and Simpleton rush into one hazardous situation after another; they get the upper hand by putting their dimwittedness on display, taking every word of advice that they hear literally; but they also escape harm because they are so naive that they confound their opponents. It may be true that they succeed in accomplishing the tasks laid out for them, but there is more than a touch of vaudeville to their every move.

The burlesque effect produced by tales chronicling the deeds of fearless heroes is perhaps most pronounced in "The Fairy Tale of One Who Went Forth to Learn Fear." The hero of that tale tries in vain to learn to be afraid, or more precisely, to shudder. Through one hair-raising episode after another he preserves his equanimity and coolly turns the tables on his would-be terrorizers. In one last desperate attempt to discover what it is to feel fear, he spends three nights warding off and ultimately exorcising the demons haunting a castle. His reward is the hand of a princess, but still he feels no fear. Only in his marriage bed does he finally learn to shudder, when his resourceful wife pulls off his covers and pours a bucketful of live minnows on him. Bruno Bettelheim is surely right to read psychosexual implications into the final act of the tale, particularly since the art of shuddering rather than the actual experience of fear constitutes the overt tale value. But the hero's inability to feel fear ought not to be construed as a negative trait; Bettelheim asserts that "the hero of this story could not shudder due to repression of all sexual feelings."[14] It is precisely the absence of the capacity to fear that enables the sprightly hero to withstand the horrors of a haunted castle and consequently to win the hand of his bride. Indeed, the inability to fear comes so close to courage here that the protagonist, for all his unflinching artlessness, begins to take on heroic attributes. Unlike his humble and helpless kinsmen in classical fairy tales of three sons, he breezily accomplishes one task after another without receiving aid from foreign agents. Were it not for the comic overtones to his adventures, it would seem entirely appropriate to place him in the class of heroes who live by their courage and wits.

If naiveté and courage are virtual synonyms in the folkloric lexicon, naiveté and cunning are also not far apart in meaning.[15] The more hopelessly naive and obtuse the hero of a tale, the more likely it is that he will triumph over his adversaries and that his adventures will be crowned with success. The Brave Little Tailor, who decorates himself for having dispatched seven flies with one blow, seems to stand as the very incarnation of fatuous vanity. Yet his bravado endows him with the power to outwit giants, to complete the tasks given by his bride's belligerent father, and to subdue a blue-blooded wife who is repelled by the thought of a marriage below her social station. In this tale, the line dividing naiveté from shrewdness and bravado from bravery has been effaced. The naive hero without fear and intelligence becomes virtually indistinguishable from the trickster.

By now it should be clear that the humble and naive youngest of three sons is a not-so-distant cousin of the fearless and naive hero.

In fact, the hero of the Grimms' "Crystal Ball" combines the attributes of humble heroes and fearless fools; he possesses the simplicity and humility that go hand in hand with his familial status as the youngest of three sons, and he is also said to have "a heart without fear." It is above all his foolishly dauntless spirit that gives him the audacity to line up as the twenty-fourth suitor to seek out a princess imprisoned in the "Castle of the Golden Sun" and to undertake her liberation. And it is precisely his slow-wittedness that provides him with the means for arriving in the kingdom inhabited by the princess. He "forgets" to return a magical hat to two giants and thereby receives just the right means for transporting himself to that kingdom. In fairy tales, brashness can accomplish as much as bravery; naiveté is as effective as craft. The manifest lack of a virtue often translates into its possession. Just as Cinderella proves to be the fairest and the noblest of them all despite her shabby attire and her station at the hearth, so the simpleton of the family ultimately prevails over older and wiser antagonists.

As noted, the rigors of a fairy-tale hero's life endow him in the end with the attributes commonly associated with royalty. Even if the humble simpleton never lifts a sword and is incapable of answering a single question, let alone a riddle, he becomes a prince in more than just name. The feats of each and every woodland helper become his own deeds and accomplishments; he becomes a figure with all the qualities of dragon slayers and giant killers. Since our other class of tales, those featuring the comic adventures of heroes without fear, generally dispenses with tests of compassion, it also does away with the helpers responsible for elevating humble protagonists to heroic stature. Fearless heroes must rely wholly on their own mental and physical resources, however modest these may be. It is those resources that are put to the test in the opening paragraphs of the tale, where brashness achieves more than bravery, and artlessness proves more effective than artifice.

Since the hero without fear displays a greater measure of self-reliance than his humble kinsmen, the plot of his adventures contains the potential for greater realism. Gone are the encounters with talking animals, supernatural counselors, and other exotic agents. Instead, the hero meets hunters, locksmiths, sextons, innkeepers, and similar folk. He may not marry a peasant's daughter, but the castle in which he finally takes up residence has the distinct odor of the barnyard. Again, we are in the village rather than in an enchanted forest. Yet it would be misleading to label these tales realistic. They do not strive to hold up a mirror to the social conditions of the age or culture in which they were told. These are tall tales, stories that take advantage of exaggeration, punning, parody, and literalism to produce comic effects.

The many realistic touches in these folk tales, in tandem with their farcical aspects, point to their basic affinity with tales of tricksters, where professional fools, tradesmen, discharged soldiers, and youths of various other callings conspire to thwart their masters, creditors, or any other members belonging to the species of the overprivileged. Through ingenious disingenuousness they succeed in coming out on top. An open-ended episodic principle organizes the plot of both tall tales featuring heroes without fear and trickster stories. One absurd skirmish follows another, with no distinctive growth, development, or maturity. By contrast, the humble hero's adventures take the form of a three-act drama, with a test in the first act, tasks in the second, and a final trial crowned by success in the third. The goal may be the same for both types of heroes, but the paths bear little resemblance to each other.[16]

Tales charting the adventures of male protagonists posit from the start one dominant character trait that establishes a well-defined identity for the hero even as it proclaims his membership in the class of heroic figures. The verbal tag attached to the character ("Dummy," "the youngest of three sons," "Blockhead") ensures that he is recognized as the central character of the narrative. But in the course of the hero's odyssey, his dominant character trait begins to shade into its opposite through a process of inversion. The humble hero weds a woman of royal blood; the brazen fool proves his mettle; the naive simpleton outwits just about anyone. In fairy tales and folk tales, the youth lacking a good pedigree, a stout heart, and a sharp wit is precisely the one who wins a princess and a kingdom.

Inversion of character traits is a common occurrence in folkloric narratives. A reversal of the conditions prevailing at the start is, after all, manifestly the goal of every tale. The folktale in general, as Max Lüthi has observed, has "a liking for all extremes, extreme contrasts in particular." Its characters, he further notes, are either beautiful or ugly, good or bad, poor or rich, industrious or lazy, and humble or noble.[17] Yet much as readers and critics insist on the folktale's low tolerance for ambiguity and stress the inflexibility of the attributes assigned to heroes and villains, the frequency with which inversion appears suggests that they overstate their case. Just as "Beast" can be at once savage and civilized, so the youngest of three sons can be both simpleton and sage, humble lad and prince, coward and hero. Both character attributes and social conditions can rapidly shift from one extreme to the other.

That character traits are not as standardized or programmed as would appear becomes evident if we analyze the fate of one character who does not figure prominently in the pantheon of folkloric heroes. The eponymous protagonist of "Hans in Luck" might, in fact, well be called an anti-hero. In the course of his travels, he outwits no one; he instead becomes the victim of numerous transparently fraudulent transactions. His fortunes, rather than rising, steadily decline. And at the end of his journey, he seems no wiser and is decidedly less prosperous than he was at the beginning. Still, Hans is said to be lucky, and he feels he is among the happiest men on earth. The steps of Hans's journey to felicity are easy enough to retrace. After serving his master loyally and diligently for seven years, Hans winds his way home with a weighty emolument: a chunk of gold the size of his head. Hans happily barters this monetary burden for a horse that will speed him on his way. In the further course of his journey, he exchanges the horse for a cow, the cow for a pig, the pig for a goose, and the goose for a grindstone and rock. Even after these two worthless rocks land at the bottom of a well, leaving him nothing to show for seven years of labor, Hans remains undaunted. He literally jumps for joy and praises God for liberating him from the burdens that slowed his journey. Unencumbered by earthly possessions and with a light heart, Hans heads for his mother's home.

Conventional wisdom has it that the happy-go-lucky hero of this tale stands as the archetypal fool. The very title of the tale, "Hans in Luck," is charged with irony: only a fool would delight in parting with the hefty wages Hans receives from his master. Yet on closer inspection, it becomes clear that the story of lucky Hans may also celebrate freedom from the burden of labor. On the last leg of his journey, Hans jettisons grindstone and rock—the tools of the trade that was to secure for him a steady flow of cash; at the outset of his journey, he rids himself of the gold with which his labor was compensated. In a stunning reversal of the value system espoused in fairy tales, Hans's story not only substitutes rags for riches, but also supplants marriage to a princess in a foreign land with a return home to mother. In short, it ends where most tales begin. Instead of charting an odyssey toward wealth and marriage, it depicts the stations of a journey toward poverty and dependence. But in remaining wholly indifferent to the wages of labor and freeing himself from its drudgery, Hans displays a kind of wisdom that invalidates ironic readings of his tale's title. Bereft of material possessions yet rich in spirit, he turns his back on the world of commerce to embrace his mother.[18]

The story of lucky Hans dramatically demonstrates the impossibility of establishing a fixed set of character traits shared by male heroes. Like Hans, who is both foolish and wise, poor and rich, lucky and unfortunate, the heroes of numerous fairy tales possess attributes that imperceptibly shade into their opposites. All the same, it is clear that certain oppositions (humble/noble, naive/cunning, timid/courageous, compassionate/ruthless) are encoded on virtually every fairy tale with a male hero. It is, then, difficult to draw up an inventory of immutable character traits largely because a single figure within a tale can—and usually does—have one character trait and its opposite. But it is equally difficult, if for different reasons, to establish precise models for the plots of tales featuring male heroes. For every score of heroes who wed princesses and inherit kingdoms, there is one who returns home as an impoverished bachelor. For ten heroes who receive assistance and magical gifts by demonstrating compassion, there is one who acquires aid and magical objects

through an act of violence. For every animal bridegroom who is released from a curse through the love and devotion of a woman,
there is one who is disenchanted by the callous treatment he receives
at the hands of his bride. To be sure, there is a measure of predictability in these plots, but only if we bear in mind that every narrative
norm established can be violated by its opposite. Thus the preliminary test of good character at the start of tales with a ternary plot
structure can be replaced by a demonstration of the hero's ruthless-
ness. The story of a hero dependent on magical helpers in carrying
out appointed tasks can exist side by side with the tale of a hero who
acts autonomously and takes on the characteristics of helpers.[19]

Recognizing and appreciating the fairy tale's instability—its penchant for moving from one extreme to another—is vital for understanding its characters, plots, and thematic orientation. Fairy-tale
figures have few fixed traits; they are re-formed once they reach the
goals of their journeys, when they become endowed with the very
qualities in which they were once found wanting. Male protagonists
may adhere slavishly to the ground rules of heroic decorum, or they
may break every rule in the book; either way, their stories end with
accession to the throne. And finally, the conditions prevailing at the
start of the tales are utterly reversed by the end. The fairy tale, in
sum, knows no stable middle ground. Inversion of character traits,
violation of narrative norms, and reversal of initial conditions are
just a few of the ways in which it overturns notions of immutability
and creates a fictional world in which the one constant value is
change.

In this context, it is worth emphasizing once again some of the
disparities between folkloric fantasies and social realities. The radical reversals that lift fairy-tale heroes from humble circumstances to
a royal station were virtually unknown during the age in which fairy
tales developed and flourished, but they undeniably correspond to
childhood fantasies of past ages and of our own day. If in real life
the youngest of three sons rarely had the wherewithal to succeed in
life or to transcend his station in life, fairy tales held out the promise
that humility and other virtues might well outweigh the benefits of
an inheritance. But beyond offering consolation to underprivileged
sons who lived in an era when primogeniture was custom or law,

fairy tales more generally respond to the insecurities of every child. Even the eldest child is likely to perceive himself less gifted or less favored than his siblings and can thereby readily identify with simpleton heroes. Fundamental psychological truths, rather than specific social realities, appear to have given rise to the general plot structure of those tales.

A stable plot still leaves much room for variation. Skillful raconteurs can take the same story line and give it unique twists and turns. The tone may vary from one tale to the next, and the hero may be presented in different lights. As Robert Darnton has shown, comparing different national versions of a single tale type can be a revealing exercise. Reading through various tellings of "Jack the Giant Killer," one can register the changes from "English fantasy to French cunning and Italian burlesque." More important, there are subtle shifts in the character of the protagonist as he slips from one culture into another. Darnton has observed that the trickster figure is especially prevalent in French folklore and literature.[20] By contrast, as we have seen, the simpleton or (to put it in more flattering terms) the guileless youth figures prominently in the Grimms' collection. These differences between the folkloric heroes of the two cultures may, however, be more apparent than real, for the roguish Gallic trickster and his naive Teutonic counterpart have more in common than one would suspect. Even the names most frequently bestowed in the *Nursery and Household Tales* on the two types (Dummling for the simpleton and Däumling for the trickster) suggest that they are kindred spirits. Both the simpleton and the trickster ultimately make good by outwitting or outdoing their seemingly superior adversaries. Still, the shift in emphasis from cunning to naiveté as one moves across the Rhine is telling, suggesting that the French celebrate cleverness and audacity while the Germans enshrine the virtue of guilelessness.

If we take a closer look at German literary traditions—both oral and written—it becomes clear that the naive hero is by no means a folkloristic aberration. He fits squarely into a long tradition of such figures. Wolfram von Eschenbach's Parzival, who comes to incarnate the highest chivalric ideals, is described as *der tumme* (the young and inexperienced one). Dressed by his mother in the costume of a fool, he mounts a wretched nag to seek his fortune in the world. Although there are hints that he is something of a dragon slayer (he arrives at Munsalvæsche during the feast of Saint Michael, the vanquisher of Satan as dragon), the only dragons he slays are emblazoned on his opponent's helmet. But like folkloric heroes, Parzival knows no fear and consequently displays valor on the battlefield. Although he fails the initial test of compassion, in the course of his adventures he develops that quality and learns humility.

Remaining in the same poetic climate but moving to another era, we find that Richard Wagner's Siegfried also launches his heroic career as a naive youth without fear. The resemblances between his story and the "Fairy Tale of One Who Went Forth to Learn Fear" are unmistakable. To his cantankerous guardian, Mime, Siegfried confides that he wishes to learn what it is to fear, to which Mime responds that the wise learn fear quickly, the stupid have a harder time of it.[21] Siegfried clearly belongs in the latter category. Like the one who went forth to learn fear, he discovers that emotion in the experience of love. As he sets eyes on the sleeping Brünnhilde, he feels a mystifying quickening of emotions:

> How cowardly I feel.
> Is this what they call fear?
> Oh mother! mother!
> Your fearless child!
> A woman lies in sleep:
> She has taught him to be afraid!
>   (*Siegfried*, act 3)

No one was more surprised by the resemblances between the Grimms' fairy-tale character and the heroic Siegfried than Richard Wagner. In a letter to his friend Theodor Uhlig, he wrote: "Haven't I ever told you this amusing story? It's the tale of the lad who ventures forth to learn what fear is and who is so dumb that he just can't do it. Imagine my amazement when I suddenly realized that that lad is no one else but—young Siegfried."[22]

It would not be difficult to identify countless other guileless fools and lads without fear in German literature. From the baroque era through the romantic period to the present, naiveté is the signature of many a literary hero. The protagonist of Grimmelshausen's *Sim-*

plicius Simplicissimus may be a clever rogue, but his name is telling. Like Parzival, he moves from foolish innocence to an understanding of the ways of the world, though his story ends in disillusion. Goethe's *Wilhelm Meister's Apprenticeship*, perhaps the finest exemplar of the *Bildungsroman*, that most hallowed of German literary traditions, gives us a naive innocent who happens to be fortunate enough to stumble into the right circles. We do not have to look far in the romantic era for heroes pure in heart and innocent in spirit. Each and every one of them—from Novalis's Heinrich von Ofterdingen to Josef von Eichendorff's Florio—begins the first leg of his journey into the wild blue yonder as a charming young man wholly untutored in worldly matters.

Twentieth-century German literature has no shortage of similar types. In a belated introduction to *The Magic Mountain*, Thomas Mann makes a point of bowing in the direction of Hans Castorp's literary antecedents. Mystified by the way in which the weight of literary tradition—without his knowing it—determines his protagonist's character, he is also flattered by the company in which literary critics placed his hero. Both Parzival and Wilhelm Meister, he notes, belong to the class of "guileless fools," and his Hans Castorp is no different. His "simplicity and artlessness" make him a legitimate literary cousin of those two quester figures. Yet Hans Castorp can also display all the wisdom of an innocent: when he wants something, he can be "clever," "crafty," and "shrewd." That Mann further emphasizes resemblances "here and there" between Hans Castorp's story and fairy tales comes as no surprise.[23]

It may seem to be stretching a point to suggest that fairy tales can tell us something about what historians of the *Annales* School call *mentalités*. Yet, throughout the ages, storytellers have embroidered the narratives passed on to them with the cultural values as well as with the facts of their own milieu. Every subtle change can be significant, so long as it takes place on a large scale and does not simply represent one idiosyncratic telling of a tale. What the Grimms' collection tells us about heroes does not deviate fundamentally from what other German folkloric and literary sources declare. There is far more to naiveté than meets the eye.

5

SPINNING TALES
The Distaff Side

> Storytelling is always the art of repeating stories, and this
> art is lost when the stories are no longer retained. It is lost
> because there is no more weaving and spinning to go on
> while they are being told.
>
> —WALTER BENJAMIN, "The Storyteller"

NEARLY everyone has heard of Mother Goose, but how many people can identify *Stories, or Tales of Times Past with Morals*? Or Charles Perrault for that matter? The renowned collection of fairy tales Perrault wrote was published under that title in 1697. Both in France and well beyond its borders, the eight stories in that collection captured the popular imagination and caught fire. The title, however, never took hold. It slipped into obscurity, in some cases right along with the author of the tales. *Tales of Mother Goose* is the name by which Perrault's collection came to be known. Perrault may not be a household term, but Mother Goose's reputation as a storyteller is firmly entrenched.

Just who was Mother Goose? There are nearly as many theories on that subject as there are tales in Perrault's collection. One thing is clear: the term *ma mère l'oye* did not originate with Perrault. Mother Goose has been around since at least 1650, when one writer referred to her "fantastic and fictitious" tales. Whether she was a real person is another question. There are those who insist that Mother Goose is nothing more than a collective term for the many elderly peasant women who narrated the kinds of tales gathered by Perrault. Since these women were allegedly entrusted with less strenuous chores on the farm—among them tending geese—they became known by the name ma mère l'oye. Other scholars have proposed that the many Mother Gooses of the world actually got their name from the cackling sound heard when they sat around gossiping or telling stories. The ethnocentric theory that one Elizabeth Goose of Boston, Massachusetts, was the real Mother Goose has long been discredited. No one has ever succeeded in locating the volume *Songs for the Nursery or Mother Goose's Melodies* that the man who married one of Mrs. Goose's sixteen children is said to have printed.[1]

Neither the casual etymologies of the term *Mother Goose* nor the positivistic attempts to pin down Mother Goose's identity are particularly satisfying. Even one literalist's suggestion that *Mother Goose* refers to a fable of ancient times in which a goose instructs and entertains her goslings with stories is not especially convincing, particularly since the fable is never printed along with the supposition. Theories that connect Mother Goose with various legendary and mythological figures are somewhat more promising and compelling. It is not wholly improbable that ma mère l'oye has something to do with a French queen named Berthe, who is often represented in legends telling tales to children. That queen, endowed either with one large foot or two oversized feet (depending on the source), has also been identified as the model for a number of church statues of *la reine pédauque* (from the term *la reine pied-d'oie* or *regina pede aucae*, meaning "the goose-footed queen"). She has close ties with spinners as well as storytellers. The phrase "when Queen Bertha was spinning" (in French, *au temps que la reine Berthe filait*, and in Italian, *nel tempo ove Berta filava*) is virtually synonymous with our "once upon a time" or "in the good old days." In France, a person asked to give his word might swear by the spindle of Queen Pédauque. That Queen Berthe's foot became enlarged or otherwise deformed from spinning seems unlikely, since spinning wheels were not yet commonly employed in her day and age. Hers seems to have been a congenital defect.[2]

The German counterpart of France's Queen Berthe is the mythological figure Berchta or Perchta, a close cousin of Holda and Frau Holle. Each of these figures reigns supreme as the patron goddess of spinners in one region or another of a German-speaking country.

Berchta, like Queen Berthe, is goose-footed, but in her case it is not entirely clear whether the webbed foot is a sign of her otherworldly origins or simply a deformity that has developed during the many hours she spent keeping a spinning wheel in motion.[3]

Moving from a goose-footed queen or goddess to Mother Goose may seem a rather long step. Perrault's Mother Goose, after all, is neither regal nor stately. And she seems to have none of the physical deformities that might connect her with geese. But she too is both spinner and storyteller. The frontispiece (figure 8) to Perrault's *His-*

FIGURE 8. *The frontispiece to Perrault's collection* Contes de ma mère l'oye *announces on the placard the title of the volume.*

toires ou Contes du temps passé shows us an old woman, seated by a spindle, dressed in peasant garb. Three well-groomed and wide-eyed children are gathered around her, evidently hanging on her every word. A plaque on the wall bears the inscription "Contes de ma mère l'oye." This illustration appears to have stood model for countless frontispieces to nineteenth-century collections of fairy tales: an elderly, careworn peasant woman with a spindle or spinning wheel by her side and a cluster of attentive youngsters at her feet becomes the visual entry point to the world of printed fairy tales (figures 9 and 10). The Grimms further propagated the myth of a hardy peasant woman by including a portrait of Dorothea Vieh-

FIGURE 9. *The frontispiece for A. L. Grimm's collection of fairy tales did much to shape the myth of elderly peasant women as the true purveyors of oral narratives.*

FIGURE 10. *Carl and Theodor Colshorn's anthology of fairy tales and legends received a decorative touch in Ludwig Richter's study of a* Märchen-mütterchen *and her youthful listeners.*

mann in the second edition of the *Nursery and Household Tales*. Edgar
Taylor, the English translator of the Grimms' collection, must have
been so enamored by Dorothea Viehmann's features and by the
Grimms' description of her that he turned her—under the pseu-
donym Gammer Gretel—into the source for the entire collection.
This "good-humored farmer's wife" (there is no indication that Dorothea Viehmann was one or the other) knew "all the good stories
that were told in the country," according to Taylor. "Every evening,
about Christmas time, the boys and girls of the neighborhood gathered round her, to hear her tell some of her budget of strange stories."[4]

In the course of the nineteenth century, a number of interesting
changes took place in the iconography of telling tales. While the
spindle or spinning wheel gradually receded into the background
until it finally disappeared, the features of the narrating figure became ever softer and more benevolent. Both Ludwig Richter and
Gustave Doré, for example, give us in their representations of fairy-
tale storytellers (figures 11 and 12) women who look more like amiable middle-class grandmothers than like flinty peasant women.
Doré's figure is typical of the latter half of the nineteenth century.
His narrator is neither a genuine toiler nor a teller; a spindle is nowhere in sight and a book has appeared on her lap. With the prolif-
eration of printed collections of tales, reading took the place of recounting and fairy tales moved from the workroom, or *Spinnstube*,
into the nursery and parlor.

Attractive as the frontispiece to Perrault's first edition of the *Histoires* may be, this decorative touch is misleading on a number of
counts—at least past readings of the sketch have been misleading.
The illustration has been presumed to depict Mother Goose and to
suggest that the elderly woman telling tales by the fireside is the
real "author" of the tales in the volume, or at least one of its real authors. As shown in the vignette, this Mother Goose is thought to take
on a representative function. She stands for the countless domestic
servants who told and retold fairy tales to their young charges.
There is, it should be noted, nothing in the illustration that defini-
tively identifies the woman shown telling tales with Mother Goose.

FIGURE 11. *Ludwig Richter's frontispiece for Bechstein's* Märchenbuch *takes us from the fireside into the woods and adds all manner of sentimental touches to the representation of storytellers.*

FIGURE 12. *Gustave Doré's storyteller must rely on a written text to entertain what appear to be her grandchildren.*

As one folklorist has pointed out, that woman may simply be re-peating to her enrapt auditors the stories of one Mother Goose.[5] The illustration has also fueled the false notion that in "the olden days" fairy tales were told exclusively by elderly peasant women to children. Female servants and nursemaids in fact constituted only one segment of the population of folk raconteurs, and children (as we now know) became only with time the principal auditors of the tales. George Cruikshank's delightful illustration for Edgar Taylor's *German Popular Stories* (figure 13) tells us something about the milieu in which the Grimms' translated stories were meant to be read. And Ludwig Richter's depiction of a *Spinnstube* (figure 14) reminds us that men too counted among peasant raconteurs, just as both adults and children figured in the audience.

FIGURE 13. German Popular Stories, *for which this vignette by George Cruikshank served as a frontispiece, is evidently a big hit with men and women, old and young alike.*

Mother Goose remains a mystery. But our detour into speculations on her origins and about pictorial representations of the settings in which her tales are told reveal a number of recurrent themes and associations. Whether those speculations are valid or not, it is striking that so many of them connect Mother Goose with the art of spinning. The French Queen Berthe is renowned as an expert in that arena; the German goddess Bertha is also an adept. In the frontispiece to Perrault's *Histoires* and to numerous other collections of fairy tales, the presence of the spindle reminds us that one of the favored sites for telling folktales was the workroom or *Spinnstube*, where spinning yarn helped to while away the hours de-

FIGURE 14. *Ludwig Richter's sketch of a spinning room makes it clear that women may have held a monopoly on spinning, but not on telling tales.*

voted to spinning flax. The repetitive rhythms of work in turn impressed upon the listeners (who might themselves be budding raconteurs) the details of each narrative. The alliance of spinning with tale telling is therefore an especially congenial one, for the labor of the one is lightened by the activity of the other.[6]

From the various theories on Mother Goose's origins, it becomes clear that spinning and telling tales are more than two compatible, mutually fortifying arts. They are further affiliated in that they both have the power to disfigure the women who practice them. Spinners, as the physical deformities of France's goose-footed queen and Germany's goose-footed goddess suggest, must pay for their mastery of a craft with a physical handicap linked directly or indirectly to the craft itself. If the activity of spinning is connected with bodily mutilation, telling tales becomes associated with vocal disturbances. Women who repeat stories are perceived to cackle like geese, to ir-

ritate and to offend with their voices. Speculations about Mother
Goose's origins may not reveal much about her actual identity, but
they do tell us a great deal about the perceived threads connecting
the telling of tales with the spinning of flax.

The activity of spinning and carrying out various other domestic
tasks is so closely associated with telling tales that it is hardly surprising to find fairy-tale heroines gathering flax, pricking their fingers with spindles, cutting their hands on thread, and in general
spending countless hours at the spinning wheel. Here again, pain
becomes the emblem of the craft. Miniature spinning wheels, spindles, and bobbins of gold are the sole items of baggage taken by a
number of fairy-tale heroines on their journeys from one home to
another. (In the Middle Ages, queens were often buried with those
items.) The Grimms' collection of tales gives us spinners of every
stripe: lazy, diligent, inept, talented, clumsy, and graceful. As expected, spinning is a quintessentially female activity. (Our language,
with its use of the terms *spindle side* or *distaff side* to refer to the female line of the family and *spear side* to the male, is quite explicit on
this point. Metaphorical terms derived from *spinning*, as for instance
spinster, nearly always refer to women.) The Grimms' story "Twelve
Huntsmen" makes it clear that no man would think of even casting
his eyes on a spinning wheel. To test whether the twelve huntsmen
of the tale's title are male or female, the king proposes having them
pass by a row of a dozen spinning wheels. That the hunters fail to
take notice of the instruments proves to him that they must be men.
Had they smiled, they would have betrayed their identity as women.

Not all women in fairy tales break into a smile at the sight of a
spinning wheel. Still, there are many who accept spinning as their
lot, even as a noble occupation, while others find in it, if not their
own means of salvation, then the one activity that promises to liberate others from curses and spells. The young heroine of "Twelve
Brothers" spends seven years mutely spinning in order to disen-
chant her brothers. Like her folkloric cousin who sews her way to
salvation in "The Six Swans," she finds deliverance by withdrawing
from the world and retreating into the sphere of silent domestic activities. "The Nixie of the Pond" also gives us a heroine who restores

a bewitched creature to his normal human condition by spinning flax, this time on a golden spinning wheel. In all these tales, spinning, weaving, and sewing (along with an entire array of other household activities) appear to have the power to turn animals into men and to domesticate the most ferocious beasts.

If some tales invest spinning with the power to break magical spells, others endow that same activity with equally beneficial, though less miraculous, powers. "The Spindle, the Shuttle, and the Needle" gives us a young orphan whose sole patrimony consists of a house along with the three instruments named in the tale's title. The heroine works so hard at spinning, weaving, and sewing that "the flax in the storeroom seemed to increase of its own accord, and when she had woven a cloth or a rug, or sewed a shirt, she always found a buyer who payed amply." So modest is this paragon of diligence that she blushes to the roots of her hair, lowers her eyes, and continues spinning when a handsome young prince passes by on horseback in search of a bride. The spindle on her wheel is less inhibited: it dashes off in pursuit of the prince, draws a golden thread behind it, and ropes the not entirely reluctant young man into the girl's lodgings. The orphan's shuttle and needle perform in an equally impressive fashion: the shuttle weaves a splendid carpet and the needle flies about the house adding decorative touches to tables, benches, and windows. Overpowered by the sight of such extraordinary domestic competence, the prince proposes at once. The tale could not announce its message more clearly: excellence in the household arts singles out the most humble girl and makes her worthy of a prince. In the treasure room of the palace, she enshrines as sacred objects the spindle, the shuttle, and the needle that lifted her to her new status, thereby conveniently ensuring that these items will remain forever unusable.

Numerous other tales in the Grimms' collection celebrate the virtues of domestic talents. The beautiful, hard-working stepdaughter of a mean-spirited widow finds that spinning until one's fingers bleed pays off in the end. Frau Holle, guardian spirit of spinners, rewards her efforts in spinning, baking, harvesting, and bed-making by showering her with gold. Her ugly, lazy half-sister is punished for her slothful ways when Frau Holle empties a steaming cauldron of pitch on her. The bridegroom of "The Odds and Ends" goes so far as to trade his attractive, "but lazy and slovenly" betrothed for a serving maid with a reputation for being a "good hard worker." Vanity and laziness are cardinal vices in all these tales; modesty and industry figure as signs of distinction. And dexterity in spinning functions as the trademark of self-effacing diligence.

If male protagonists must routinely submit to character tests and demonstrate compassion, their female counterparts are subjected to tests of their competence in the domestic arena—tests that turn into tasks usually carried out without the aid of helpers. As noted earlier, fairy-tale heroines rarely display humility; rather they are placed in humble, if not downright demeaning, circumstances. King Thrushbeard forces his blue-blooded wife to try her hand at making fires, cooking, cleaning house, selling pots, weaving, and spinning; the king's daughter in "The Prince and the Princess" is obliged to spend her afternoons washing dishes; the princess in "The Six Servants," the Goose Girl, and Two-Eyes must tend swine, geese, and goats; in addition to picking peas and lentils out of the ashes, Cinderella has to get up before daybreak, carry water, light fires, cook, and wash (for these chores she receives no help at all); Thousandfurs too is burdened with "all the nasty work" and must haul wood and water, tend the fires, pluck fowls, clean vegetables, and sweep up the ashes. Even the heroine of "The Three Little Men in the Forest," who passes a character test not unlike that generally put to male heroes, must take broom in hand before becoming the beneficiary of the helpers in the tale's title. Should they succeed in escaping oppression at home, fairy-tale heroines often undertake a journey that succeeds only in landing them at the site of new forms of domestic drudgery. But by holding their tongues and exercising their muscles, they ultimately succeed in rising in the world.

Although the activity of most fairy-tale heroines is confined to the domestic sphere, a few take to the road to carry out tasks required to liberate themselves and their husbands. The pattern of the heroine's journey in "The Lilting, Leaping Lark" is in many ways typical of the redemptive journeys undertaken by female protagonists.

For seven years, the princess of that tale gives chase to her husband, who has been changed into a dove. After losing track of him, she makes her way up to the sun in search of guidance and wisdom but receives for her efforts nothing more than a small box. A trip to the moon yields an egg that is to be broken should the princess find herself in distress. A conference with the four winds results in some concrete information about her avian spouse along with a third gift. When the princess finally arrives at the castle of her beloved, she learns that he has reverted to human form and is planning to celebrate his wedding feast. Slipping on the dress in the box given her by the sun, she succeeds in arousing the envy of her rival and strikes a bargain with her: the dress in exchange for the chance to spend one night in the bedroom of the prince. Once there, she reveals her identity, but in vain, for a servant of the false bride has administered a sleeping potion to the unsuspecting groom. The egg from the moon contains a second dazzling gown—one that once again provokes the envy of the false bride and leads to further negotiations resulting in a second night with the prince. On the second try, she succeeds in recounting her past to the prince who, upon recognizing her voice, is freed from the spell that bound him to the false bride.

In countless tales, one finds female protagonists making journeys to the sun, the moon, and to the winds or stars. These cosmic excursions produce gowns that are tendered as bribes to a false bride in exchange for the chance to arrange an intimate meeting with her groom. But the sun, the moon, and the stars (or variants thereof) also appear as a trio in fairy tales where the heroine never ventures from home or travels no farther than the next farm or castle. Thousandfurs tries to stall for time when her father presses her to set a date for their marriage by demanding three dresses: "One as golden as the sun, one as silvery as the moon, and one as glittering as the stars." When she recognizes that there is no hope of bringing her father to his senses, she bundles the three dresses in a nutshell, wraps herself in a coat of furs, and blackens her face and hands with soot. Donkey-Skin (Peau d'Ane), the French cousin of Thousandfurs, has similar tastes when it comes to her wardrobe. From her father she demands a dress the color of the sky, another the color of the moon, and a third as bright as the sun. When her father too fails to keep his desires in check, she dons a donkey-skin, takes to the road, and ends her journey on a farm laboring as a scullery maid. Cinderella's attire does not have explicit cosmic attributes, but the three dresses that rain down from the hazel tree planted on her mother's grave bear a distinct resemblance to the clothing worn by Thousandfurs and Donkey-Skin. The heroine of "The Prince and the Princess" receives from her mother three walnuts that contain dresses also used to arouse jealousy. In "The Cast-Iron Stove," a princess is given three nutshells housing three dresses that are successively slipped on in order to stir the envy of her rival for the hero's affections.

Time and again in the Grimms' collection, we encounter heroines who are reduced to tending swine, washing dishes, or scrubbing floors, but who are ultimately liberated from their lowly condition by clothing themselves in frocks that arouse the admiration of a prince and that drive rival princesses into jealous rages. Through a combination of labor and good looks, the heroine gets her man. Social promotion depends primarily on proof of domestic skills—the equivalent of the male's demonstration of compassion. But it also turns to some extent on the receipt of gifts from nature, gifts that endow the heroine with nearly supernatural attractiveness. If the helpers in stories with male leads transfer their strength, wits, and courage to the hero, the helpers in tales with female leads bestow beauty on the heroine. That beauty, symbolized by the gowns, yokes the cosmic and the domestic in that it is the joint product of nature and of human labors (spinning and weaving). Supernal beauty and down-to-earth hard work are linked to create the fairy-tale heroine's passport to success.

Most fairy tales extol the value of diligence in spinning (and other household arts), yet there are a few texts in the *Nursery and Household Tales* that present it as a tediously oppressive activity to be avoided at all costs. "Frau Holle" already contains hints that spinning goes hand in hand with physical mutilation. And it is hard to have pleasant associations with spindles after reading "Briar Rose."[7] But other tales—these generally do not number among the classical fairy tales—are more explicit in their condemnation of spinning and their defense of sloth. In one such popular tale (of which a variant form appears in the Grimms' collection), the heroine avoids spinning by seeking out three misshapen hags, confronting her husband with them, and attributing each of the women's deformities to one step in the process of spinning. "The Horrid Spinning of Flax" recounts the same trick, which succeeds in liberating a queen and her three daughters from the "tortures" of spinning, tortures imposed on them by the tale's monarch. It is easy to see why the Grimms dropped this tale when they prepared the second edition of the collection. Sharp wits, these tales seem to say, are all that are needed to escape a life of drudgery at the spinning wheel and to secure a life of indolence and indulgence.[8]

Idleness and indulgence are paired in one other spinning tale among the texts in the Grimms' collection. "The Lazy Spinner" recounts the various ruses to which a woman resorts in order to escape the miserable lot of a spinner. She begins by making one excuse after another to her husband, who is forever supplying her with flax in his eagerness to keep her occupied. When he heads straight for the forest to cut wood for a missing reel, she follows him, hides in a tree, and warbles a warning from above: "He who cuts wood for reels shall die, and she who winds shall perish." This and other artifices conspire to prevent the husband from ever mentioning yarn or spinning in his wife's presence. "You'll have to admit that she was a hateful woman" (*eine garstige Frau*). This is the final declaration of the tale, a judgment that probably came straight from the pen of Wilhelm Grimm. The version printed in the first edition of the *Nursery and Household Tales* ends with the husband's decision to stop pressing his wife to get on with her household chores. Only in a later edition does the intrusive voice of a judgmental narrator call on the reader to join in condemning the woman's behavior. Laziness coupled with deceit was a combination that ran counter to the values inscribed on so many tales gathered in the collection.

If we review the various stories in the *Nursery and Household Tales* that incorporate spinning into the plot line, it becomes clear that the occupation of spinning assumes a privileged position only in texts furthest removed from reality. If a spindle dances, you can be sure that it will bring good fortune. If a distaff is placed in the service of disenchantment, it will perform many useful offices. But once we leave behind the supernatural arena of classical fairy tales and move to the earthy realism of anecdotes, jests, and humorous folktales, spinning becomes an occupation that elicits little more than moans and groans. A clever heroine will devote all her mental and physical resources to finding avenues for escaping the drudgery of sitting at a spinning wheel.

Fairy tales, with their extravagant touches and surreal events, have a special appeal for children. Tales of magic and enchantment are precisely those most frequently selected for "children's editions" of the *Nursery and Household Tales.* These are also, perhaps coincidentally, the stories that endorse conventional ethical values and social norms. Wilhelm Grimm saw to it that they were encoded with tributes to thrift, honesty, obedience, diligence, patience, and other noble civic virtues. He rarely resisted the temptation to highlight certain values, to add moralistic glosses, and to elaborate specific lessons in the tales themselves. After all, with time, he came to recognize the book's value as a moral guide through the dark thickets of nineteenth-century social unrest. He was not above lifting a tale such as "The Spindle, the Shuttle, and the Needle," with its hardwork ethic and pro-spinning message, from a literary source. Sacrificing folkloristic authenticity to ideological purity failed to prick his scholarly conscience.[9]

Once we turn from fairy tales to humorous folk tales set in villages, a different ethos prevails, one that makes a fine art of escaping work. Here, Wilhelm Grimm may not have been restrained in exercising his editorial powers, but he appears to have been far less biased in favor of bourgeois values.[10] (He did not let the "lazy spinner" escape without a sharp authorial reprimand, but he allowed a number of brash rebels and rogues to get away with subverting the work ethic and undermining authority in its most regal form.) The values encapsulated in biographies of discharged soldiers, for example, deviate dramatically from those embedded in fairy tales. In

"Six Who Made Their Way in the World" and again in "The Blue Light," discharged soldiers get the better of the ungrateful monarchs who exploited their valor in times of war, but left them penniless once hostilities ceased. From one edition to the next, the monarchs come under heavier fire. Here are the opening sentences of the first printed version of "The Blue Light": "Once upon a time there was a king who had a soldier as a servant. When he became old and useless, he was sent off with nothing." The final edition of the *Nursery and Household Tales* elaborates further on the soldier's sacrifices and on the king's cruelty, heightening the contrasts between the two.

> Once upon a time there was a soldier who had served his king faithfully for many a year. But when the war was over and the soldier could no longer serve because of the many wounds he had received, the king said to him: "You can go home. I don't need you any more. You won't be getting any more money, because I pay wages only to those who give me something in return."

The hero of "Six Who Made Their Way in the World" serves his king well, but once the war is over he receives no more than a trifling sum for his efforts. "Hold it," he says. "They can't do this to me! If I find the right people, the king will have to hand over to me the wealth of the entire land." And he proceeds to make good on his resolution. By the end of the story, we find him winding his way home with seven thousand wagonloads of gold. The defeated monarch of the tale is forced to concede that the hero and his five companions are simply too much for him; the strength of their show of solidarity has humbled the once arrogant monarch and reduced him to the modest circumstances he sought to inflict on his faithful servants.

In a fairy tale such as "The Frog King or Iron Heinrich," the paternalistic authority of kings is sacred. Folk tales in the Grimms' collection, with their emphasis on class conflicts rather than family conflicts, are far more likely to cast aspersions on authority dressed in monarchical garb. In this context, we must not forget that although the Grimms may have espoused conservative social values, they also belonged to the "Göttingen Seven," that courageous group of professors who were dismissed from their posts for protesting the scrapping of the constitution by the king of Hanover.[11]

Folk tales are just as effective in belittling the rich and powerful (the very ranks to which fairy-tale heroes aspire) as they are in exposing the failings of monarchs. "Clever Gretel" recounts a cook's skill in outsmarting her master and depriving him of a pair of plump roasted chickens. A poor peasant hangs out a shingle declaring that he is Dr. Know-it-all and soon gets the better of his social superiors. "The Peasant's Clever Daughter" proves that a young girl of humble origins can outwit a king. "The Young Giant" shows us a character whose goal in life is to bamboozle and humiliate one miserly employer after another. Wilhelm Grimm did not let slip opportunities to add sardonic comments on the values implicitly endorsed by these stories. There is, for example, more than a touch of irony in the coda to "The Wise Servant," which teaches how to dodge household chores in one quick, easy lesson. "Don't worry about your master and his orders," the tale declares. "Do whatever enters your head, whatever you feel like. Then you'll be acting as wisely as wise Hans."

Despite asides here and there on the impropriety of hoodwinking one's superiors, the stories of village life compiled by the Grimms are remarkably bold in their indictment of the monied and powerful. Again and again they show the common man turning the tables on the wealthy or at least exposing their vulgar, fatuous ways. The underdog usually gets the upper hand by using his wits, but occasionally he obtains what he wants by engaging in utterly inane behavior.[12] Either way, he succeeds in unmasking the privileged and in demonstrating their innate inferiority. In folk tales set in the village or on the road, the hero works hardest when he is hatching plots to humiliate his master or other representatives of local authority. Deceit, chicanery, and slyness are paraded before the reader as the highest virtues; without them, survival, let alone prosperity, would simply be out of reach. Fairy tales may tacitly endorse the prevailing social order (usually a feudal society with an overlay of bourgeois values) and subscribe to all the virtues required to uphold it, but folk tales attack the sanctity of that order and subvert the very essence of the work ethic.

In this context, then, it is not surprising to find that spinning oc-
cupies a highly ambiguous status—not just in the Grimms' collection, but in Western folklore as a whole. It can take the form of both
a blessing and a curse. Like manual labor in general, it goes hand in
hand with industry and achievement, but it is also associated with
physical oppression and enslavement. In fairy tales, spinning skills
are a girl's best dowry, in some cases the only ones she needs. In folk
tales of a more realistic bent, spinning rarely builds character; it de-
forms the body and dulls the mind. To avoid it, a heroine is entitled
to resort to almost any means. The conflicting messages communi-
cated by fairy tales and folk tales are not mutually exclusive. Rather,
they accord with the contradictions of peasant life. Hard work was
one of the perceived methods of getting ahead or at least staying
even, but it also proved disfiguring and could impede the very goals
it set out to achieve.

In the Grimms' collection, there is one tale that conjoins the pro-
spinning ideology of magical fairy tales with the anti-work ethic of
humorous folk tales. The miller's daughter in "Rumpelstiltskin"
works her way up the ladder of social success through her alleged
accomplishments as a spinner, yet she also manages to avoid sitting
down at a spinning wheel. Whether we look at German, Scottish, or
French versions of the tale, the king whom the heroine marries
makes it clear just why he finds this humble girl so irresistible. In
one tale he congratulates himself on finding a wife whose spinning
will generate a steady stream of income. In another, he reassures
himself that her talents will protect him from financial ruin should
he lose his crown. In a third he reveals his high hopes about the rev-
enues his wife will produce by spinning silk. And in still others, he
rejoices at having found so "energetic," "diligent," and "able" a
bride.[13]

In some versions of "Rumpelstiltskin," the king's greed is stirred
by more than the prospect of finding an able-bodied worker. The
Grimms' final version of "Rumpelstiltskin," for example, features a
heroine who evidently can spin straw to gold, a talent that the story's
monarch finds "most appealing." That tale, rather than linking a
heroine's labor with supernatural beauty, allies hard work with
supernatural powers to produce desirability. While wealth is the ex-

plicit goal of most fairy-tale heroes, it usually stands on no more than an equal footing with a happy marriage. Few tales in the Grimms' collection are so crass as "Rumpelstiltskin" in depicting purely economic motives for marriage.

Rumpelstiltskin goes by many names. Titeliture, Doppeltürk, Purzinigele, Batzibitzili, Panzimanzi, and Whuppity Stoorie are just a few of his sobriquets. Whether he makes an appearance as Ricdin-Ricdon in a French tale or as Tom Tit Tot in an English tale, his essence and function remain much the same. Not so with the heroine. Although she is almost always a young girl of humble origins, her other attributes and abilities change dramatically from one tale to the next. The challenges to which she must rise also vary from tale to tale. In a random sample of seventeen versions of Rumpelstiltskin, for example, eleven turn on the issue of spinning vast quantities of flax in a ludicrously brief span of time; six are concerned with transforming straw or flax into gold.[14]

Let us begin by looking at tales that demand the fulfillment of quantitatively impossible tasks—spinning heaps upon heaps of flax. The heroines of these stories find themselves in a fix because a foxy parent is determined to get rid of a daughter who is old enough to marry. What quicker way to find a bridegroom, these tales imply, than to advertise a girl's diligence as a spinner. Indeed, diligence alone seems to make the heroine not just desirable, but virtually irresistible. The local monarch is invariably persuaded to marry a young woman who in reality is hopelessly lazy and often gluttonous to boot. In Italy, she devours seven pots of noodles; in England, she polishes off seven dishes of pudding; and in Russia, she bolts down seven loaves of bread.

A few of the heroines in tales pertaining to flax spinning start out as hard workers whose parents, for one reason or another, are anxious to disencumber themselves of a daughter. In such cases, the cast of fairy-tale characters is rapidly reshuffled to yield a diligent daughter, an unnaturally hostile mother, and a relentlessly demanding mother-in-law as replacements for the lazy daughter, deceitful parent, and gullible king. Still, the plot line remains intact. No matter how capable the understudy for the lazy heroine, she too shudders at the unending bundles of flax hauled into the palace by her prospective mother-in-law. In the end, she is also obliged to enlist the services of a Rumpelstiltskin to appease a regal figure. Lazy or diligent, the protagonist finds herself trapped in a perilous situation, one that requires her to resort to trickery and deceit in order to deliver on the promises made by a parent and to escape the sure death that awaits her if she cannot make good on those promises.

A second set of tales recounts the trials of a young girl (usually a miller's daughter) whose father boasts that his daughter can transform straw to gold. Here, the heroine faces a task that requires more than herculean effort—nothing short of magic can save her from this predicament. Nonetheless, the constellation of characters is the same as in the first set of tales; only here, the attribute associated with the daughter has shifted from laziness to beauty, and the parental lie has been reformulated: the daughter is said to have supernatural powers rather than superhuman ones. Of the several versions of "Rumpelstiltskin" recorded in draft forms for the *Nursery and Household Tales*, one deviates from this norm by narrating the fortunes of a young girl "cursed" with the gift of spinning flax to gold. The text is brief, with only a few broad strokes used to establish the grounds for making a pact:

> A little girl was given a knot of flax to spin, but ended up spinning threads of gold, not a single flaxen thread did she pull from her wheel. She was so sad that she went up to the roof, where she spent three days spinning, still there was nothing but gold. Then a little man came along: "I'll help you out of your plight, a young prince will come by and marry you, but you must promise me your first-born child."[15]

This tale, unlike its more cynical and psychologically realistic counterparts, is not built on logical premises. It gives us nothing more than an outline of the most fundamental fairy-tale situation: helplessness/deliverance. Once the girl reaches the point of desperation (three days are always sufficient to test a fairy-tale figure's strength), help is at hand. The details of plot are inconsequential; they simply flesh out the basic situation.

The prelude to "Rumpelstiltskin" can take two basic forms. When it operates with the opposition lazy/diligent, it shifts into the comic mode of the folk tale, indulging in irreverent humor (often at the expense of the tale's monarchs). Here the story's primary aim is to engineer a marriage between the heroine and her social and economic superior, and that goal is accomplished through trickery and deceit. The mother who boasts that her daughter can spin five skeins a day (when in reality her sole achievement consists in having devoured five pies at a sitting) has something of the shrewdness associated with the "brave little tailor," who prides himself on having dispatched "seven at one blow." But while the mother is obliged to advertise her daughter's capacity for hard work in order to arrange a fairy-tale marriage for a folk-tale heroine, the tailor attains his social promotion by broadcasting his brawn and using his brains. The folk heroine of "Rumpelstiltskin" can get ahead in life only when a parent is clever enough to hoodwink a monarch and when a helper comes to her rescue.

When the prelude to "Rumpelstiltskin" operates with the opposition natural/supernatural, the tale slips into the melodramatic mode of fairy tales, depicting situations in which the stakes are always high and a heroine whose morale is always low. Here the goal is also once again marriage, but with little purposeful maneuvering on the part of the tale's protagonists. The father boasts about his daughter's supernatural powers, yet no ulterior motives are attributed to him; a girl can spin flax to gold, but she has no particular aspirations in mind. The clever ruses and resourceful deceptions that drive the plots of folk tales rarely advance the action of fairy tales. Still, both the folk-tale and fairy-tale versions of "Rumpelstiltskin" rest on the premise that a daughter who produces wealth, whether through her own labor or through magical means, is a girl who can make a good marriage.

At the heart of all versions of "Rumpelstiltskin" is a contract made between an innocent young girl and a devilish creature. Motivating that contract—the tale's stable center—requires nothing more than positioning the heroine in a situation where she finds herself in desperate straits. Whether there is any logic to her neediness is irrelevant. Psychological realism has never been the strong suit of folkloristic narratives, particularly those that veer off in the direction of the supernatural. What counts is the heroine's perceived need for intervention; that need, no matter what form it takes, elicits a helper. The industrious and gifted heroines in this tale type do not take long to recognize the impossibility of the task facing them and consequently throw up their hands in despair or burst into tears. The hopelessly self-indulgent and less persevering heroines simply shrug their shoulders and resign themselves to their fate. "The devil may spin for all I care," asserts one young woman.[16] No sooner has she spoken these words than Terry-top, the Cornish Rumpelstiltskin, materializes to accept the invitation to sit down at the spinning wheel. The pact between maiden and unearthly creature is quickly sealed.

The very labor celebrated as captivating, as the activity designed to win the heart of a king, is carried out by one of the least attractive of fairy-tale figures, a misshapen gnome of questionable origins. For all his less than charming physical attributes, Rumpelstiltskin has succeeded in eliciting a good measure of sympathy from readers. "It is not the miller who boastingly vaunts his daughter into peril, or the avaricious, cruel king who marries her, but the little man who helps her and wants only a child for himself who is singled out for punishment," complains one critic. In a world where fathers tell brazen lies about their daughters in order to marry them off, where marriages require prenuptial agreements that read like labor contracts, and where young girls agree to give up their first-born child in return for a favorable marriage, Rumpelstiltskin comes off rather well. He works hard to hold up his end of the bargain, shows genuine compassion when the queen regrets the agreement into which she has entered, and is prepared to add an escape clause to their contract even though he stands to gain nothing from it. To be sure, he has taken advantage of the desperate heroine's shortsightedness, but he still is as much helper as villain.[17]

The entire cast of male protagonists in "Rumpelstiltskin" can be seen as a set of mixed characters: guardians, protectors, and benefactors become each in turn the heroine's adversaries.[18] The father imperils his daughter's life by trying to impress the king, the king obliges the heroine to spin straw to gold under penalty of death, and Rumpelstiltskin demands her child in payment for his services as spinner. Each crisis in the various phases of the heroine's life is marked by the transformation of a helper into a villain and the emergence of a new helper as a countervailing force to the turncoat. The heroine's life turns into a succession of crises in which she is put at risk by the very figure who liberated her from the previous crisis. And in nearly every case it is deceit that gets her into trouble or deceit that saves her. In the end the queen herself uses what can be seen as deception in order to dodge the terms of the contract. Once she has ascertained Rumpelstiltskin's name, she finds it hard to resist the temptation to engage in the cruel game of playing dumb as she rehearses various names.

With the revelation of Rumpelstiltskin's name, the immediate threat facing the queen is lifted, but it is not clear that the burden of spinning will be banished from her life forever. The queen's husband, who is often not party to the secret of his wife's miraculous achievements, might well be tempted to seek further demonstrations of her prowess at the wheel. Who is to say that Rumpelstiltskin's demand for fulfillment of the terms of his bond represents the last in the succession of crises marking the heroine's life? Some folklorists have suggested that a tale known as "The Three Spinners" functions as a sequel to "Rumpelstiltskin," a finishing touch that puts a decisive end to the demands made on the queen. The close relationship between the two tales has long been recognized; in Aarne and Thompson's register of tale types, they stand side by side.

The Grimms' version of "The Three Spinners" begins with these words: "Once upon a time there was a lazy girl who didn't want to spin." This opening line immediately establishes the heroine's kinship with the female protagonists of "Rumpelstiltskin" and its variants. The entire first part of "The Three Spinners" seems modeled on the plot line of one version of "Rumpelstiltskin." The lazy young protagonist finds her way into a palace after her mother brags to the queen about her daughter's unnerving obsession with spinning. The lie proves effective, for the queen is delighted with the prospect of a daughter-in-law so enamored of the work ethic. "You may be poor," she bluntly avows, "but what does it matter? You're a good hard worker, and that's all the dowry you need." Faced with the task of spinning flax piled from floor to ceiling in three cavernous rooms, the poor girl despairs, sure that all is lost. Help surfaces in the form of three old women: one with a broad foot grotesquely flattened from treading, another with a lower lip hideously enlarged from licking thread, and a third with a thumb broadened out of shape from twisting thread. The three weird crones carry out the girl's charge in exchange for an invitation to her wedding and a promise that they will be introduced there as cousins and treated as intimates. At the wedding celebration, the bridegroom is so appalled by the unsightliness of the deformed cousins that he forbids his wife to spin that "horrid flax."

Until the moment the three spinners shuffle into the palace to offer their services, we might easily mistake this tale for yet another variant of "Rumpelstiltskin." But their appearance marks the point at which "The Three Spinners" parts ways with "Rumpelstiltskin." These ladies may know how to spin and they may be prepared to rescue the girl from her plight, but they have little else in common with the figure of Rumpelstiltskin. The terms of their contract are more than reasonable: for their labors they demand nothing but kindness. To be sure, the beneficiary of their favors risks offending her prospective husband with her "repulsive" (the term is his) acquaintances, but the conditions are still generous. Rather than demanding "something living" (as does Rumpelstiltskin) and proposing an exchange that imperils what will prove to be dearer to the queen than her own life, the crones simply test the heroine's character and inadvertently furnish her with a second reward once she passes the test. For once, a heroine gets what she wants by a show of good character.

Illustrators of "Rumpelstiltskin" have never been kind to the diminutive creature for whom the tale is named. Invariably clad in black, he is burdened with a physiognomy that displays devilish features to the world. His physical appearance, in tandem with his harsh contractual terms, colors the story with somber overtones.

The three spinners, by contrast, add a light touch to the story of the lazy girl's predicament. Once they appear, the story veers off into the burlesque, steering clear of the tragic or near tragic. With their broad feet, drooping lower lips, and fat thumbs (some versions give them wide hips and sagging bottoms from their sedentary ways), they offer comic relief from the pressing circumstances of the heroine. When they arrive at the wedding in order to hold the heroine to her end of the bargain, they cut strange figures in their outlandish costumes. It goes without saying that the bridegroom's dawning awareness of the direct link between the trio's deformities and their roles in the spinning process adds a humorous twist to the story. Valuing looks above labor, he proudly declares: "My beautiful bride shall never touch a spinning wheel again." As if waving a magic wand, he liberates his wife forever from the tyranny of labor in its most disfiguring form. As noted earlier, a variant of "The Three Spinners" gives us a heroine who outfoxes her husband by hiring three women with precisely the deformities that could be attributed to too many hours at the spinning wheel but are not. This version is even more explicit in subverting the work ethic and in celebrating the triumph of a clever mind over domestic matters. "And if she hasn't died, she's still lazing about somewhere," one version of the story ends. With their humorous tableaux and their displays of specious reasoning, both tales contrast starkly with the dead seriousness of the central scene in "Rumpelstiltskin."

"The Three Spinners" has less in common with the second part of "Rumpelstiltskin" than might appear at first blush. One tale gives us comic distortion, and the other gives us repeated narrow brushes with tragedy. That the two stories were once part of a larger whole (with Rumpelstiltskin responding to the queen's immediate needs and the three spinners providing a long-term solution to her problems) seems unlikely, despite the existence of a few such spliced texts. One narrative takes advantage of exaggeration to create a tall tale, the other mobilizes a supernatural agent to set its plot in motion. But "The Three Spinners" belongs unequivocally to the comic mode of folk tales, while "Rumpelstiltskin" moves along the melodramatic lines characteristic of fairy tales. Joining the two texts produces a distinctly jarring effect.[19]

"The Three Spinners" must have been close to the hearts of its tellers. It is a folk tale whose subject is the evasion of the very type of labor carried out while it was being told. It may initially commend hard work as a trait leading to a good match, but it is utterly realistic about the consequences of a life of labor. By imprinting the bodies of the three spinners with the trademarks of toil, the tale makes it eminently clear that beauty and hard work are incompatible. In proper folk-tale fashion, however, the heroine of "The Three Spinners" manages to earn a reputation as a diligent laborer even as she remains a beauty by escaping a lifetime of drudgery. Her story nonetheless illustrates the ambiguities associated with the household arts and reveals that the contradictions of life in an earlier age, however keenly felt, could be treated with irreverent humor.

"Rumpelstiltskin" lacks the homespun humor of "The Three Spinners." At its center stands the compact with its harsh terms: labor in exchange for "something living." The terms of the contract between the heroine and Rumpelstiltskin evidently did not always pit labor against life. One of its many variants is sketched out in the first edition of the *Nursery and Household Tales*. The resemblances to "Rapunzel," even in this brief outline, are unmistakable.

> A woman passes by a garden where there are beautiful cherries, she develops a craving for them, steps into the garden, and eats them; a black man rises up out of the ground, and she has to promise him her child. When it is born, he slips past all the guards that the woman's husband posted and won't allow the woman to keep her child unless she can guess his name. The husband follows him, watches him descend into a cave decorated with cooking spoons, and hears him call himself *Fleder Flitz*.

The exchange in this tale, as in "Rapunzel," is remarkably uneven. For something utterly trivial, the "black man" demands what is closest to the queen's heart. To be sure, satisfying a whim can cost dearly, and fairy tales make that point so often that it has taken on the character of a motif. Still, the terms of the contract are so asymmetrical that it becomes difficult for most readers to suspend disbelief. How is it that the black man is entitled to demand the woman's child? The plot withholds vital information of that nature yet in-

cludes details—the cooking spoons lining the cave—that fail to add
up. Scholars will be quick to remind us that the absence of logic and
causal connections point to this tale's folkloristic authenticity—it
gives us the poetry of the folk in pure, unadulterated form. That
poetry does not necessarily observe either the laws of nature or the
conventions established by human nature. Only when folklore began to enter written literature through various channels did it begin
to assimilate the logic of realistic narratives. Externally motivated
episodes gradually drove out poorly motivated events or wholly unmotivated ones.[20]

Were we to document the fortunes of "Rumpelstiltskin" over the
centuries, we would probably find that a tale about a pact between
mortal and demon evolved into a sequence of narratives, each offering ever more plausible grounds for the heroine's decision to enter into an agreement with so sinister a creature. Above all, a child—
a product of the queen's labor—comes to be exchanged for something that is its equivalent, if only in lexical terms: the product of the
demon's labors. These labors become ever more closely affiliated
with spinning, turning "Rumpelstiltskin" into a story that thematic-
izes the very labor that gave birth to it. The exchange between
mortal and demon becomes more evenly balanced and less improbable.[21]

It was perhaps inevitable that the language and the plot of many
fairy tales and folk tales would become contaminated by the context
in which they were told. Josef Lukas's anthology of European spinning tales reveals that almost any classical folkloristic narrative can
be retold in such a way that spinning figures prominently in the
plot.[22] An animal groom takes on the form of a silkworm, an impossible task is cast in terms of spinning, or a prohibition is violated
when a young girl spins on Sunday. But few fairy tales assimilated
the craft of spinning in so thoroughgoing a fashion as "Rumpelstiltskin." Once the pact between girl and gnome was defined by the
terms spinning in exchange for human life, it was easy to frame the
story with ready-made motifs drawn from folk tales. The protagonist finds herself in dire straits because of a parent's pragmatic desire to marry her off rather than because of an irrational whim on

her part. And the conclusion to "Rumpelstiltskin," instead of leaving us in suspense about the queen's future, is rounded off by an amusing anecdote detailing her tactics for ensuring a trouble-free existence. By using motifs from folk tales, "Rumpelstiltskin" could become a curious hybrid of fairy tale and folk tale, containing the magic of one even as it indulged in the humor of the other.

The rules of fairy tales remind us that labor in and of itself has never been enough to secure a king and half his kingdom. Who has ever heard of a miller grinding his way to wealth or a tailor sewing his way to riches?[23] Rumpelstiltskin's gift of spinning prodigious quantities of flax or of turning common fibers into filaments of gold is what warrants a pact. Because he carries out superhuman tasks or performs supernatural acts, the heroine finds herself elevated to a higher social rank. Ultimately, spinning has little value. In order to prove effective, it must have a magical quality attached to it.

"The Three Spinners" and "Rumpelstiltskin," which appears over time to have assimilated the prologue to "The Three Spinners," initially promote the virtues of diligence and hard work. They thereby appear to contain a pro-spinning bias. Skill at the spinning wheel is what draws the attention of the kings in each of these two tales to the humble heroines. Both stories, however, also subvert the message that skill at the spinning wheel enhances marriageability by emphasizing that spinning can never be performed with sufficient speed or with the right magical touch to satisfy a king. In the end, three hideous women deformed by their trade or a misshapen gnome must carry out the labors demanded by royal personages. The end product of the spinning process may get the heroine a husband, but the process itself is guaranteed to disfigure and deform. This is the deeper message and the higher wisdom that emerged as the tales were spun throughout the ages.

III

VILLAINS

6

FROM NAGS TO WITCHES
Stepmothers and Other
Ogres

"Once upon a time there was a princess who loved her father very much because she had a repressed Electra complex. She was so beautiful that her stepmother, who had
strong sadistic impulses, fell prey to sexual jealousy and
ordered a hunter to take Snow White into the forest."

—WILLY PRIBIL,
"Snow White in the Manner of Sigmund Freud"

AMONG the most familiar facts of anthropology, wrote Sir James
Frazer in *The Golden Bough*, are the "awe and dread with which the
untutored savage contemplates his mother-in-law."[1] Mothers-in-law
may never have enjoyed a reputation for warm-hearted benevo-
lence, but Frazer's mixture of "awe and dread" seems exaggerated.
If we turn from real life to fairy tales (many of which have roots in
primitive cultures), it quickly becomes apparent just why a mother-
in-law might strike terror in the heart of an "untutored savage." Of
all the fiends in the *Nursery and Household Tales*, few can match the
savage bloodthirstiness of the protagonist in "The Mother-in-Law."
That story has never numbered among the more popular of the
Grimms' tales; in fact, it is virtually unknown, in part because it appeared only in the first edition of the collection and was subsequently relegated to the volume of scholarly annotations. The
shocking events in "The Mother-in-Law" are narrated in a dry, matter-of-fact tone. A king rides off to war, entrusting the care of his
wife and children to his mother. No sooner have the gates slammed
behind him than his mother (the mother-in-law of the tale's title)

locks the wife with her two boys in a dungeon. A few days later, she develops an irresistible craving for human flesh, summons the chef, and instructs him to slaughter and dress one of the two boys. "What kind of sauce should I prepare?" asks the cook. "A brown one," she answers. The desperate mother of the boys persuades the cook to substitute a pig for her son on each of the two occasions that her mother-in-law is overpowered by the urge to devour a grandchild. But the elder woman finds the cook's pork dishes so tasty that she orders him to serve the queen herself for the next meal. Fortunately for the intended victim, a young hind is on hand as a substitute. Still, the queen finds herself in a new predicament when her boys' sobs threaten to betray their presence in the castle. Here the story breaks off, leaving us in suspense about the queen's fate.[2]

We do not have to look far to find out exactly how the queen fares in the struggle with her mother-in-law. If we read Charles Perrault's version of "Sleeping Beauty," we discover that he begins the story of the wicked mother-in-law precisely at the point where most latter-day versions of the story end. Perrault's mother-in-law (the mother of the prince who wakens Sleeping Beauty with his "tender gaze") comes from "a race of ogres." When children come near her, she has "the greatest difficulty in the world keeping herself from pouncing on them." Her resemblance to the Grimms' mother-in-law is unmistakable. There may be some differences in detail (she sends her son's wife and children to a country mansion in the woods), but there is virtually no change in her character. In the tones of an ogre "who longs for raw meat," she directs the cook to serve up the queen's daughter in "a piquant sauce" (we are, after all, in France). After having satisfied her appetite for the queen and her two children, she prowls about the castle one day with the hope of coming on the scent of more human flesh, only to hear her grandchildren weeping. Enraged by the discovery of the cook's deception, she fills a huge vat with vipers, toads, and serpents and is about to hurl her kin and their accomplices into it when the king arrives. She ends by throwing herself into the vat, where she is devoured immediately by the reptiles. The king regrets her death ("after all she was his mother") but finds ample consolation in his wife and children.[3]

Perrault's tale is, in turn, not without its literary antecedents. Giambattista Basile's racy seventeenth-century Neapolitan version of the tale in *The Pentamerone* tells of a king who comes upon a "sleeping beauty," then rapes and abandons her. Nine months later, the young woman gives birth to twins. Basile's king is already married, and his wife is consumed with rage at the discovery of her husband's dallying with another woman. So intense is her jealousy that she orders the king's illegitimate children killed and directs her cook to prepare a hash of their flesh. Like other cooks in tales of sleeping beauties, this one too cannot bring himself to slaughter the children and ends up killing two young goats for the dish of hash that the queen sets before the king.[4]

It is not difficult to understand why the Grimms decided to eliminate "The Mother-in-Law" from their collection. The subject matter is decidedly unsavory—what was fit for the scholars to whom the first edition of the *Nursery and Household Tales* was directed was not necessarily suitable for the children who came to constitute the primary audience of subsequent editions. The tale is also a fragment and, as a brief glance at Perrault's "Sleeping Beauty" reveals, a French one at that. "The Mother-in-Law" consequently went the way of "Bluebeard," "Puss-in-Boots," and other stories that bore too close a resemblance to their French literary sources.

There are three types of ogres in the *Nursery and Household Tales*. The first comprises beasts and monsters; these include wolves and bears, but also the man-eating giants who threaten to devour the hero as he makes his way through the world. The second group consists of social deviants; among them are the robbers and highwaymen who waylay innocent young women, murder them, chop up their corpses, and cook the pieces in a stew. The third (and this group easily outnumbers the members of both other categories) is composed of women. These are the various cooks, stepmothers, witches, and mothers-in-law with voracious appetites for human fare, sometimes even for the flesh and blood or for the liver and heart of their own relatives. Snow White's stepmother, the witch in "Hansel and Gretel," and the cook in "Fledgling" belong to this class of cannibalistic fiends. The term applied almost uniformly to these female ogres is the German *Menschenfresserin* (devourer of humans), a word far more expressive than the English *ogre* generally used to translate it.

How is it that these figures continue to occupy so prominent a position in a collection of tales for children? Surely these stories, of all the stories in the Grimms' collection, have the least factual basis, even in the realities of past ages or of savage practices, or so it would seem. Another text in the first edition of the *Nursery and Household Tales* (this one too failed to enter the pages of subsequent editions) suggests that cannibalism was not unknown in times of famine.[5] The Grimms' "Starving Children" is neither fairy tale nor folk tale, but the summary of a seventeenth-century written account of a mother who threatened to kill and devour her daughters that she might survive a famine. In the end, the girls die of starvation and the mother simply disappears. It is unclear whether she planned to carry out her threat; the account may be embellished by the all-too-lively imagination of its reporter. It is telling, however, that the Grimms elected to include this kind of account in their collection. Clearly, for them there was no distinct dividing line between the fiction of fairy tales and the facts of everyday life, or at least the most sensational aspects of everyday life.

The many faces of maternal evil in fairy tales represent the obverse of all the positive qualities associated with mothers. Instead of functioning as nurturers and providers, cannibalistic female villains withhold food and threaten to turn children into their own source of nourishment, reincorporating them into the bodies that gave birth to them. Like the Jungian *magna mater*, they take ferocious possessiveness to an extreme. "Now the children are in my body," one mother-in-law triumphantly declares.[6] These figures work hard to earn the trust of their victims with magnanimous maternal behavior, then reveal their true colors as cannibalistic monsters. The old witch in "Hansel and Gretel," for example, uses her tasty house to lure the children to her, then sets a feast of milk and pancakes, sugar, apples, and nuts before them. But she "only pretended to be friendly," we learn. "She was actually a wicked witch who . . . killed, cooked, and ate any child who fell into her hands."

Not all female villains in the Grimms' fairy tales indulge a taste for human flesh. Many are experts in the art of weaving spells: these are the witches and enchantresses for whom uttering curses rather than devouring children is the preferred mode of oral expression. Nearly all the stock characters of fairy tales—not just female villains—are blessed (or cursed) with the gift of casting spells. When one fairy-tale father, for example, denounces his sons in a moment of irritation for their frivolous ways and utters the fateful wish that they turn into ravens, he finds himself suddenly endowed with magical powers. No sooner has the wish escaped his lips than he hears the beating of wings and silently watches seven ravens fly into the distance. Variants of the tale of the seven ravens suggest that such rash imprecations, whether uttered by fathers or by mothers, are instantly translated into reality. In "Twelve Brothers," it is the sister of the twelve boys who bears the blame for their transformation into ravens, though some versions implicate the children's stepmother in the guilty act. In yet another tale of enchanted male siblings ("Six Swans"), a woman turns her stepsons into winged creatures when she flings six magical shirts over them. While the spells cast in all three tales are equally effective, only one of the three transformations arises from a willful act of premeditated evil. It is the stepmother alone who deliberately takes advantage of magical powers to harm her six stepchildren. Nearly the entire cast of characters in fairy tales may possess supernatural powers, yet it will be obvious to the habitual reader of these tales that stepmothers are the principal agents of enchantment.

Stepmothers stand as an abiding source of evil in countless fairy tales, and it is no accident that they rank among the most memorable villains in those tales. Folklorists would be hard pressed to name a single good stepmother, for in fairy tales the very title "stepmother" pins the badge of iniquity on a figure.[7] One can safely argue that the phrase *wicked stepmother*, which has a nearly formulaic ring to it, is pleonastic.

The vast majority of the Grimms' stepmothers actively persecute not their stepsons, but their stepdaughters, who consequently take on the role of innocent martyrs and patient sufferers. If the stepmothers are not literal witches, they possess qualities that place them firmly in the class of ogres and fiends. As alien intruders, they disturb the harmony among blood relations. They may not always have the power to perform a metamorphosis from woman to beast, but they can turn even the most aristocratic and beguiling girl into the humblest of scullery maids. By contrast to the sorceresses who work behind the scenes in tales of enchanted young boys, they remain visible, palpable presences in fairy tales that chart the shifting fortunes of heroines who have lost their biological mothers and await rescue by dashing young princes or kings.

Biological mothers, as noted earlier, seldom command a central role in the fairy tales compiled by the Grimms, in part because Wilhelm Grimm could rarely resist the temptation to act as censor by turning the monstrously unnatural cannibals and enchantresses of these tales into stepmothers, cooks, witches, or mothers-in-law.[8] As the audience for the tales changed, the need to shift the burden of evil from a mother to a stepmother became ever more urgent. Yet the tactic had a way of backfiring. In the 1856 preface to his *New Book of German Fairy Tales (Neues Deutsches Märchenbuch)*, Ludwig Bechstein made a point of deviating from the practice established by Wilhelm Grimm and others.

> There is nothing that children would rather read than fairy tales. Among the thousands of children who every year get their hands on books of fairy tales, there must be many so-called *stepchildren*. When such a child—after reading many a fairy tale in which stepmothers appear (the stepmothers are all uniformly evil)—feels that it has been somehow injured or insulted . . . by its own stepmother, then that young person makes comparisons and develops a strong aversion to his guardian. This aversion can become so intense that it disturbs the peace and happiness of an entire family.[9]

Whether a figure is designated as a stepmother or a witch, she takes on a single well-defined function in fairy tales—one that is limited to the sphere known as villainy and that magnifies and distorts all the perceived evils associated with mothers. Wicked stepmothers and cooks find their way into the homes of fairy-tale heroes; witches masquerading as magnanimous mothers are nearly ubiquitous in the woods; and evil mothers-in-law make their presence felt in the castles that serve as a second home for fairy-tale heroines. That these figures share not only a common function but also a single identity becomes clear on closer inspection of the tales in which they imperil innocent young children.

Let us begin by taking a more careful look at stepmothers and cooks. Snow White's stepmother is perhaps the most infamous step-mother of them all. But is she really a stepmother? In the first edition of the *Nursery and Household Tales*, Snow White's mother never dies; her vanity and pride turn her into an ogre who orders her daughter murdered; she then devours what she believes to be the girl's lungs and liver. Only in the second edition of the Grimms' collection does the real mother die and is replaced by a wicked step-mother. "Mother Holle" underwent a similar transformation. The first version of the tale featured a widow with two biological daughters, and the second version traced the fortunes of a widow with one favored, biological daughter and one ill-treated stepdaughter. What easier way is there to depict maternal abuse of children and at the same time preserve the sanctity of mothers than by turning the evil mother into an alien interloper whose goal is to disturb the harmony of family life? As for the evil cooks in the *Nursery and Household Tales*, more often than not they turn out to be stand-ins for stepmothers. In "Fledgling," one such figure plans to throw the adopted foundling of the household into a vat of boiling water—presumably he will constitute the main course for that night's dinner. Almost all other versions of that tale type place an evil stepmother in the role of the old cook. Think of "The Juniper Tree," in which a stepmother murders her stepson by decapitating him. (In passing, it should be noted that nearly every variant of the famous refrain of that tale ["My wicked mother slew me, / My dear father ate me."] attributes the murder to a mother rather than to a stepmother, even though the actual perpetrator in the story is usually a stepmother.)[10] Here the folkloric imagination—not just the Grimms—is responsible for the replacement of a mother by a stepmother. To some extent, Wilhelm Grimm, with his editorial practices, may simply have been falling in line with a general tendency to sanitize the tales for consumption by children. In surveying the Grimms' collection of tales, it becomes clear that both stepmothers and cooks are almost always thinly disguised substitutes for biological mothers.

Witches and mothers-in-law display the evil impulses and instincts of cooks and stepmothers, and they clearly perform the same function in fairy tales. Heroines who emerge from the forest to live happily ever after with the kings who discover them there often find their domestic bliss disturbed by a rival. In "Twelve Brothers," that particular figure is characterized first as the heroine's mother-in-law, then as her stepmother.[11] In fairy tales, these two figures are clearly interchangeable. "Little Brother and Little Sister" gives us a witch who masquerades as a stepmother so that she can insinuate herself into a household. At home she subjects the children to daily abuse; in the forest she continues to tyrannize them by enchanting their sources of drinking water. In "Hansel and Gretel," it is probably not coincidental that the two siblings return home to find that their cruel stepmother has vanished once they have conquered the evil witch in the woods.[12] It quickly becomes clear that stepmother, evil cook, witch, and mother-in-law are different names for one villain whose aim is to banish the heroine from hearth and home and to subvert her elevation from humble origins to noble status. What at first blush appears to be a conspiracy of hags and witches is in the final analysis the work of a single female villain.

To some extent, the female villains of fairy tales have a dual identity. As stepmothers, evil servants, and hostile mothers-in-law, they remain firmly anchored in the world of family life and figure among the facts of everyday life. Conflicts and tensions between them and the tales' protagonists reflect nothing more than the observable realities of human life. These female villains—whether wearing the hat of cook, stepmother, witch, or mother-in-law—have repeatedly been labeled folkloristic projections of the "bad mother." Bruno Bettelheim, Marthe Robert, and other psychoanalytically oriented critics have admired the deft way in which these stories split mother images into two components: the good (and usually absent) mother and the evil stepmother. As Bettelheim points out, "the fantasy of the wicked stepmother not only preserves the good mother intact, it also prevents having to feel guilty about one's angry wishes about her."[13] But what is especially remarkable about fairy tales is the extent to which they inflate maternal evil. The alien meddlers who make their way into households and attempt to divide a heroine from her father or husband are painted in the worst imaginable colors. As terrifying ogres and evil enchantresses, they take on almost mythical dimensions.

The female villains of fairy tales operate in three distinct arenas of action that emerge in chronological sequence. The main contours of the opening situation in tales featuring these villains are reasonably predictable. The child or children whose biological mother has died become the victims of a brutal, scheming stepmother. One fairy-tale brother confides to his sister: "Ever since mother died, we haven't had a single happy hour. Our stepmother beats us every day, and when we go to see her, she kicks us and sends us away. We get nothing but hard breadcrusts to eat. Even the little dog under the table is better off than we are." Small wonder that these abused youngsters resolve to escape the oppressive atmosphere at home even at the cost of facing the perils of "the vast world." Those who fail to move into voluntary exile are, like Hansel and Gretel, banished from home owing to a stepmother's relentless bullying of her husband. But even those who patiently endure villainy at home find themselves expelled from the family circle, living like servants at the hearth rather than like children at home. At home or in the woods, the once unrivaled princes and princesses of the household find themselves dethroned, living a lowly existence in exile. Whether literally of royal parentage or regal simply by virtue of their status as children, the adolescent protagonists of fairy tales find that their legitimate rights have been abrogated and that their positions have been usurped by those perennial pretenders to the throne known in fairy tales as older brothers and as stepsisters.[14]

If home represents the first station in the hero's sufferings, the enchanted world of the forest stands as the locus of his second series of struggles. But in the woods the hero is no longer pitted against a powerful human adversary; instead he finds himself locked in combat with a superhuman opponent armed with supernatural powers.

The villainous stepmother reemerges in the woods as a monster equipped with powers far more formidable than those she exercised at home. If she proved successful in deposing her stepchildren and banishing them from the household by constantly badgering and hectoring either children or spouse, in the woods she appears above all to be a master in the art of transforming humans into animals. Her power to turn children into beasts is generally exerted on stepsons; the task of disenchantment falls to stepdaughters. Little Brother rather than Little Sister is turned into a deer when he drinks from waters enchanted by his stepmother; Hansel, not Gretel, is encaged like an animal and fattened up for a feast of flesh; the six swans in the tale of that title are all male; and of the thirteen children in "Twelve Brothers," only the boys take wing after being turned into ravens. In this context, it is worth noting that there are relatively few female counterparts to the many enchanted males in the cycle of tales known as animal-groom stories. To be sure, female heroines are not immune to spells cast by witches and fairies, but, like Snow White and Sleeping Beauty, they remain eternally human and beautiful even in their dormant, enchanted states. That brothers and prospective bridegrooms are turned into animals by older women may be read as a telling commentary on women's attitudes toward male sexuality, just as the choice of a catatonic Snow White and Sleeping Beauty as the fairest and most desirable of them all may offer a sobering statement on folkloristic visions of the ideal bride.[15]

While the curses uttered by stepmothers take effect almost instantaneously, the process of disenchantment is long and arduous. In tales of metamorphosed males, the sisters or prospective brides of the degraded heroes are burdened with the task of disenchantment. Yet as one mentor after another warns these heroines, the conditions of that task are so difficult as to be virtually impossible to fulfill. Only Gretel, who keeps her wits about her, succeeds in liberating her brother within a reasonable period of time. The sister of the six swans requires a more typical time span, spending year after year perched on a tree branch sewing shirts. She releases her brothers from the stepmother's curse only after six years have passed. Given

the duration of the brothers' bewitchment, it is not altogether surprising to find that the heroine of the fairy tale matures, marries,
and establishes a family of her own by the time the prescribed length
of her trial has elapsed.

While the brothers of fairy-tale heroes patiently wait in the woods
for liberation from their enchanted state, the heroines have moved
on to a third arena of action. Rescued or, more often than not, kid-
napped by the hunting party of a king, they are spirited off to a castle and in due course married to the sovereign of the land. Yet many
of these heroines, who are bound by vows of silence or solemnity,
cannot yet live happily ever after, at least not so long as their brothers remain enchanted. Furthermore, even at the castle that has become their second home, they become once again the victims of
plotting females, be they treacherous mothers-in-law or ever vigilant stepmothers who have heard of their stepdaughters' accession
to a throne. Since the young queens frequently become mothers
themselves, the murderous schemes of their stepmothers take on an
added dimension of peril. The children of the new royal couple
seem destined to share the lot of their mothers, to relive the fairy
tale whose plot will come to an end with the death of their biological
mother. Once a stepmother succeeds in murdering her stepdaughter (as in "Little Brother and Little Sister") or in conspiring to have
her put to death (as in "Twelve Brothers" and "Six Swans"), she
paves the way for the marriage of her own, biological daughter to
the newly widowed king and thereby precisely re-creates the kind of
family situation that prevailed at the tale's beginning. That new
royal family, like the nuclear family described in the opening paragraphs of fairy tales, would consist of a father, a stepmother, and
one or more children from the father's first marriage. It can only be
a matter of time until the sole missing elements, the children of the
second union, appear on the scene to assist in reenacting the drama
played out in the first part of the fairy tale.[16]

Before anyone can live happily ever after, this vicious cycle of
events must be arrested. To avoid the danger of endless repetition
of one plot, the stepmother must perish along with her mischievous
progeny. Not until she has been conquered and done away with is it

possible to break the magic spell that bedevils the stepchildren of
fairy tales and that threatens to doom one generation after another
of their progeny. Once a fairy-tale heroine succeeds in reversing the
effects of her stepmother's villainy, either by completing the tasks
assigned to her or by returning from the dead to broadcast the harm
done to her, the process of disenchantment is complete. To emphasize the definitive end to the stepmother's reign of terror, the fairy
tale describes her demise in graphic and morbid detail. Drowned,
burned to ashes, torn to pieces by wild animals, or placed in a casket
filled with boiling oil and poisonous snakes, she dies in both body
and spirit, no longer representing a threat to the recently established royal family. And once the biological mother of that family
reigns supreme, the king and even his children are destined to live
happily ever after.

In tales ending with the wedding of a royal couple, stepmothers
are repeatedly implicated in the evil that befalls their stepchildren,
just as they eternally attempt to obstruct their elevation to a higher
social rank. These heartless creatures stand in sharp contrast to
their relatively artless spouses, whose only serious defect appears to
be lack of discrimination in choosing a marriage partner. Even that
defect is eliminated in some tales featuring evil stepmothers: occasionally it is the heroine who is deceived by the friendly face put on
by a woman and who naively persuades her father to remarry. The
fathers of fairy-tale heroines may appear passive to a fault, but it is
surely to their credit that they rarely take the lead in abandoning
their children or in treating them like servants. It is the stepmother
of Hansel and Gretel who hatches the plot to desert the children in
the forest; only after being subjected to a good measure of brow-
beating does their father acquiesce in her plans. Cinderella's father
never conspires to debase his daughter, for his wife and stepdaughters are experts in the art of humiliation. And the father of Snow
White (mentioned by the Grimms only in the context of his remarriage and even then solely to motivate the presence of the stepmother) never once interferes with the elaborate web of evil that his
wife spins in order to remain "the fairest of them all." Although the
fathers of these fairy-tale figures are supremely passive or positively

negligent when it comes to their children's welfare, they remain benevolent personages largely because benign neglect contrasts favorably with the monstrous deeds of their wives.[17]

In the Grimms' collection there is one conspicuous example of a father whose perversity rivals the malice harbored by his female counterparts in fairy tales. Stepmothers may sin by withholding love and affection from their stepchildren, but this father errs in the excessive love and devotion he feels for his biological daughter. The father of young Thousandfurs (Allerleirauh), in the tale that bears her name, promises his wife on her deathbed that he will remarry only if he finds a woman whose beauty equals that of his quickly fading spouse. When the king's envoys return from a worldwide search for a second wife to announce that they have failed in their mission, the king's eye lights on his daughter, and he is overcome by passion (*eine heftige Liebe*) for her. The king's counselors may be stunned by their sovereign's proposal to marry his own daughter, but they are not nearly so shocked and dismayed as Thousandfurs herself, who, after a variety of delaying tactics, ultimately flees the castle to escape her father's erotic advances.

On the surface of things, it would appear that plots concerned with wicked stepmothers belong to a tale type separate from plots featuring fathers driven by incestuous desires. In practice, these two plots do indeed run on different tracks: a stepmother's insufficient love and a father's excessive love for a child appear to be incompatible. Yet what the folk have worked hard to keep apart, folklorists have sought to bring together. Antti Aarne's authoritative register of tale types, for example, assigns a single number to two such representative plots (*Cinderella* is 510A; *The Dress of Gold, of Silver, and of Stars*, of which "Allerleirauh" is a variant, is 510B). Clearly, Aarne must have intuitively recognized a kinship between these two types of tales, though he never explained just how the two could coexist as a single drama. Another folklorist determined that two distinct motifs are associated with the tragic loss of the heroine's appendages in "The Girl without Hands." One involves the sexual jealousy of any one of the following: a biological mother, a stepmother, a mother-in-law, or a sister-in-law; the other is concerned with a father's love for a daughter or (as is the case with the version in the *Nursery and Household Tales*) a father's forging of a pact with the devil.[18]

In German tales depicting social persecution of a girl by her stepmother, the central focus comes to rest on the unbearable family situation produced by a father's remarriage. But while the father's responsibility for creating turmoil by choosing a monstrous marriage partner recedes into the background or is entirely suppressed as a motif even as the father himself is virtually eliminated as a character, the foul deeds of his wife come to occupy center stage. Her repulsive attributes and sadistic acts are described in painful detail. We learn how she throws her stepdaughter into a river, instructs a hunter to kill her and to recover her liver and lungs for dinner, inadvertently decapitates her own daughter, or, as "The True Bride" tells us, makes life "wretched in every way."

In tales depicting erotic persecution of a daughter by her father, on the other hand, mothers and stepdaughters tend to vanish from the central arena of action. Yet the father's desire for his daughter in the second tale type furnishes a powerful motive for a stepmother's jealous rages and unnatural deeds in the first tale type. The two plots thereby conveniently dovetail to produce an intrigue that corresponds almost perfectly to the Oedipal fantasies of female children. In this way fairy tales are able to stage the Oedipal drama even as they disguise it by eliminating one of its two essential components.

If we survey extant versions of the two tale types, it becomes evident that intimations of a father's passion for his daughter are generally discreetly kept to a minimum, while the evil deeds of a stepmother are invariably writ large. A comparison of Perrault's "Donkey-Skin" (the French counterpart of "Thousandfurs") with Perrault's "Cinderella" offers a typical contrast. In "Donkey-Skin," the king's unrestrained passion for his daughter is explained as nothing more than a temporary aberration caused by excessive grief over the loss of his wife. The king becomes confused, imagines himself a young man, and labors under the delusion that his daughter is "the maiden he had once wooed to be his wife."[19] Perrault is clearly at pains to frame excuses for the advances the king makes to his daughter. In "Cinderella," by contrast, he strains his verbal resources to summon up negative terms ("haughty," "proud," "mean," and so on) to describe Cinderella's stepmother. Even when they violate basic codes of morality and decency, fathers remain noble figures who rarely commit premeditated acts of evil. Stepmothers, however, are unreconstructed villains, malicious by nature and disposition.

It may be true, as Bettelheim has asserted, that fairy tales enacting Oedipal conflicts split the mother figure in two: one mother who stands by her child and another (step)mother who stands in the way of the female child's attempts to secure the love of her father. Most fairy tales depicting the fortunes of heroines persecuted by stepmothers portray benevolent female figures in the form of wise women, or, failing that, enact a deceased mother's undying love for her child by bringing Mother Nature to the heroine's rescue. Cinderella, the Goose Girl, Thousandfurs, and a host of other oppressed female protagonists benefit either from nature's munificence in the form of animal helpers or from the natural sanctuaries found in the hollows of trees and in the forest.[20] Yet while the good mother generally appears incognito as a dove, a cow, or as a tree (and then only ever so briefly), the evil stepmother becomes an overpowering presence in the tale. She stands as the flesh-and-blood embodiment of maternity, and it is this figure of manifest evil that is most openly associated with women as mothers.

If the Grimms' fairy tales tend to permit all manner of explicit social persecution by jealous stepmothers (whose true identity is only thinly concealed by the prefix *step*-), they also tend to avoid direct depiction of erotic persecution by fathers and to shun amorous entanglements with them. Some heroines make a point of returning home to their fathers and sharing their new-found wealth with him and with him alone. And in one version of "Snow White" recorded by the Grimms, it is the father and not a prince who discovers his daughter's coffin on his way through the woods and who mobilizes medical help to reanimate her. But on the whole, fathers in the Grimms' tales either absent themselves from home or are so passive as to be superfluous. We have already seen the lengths to which Wilhelm Grimm was prepared to go in order to mask incestuous desire in "The Girl without Hands." Only in "Thousandfurs" was a father permitted to stand as the active source of evil at home, with the consequence that the theme of incest was broached and pushed to its limits. Even the most restrained commentators on "Thousandfurs" speculate on the possibility that the heroine ends up marrying the very king who sent her into exile. The Grimms may have attempted to describe the marriage in ambiguous terms ("so as to avoid being offensive," one critic insists), but one possible aspect of that marriage cannot be entirely suppressed. This critic neglects to note what is perhaps most remarkable about "Thousandfurs." In its original version, it confronts the problem of incestuous desire in a wholly matter-of-fact fashion and at the same time points to a resolution of that problem.[21]

At times it appears as if the tellers of these tales, or those who set down the tales in their written versions, were bent on excising all explicit references to the source of rivalry that divides mothers from daughters in childhood fantasies. As folklorists remind us, censorship of material in oral literary forms is generally exercised by the audience, which determines the vitality of certain plots by voicing approval of them or simply selecting them for retelling.[22] The same seems to hold true for written tales, though perhaps less consistently. In our own culture, we find in the process of selection a bias working manifestly in favor of the rags-to-riches tale that contains a powerful, wicked older woman. "Cinderella," "Snow White," and "Sleeping Beauty" are the tales from Perrault and from the Grimms that continue to thrive even on non-native soil, while stories such as "Thousandfurs" and "Donkey-Skin" are virtually unknown.[23] Of the two components that shape female Oedipal plots—the fantasy of an amorous father and the fantasy of rivalry with the mother— only the latter has become a prominent, virtually undisguised theme in popular tales depicting the marriage of female protagonists. While (step)mothers are habitually demonized as nags at home and witches in the woods, fathers qua fathers tend to fade into the background or to be absent from the tale.

It is important to bear in mind that the passive or absent father was not always the rule in fairy tales. As Marian Cox's nineteenth-century study of 345 variants of "Cinderella" makes clear, at least two widespread and pervasive versions of that tale attributed the heroine's degradation either to what Cox describes in characteristic Victorian language as an "unnatural father" or to a father who attempts to extract from his daughter a confession of love. Of the 226 tales belonging unambiguously to one of three categories labeled by Cox as (1) ill-treated heroine (with mothers, stepmothers, and their progeny as victimizers), (2) unnatural father, and (3) King Lear judgment, 130 belong to the first class, 77 to the second class, and 19 to the third. Thus in the tales examined by Cox, the versions that cast (step)mothers in the role of villain only slightly outnumber those that ascribe Cinderella's misfortunes to an importunate father. Cinderella and her folkloristic sisters are therefore almost as likely to flee the household because of their father's perverse erotic attachment to them or because of his insistence on a verbal declaration of love as they are to be banished to the hearth and degraded to domestic servitude by an ill-tempered stepmother.[24]

Although folklorists have correctly pointed out that it is impossible to reconstruct the *Urmärchen*, or authentic parent tale (if ever there was one), that gave rise to the countless versions of "Cinderella" existing the world over from China to North America, it is important to recognize that one basic tale type has attached to it two components that are now perceived to be competing and mutually exclusive. The jealous mother and amorous father, as Cox's neat divisions make clear, rarely coexist in one tale. In "Aschenputtel," the Grimms' version of "Cinderella," the father makes only the briefest cameo appearance to give his daughter a branch which, once planted, turns into a tree that showers Cinderella with royal apparel for the ball. From an accomplice in Cinderella's degradation, he has turned into an unwitting, yet benevolent, helper in the tests that await her. In "Thousandfurs," by contrast, the only mother figure in the tale expires in the introductory paragraph.

In tales that emphasize a stepmother's cruelty, the role of the biological father tends to be peripheral. Indeed, the father does not appear at all in a number of stories that conform to the rags-to-riches pattern found in "Cinderella." "Snow White" stands as an especially prominent example of such a tale, although even this most chaste and guileless of fairy-tale heroines is subjected to paternal advances in some versions of the story, even as her father's manifest delight in her beauty stands as the source of marital discord in other versions.[25] In the Grimms' version of the tale, which refers to the father only once and then merely to proclaim his marriage, astute observers have nonetheless identified vestiges of the father's original function: "His surely is the voice of the looking glass, the patriarchal voice of judgment that rules the Queen's—and every woman's—self-evaluation."[26] Once the disembodied voice in the mirror is recognized as that of the wicked queen's husband, it becomes clear that the struggle between Snow White and her mother could well be motivated in psychological terms by rivalry for the love and admiration of an absent husband and father.

The voice in the mirror is not the sole means by which the father makes his presence felt in the tale. In his study of fifty-seven variants of "Snow White," Ernst Böklen notes (with evident consternation) that some versions of the tale openly depict the father as a co-conspirator in his wife's intrigues.[27] It is the father who, in an attempt to pacify his disagreeable spouse, leads Snow White into the woods and abandons her there. Böklen's study of such variants gives added weight to the view voiced by Bettelheim that, in the Grimms' tale, the hunter who spares Snow White's life yet abandons her in the woods may represent a disguised father figure. Torn between his loyalty to a wife and affection for a daughter, he "tries to placate the mother, by seemingly executing the order, and the girl, by merely not killing her."[28] In short, despite the complete suppression in this tale of explicit references to the figure for whose affection mother and daughter vie, the logic of the Oedipal subplot dictates the presence of male figures who find themselves divided in their allegiances to a mother and her daughter.

Here a word of caution is in order. In "Snow White," we have seen just how easy it is to discover a father figure lurking behind every male voice and body. For some critics, the father has slipped into the mirror, for others he has been taken into the service of the queen, and for still others he has transformed himself into a handsome young prince. In "Little Red Riding Hood," the father has been identified as both wolf and hunter in disguise. In view of the fairy tale's often single-minded focus on family life, this perceived duplication, even multiplication, of fathers in each tale is not wholly off the mark. Still, it is wise to keep in mind that a handsome young prince generally functions as an alternative to the father rather than as his double.

In reviewing the Grimms' tales of oppressed female protagonists, it becomes evident that these stories dramatize female Oedipal conflicts in unique fashion. With the exception of "Thousandfurs," they suppress the theme of paternal erotic pursuit even as they indulge freely in elaborate variations on the theme of maternal domestic tyranny. For the one story in the *Nursery and Household Tales* that openly depicts a father's persecution of his daughter, there are twelve that recount a girl's misery at the hands of her stepmother. Enshrining the stepmother as villain brings with it the added advantage of exonerating both biological parents from blame for the miserable conditions at home. One might reasonably argue that cruel stepmothers, absent fathers, and child abandonment counted far more significantly than father-daughter incest among the social realities of the age in which the Grimms recorded German fairy tales.[29] Yet fairy tales have never been treasured as mirrors of reality; only in their opening paragraphs and in their decorative details do they offer a world that bears some resemblance to the realities of family life.[30] Once the protagonists of these tales leave home, they pass through the looking glass and arrive in a world of inner realities. Although those childhood fantasies are remarkably stable in contrast to social realities, they are nonetheless reshaped and modified by the cultural setting in which they are told and retold. In our own age, it is easy to see why fairy tales, which evolved only late in their development into stories for children, favor the theme of maternal malice over the forbidden and forbidding theme of incest.

7

TAMING THE BEAST
Bluebeard and Other
Monsters

Curiosity is a valuable trait. It will make the simians learn
many things.
—CLARENCE DAY, *This Simian World*

"OF ALL the irrational incidents of folk-tales," one anthropologist
grumbles, "none is more irrational than that in which a human
being is wedded to a beast." The erotic persecution of fairy-tale heroines by their fathers, another critic of fairy tales adds, may be
"needlessly repulsive to the feelings of every European nation," but
it at least appears to have its roots in a stage of civilization when marriage between a widowed father and his orphaned daughter was not
necessarily taboo. That critic may not have his facts right, but he has
asserted the principle correctly. Few would be prepared or, for that
matter, would want to concede a factual basis for marriages between
princesses and pigs, girls and bears, or peasant women and hedgehogs. Yet such couplings are prominent in fairy tales. That marriage vows are, in some cases, not exchanged until after a beast has
been disenchanted does not diminish the oddity of such matches.[1]

As irrational as these tales may seem (even to an anthropologist),
most collectors and interpreters of folklore have never had much
trouble identifying their aims and messages. Take the case of the
lessons afforded by the two most celebrated tales of beast marriages.
In one, the heroine marries Bluebeard, a beast in all but the literal
sense of the term; in the other, the heroine weds Beast, a beast in all
but the figurative sense of the term. There is no lack of consensus,
as we shall see, about the moral offered by each story. One warns us

about curiosity and its consequences; the other alerts us to the dangers of disobedience. So we are told.

Let us look first at "Bluebeard," in the version formulated by Charles Perrault. In Perrault's tale, which was included in variant form in the Grimms' first edition but subsequently eliminated on the grounds that it showed too many signs of its French origins, the newly wed heroine learns from her husband that she may open everything, go anywhere, and do whatever she pleases. Under no circumstances, however, may she enter "the small room at the end of the long passage on the lower floor" (the directions could not be more explicit). Needless to say, the many attractions of Bluebeard's castle fail to divert the heroine's attention from the one "inconsequential" room, and she soon gives in to the temptation to unlock the forbidden chamber. To her horror, upon opening the door to the room, she sees a pool of clotted blood in which are reflected the corpses of Bluebeard's wives, each with her throat slashed. Overcome by terror, she makes the nearly fatal error of dropping the key into the pool of blood, thereby staining it and furnishing her husband with telltale evidence of her transgression. Rescue at the eleventh hour by her two brothers saves her from sharing the fate of Bluebeard's earlier victims.

The Grimms' version of this tale ("Fowler's Fowl") is no less grisly.[2] Their Bluebeard is a sinister magician who masquerades as a frail beggar in order to kidnap unsuspecting girls. To each he issues a key to the forbidden chamber and an egg that, on pain of death, must not be dropped. Only the youngest of three daughters succeeds in tricking the wizard by depositing the egg in a safe place before exploring the forbidden chamber. Her sisters drop their eggs when they come in view of a bloody basin filled with mutilated corpses. After deceiving the wizard, the heroine resurrects her slaughtered sisters by deftly reassembling their dismembered parts. She subsequently engineers the downfall and death of her betrothed. Unlike her French counterpart, she takes on the role of savior for her unhappy predecessors and through her own quick-wittedness escapes the fate of her sisters.

Perrault leaves no room for doubt about the lessons of "Bluebeard." He takes pains to present the character of his heroine in an unattractive light: she is so tormented by curiosity that she "rudely" leaves her guests to themselves. Then, in a most undignified manner, she hastens to the forbidden chamber, nearly breaking her neck as she races down the stairs. At the door, she reflects ever so briefly on the consequences of "disobedience" but fails to resist the "temptation" to open the door. Using the sledgehammer tactics adopted by many a writer of his generation, Perrault spelled out the tale's *moralité* in a coda to his text: "Curiosity . . . often brings with it serious regrets."[3] Rather than appending morals to their fairy tales and thereby creating the impression that self-conscious educators had tampered with their content, the Grimms deftly integrated character judgments and moralizing pronouncements into the body of their texts. The heroine of "Fowler's Fowl" does not come under fire for being curious, but one sister is described as "plagued by curiosity," and the other is "led astray by curiosity." That Wilhelm Grimm made the point about the evils of female curiosity becomes clear when we look at the first edition of the *Nursery and Household Tales*: not a word is said in that version about curiosity. In much the same way, the story of "Mary's Child" was turned by Wilhelm Grimm into an object lesson on the hazards of curiosity. The first version states only that the heroine is unable to curb her curiosity. The final version intensifies the desire to transgress. Curiosity "picks and gnaws" at the young girl, leaving her no peace.

Nearly every nineteenth-century printed version of "Bluebeard" singles out the heroine's curiosity as an especially undesirable trait. Ludwig Bechstein, whose *Book of German Fairy Tales (Deutsches Märchenbuch)* outsold the *Nursery and Household Tales* for many decades, saw to it that Bluebeard's wife found it hard to live happily ever after: "It took a long time before she was able to recover from the consequences of her curiosity." Still, folkloristic and quasi-folkloristic versions of "Bluebeard" remain, in comparison with literary versions, relatively restrained in their condemnation of the heroine's inability to suppress her curiosity. When the Grimms' romantic contemporary Ludwig Tieck, for example, dramatized the tale, he also framed one of the most severe indictments of the heroine's character. In his rendition, even Bluebeard's wife is appalled by her inability to resist temptation: "O curiosity," she declaims, "damned, scandalous curiosity! There's no greater sin than curiosity!" Her self-accusations are uttered in full view of the scene of carnage for which her husband bears responsibility. Bluebeard confirms his wife's appraisal of her high crimes (by contrast to his misdemeanors).

> Cursed curiosity! Because of it sin entered the innocent world, and even now it leads to crime. Ever since Eve was curious, every single one of her worthless daughters has been curious. . . . The woman who is curious cannot be faithful to her husband. The husband who has a curious wife is never for one moment of his life secure. . . . Curiosity has provoked the most horrifying murderous deeds.

This is surely a case of the pot calling the kettle black. Whether intentionally or not, Tieck revealed the extent to which both folkloric and literary recastings of "Bluebeard" blame the victim for the crimes of the villain. Sam Weller, faithful servant to Mr. Pickwick and eponym of the Wellerism, makes the same point in his characteristic succinct fashion: " 'I think he's the wictim of connubiality, as Blue Beard's domestic chaplain said, with a tear of pity, ven he buried him.' "[4]

Perrault's "Bluebeard," which stressed the heroine's curiosity even as it toned down her husband's barbaric crimes, must have guided the pens of many retellers of the tale. How else is one to explain the striking predictability of judgmental comments made by various narrators of "Bluebeard"? Even critics seem to speak with one voice in their commentaries on the tale. "Succumbing to temptation," one representative interpretation tells us, is the "sin of the Fall, the sin of Eve." It is hardly surprising to find Perrault's illustrators making the same connection, embroidering their portrayals of Bluebeard's wife with vignettes from Genesis (figure 15). One critic after another falls in line with the view that "Bluebeard" proclaims the inability of women to resist temptation and cautions against the perils of idle female curiosity. We will see that for Bluebeard's wife, as for Eve, that curiosity takes on a both cognitive and sexual dimension. Only occasionally has a reteller or critic of the tale recognized

FIGURE 15. *As Bluebeard's wife steals away to the forbidden chamber, she leaves behind her curious female guests, who are opening chests, cupboards, and doors, and passes a tapestry showing Eve succumbing to temptation.*

that Bluebeard might be engaging his wife in a "charade of innocence and vice" or that obedience to Bluebeard's command might not be a virtue. A nineteenth-century Scottish version summarizes in its title the nearly collective critical wisdom of the past three centuries on this tale: "The Story of Bluebeard, or, the effects of female curiosity."[5]

Recent commentators on "Bluebeard" have also followed Perrault's lead and are equally uncharitable to the young bride. Cognitive curiosity, as we saw in the case of Tieck's "Ritter Blaubart," is turned with ease into sexual curiosity. Is it any wonder that Anatole France's "The Seven Wives of Bluebeard" attempts to rehabilitate Bluebeard and to explain the heroine's breakneck speed in rushing down the stairs to the forbidden chamber by revealing that there was nothing more behind the door than a handsome young man? In "Bluebeard" as in "Fowler's Fowl," Bruno Bettelheim sees a cautionary tale armed with the message: "Women, don't give in to your sexual curiosity; men, don't permit yourself to be carried away by your anger at being sexually betrayed." For Bettelheim, the blood-stained key that Bluebeard's wife is obliged to surrender to her husband clinches the argument that she has had "sexual relations" and symbolizes "marital infidelity." The same holds true for the bloody egg. For another reader, the stained key becomes a symbol of "defloration," revealing the heroine's sexual betrayal of her husband during his absence. For a third, the bespattered egg marks the heroine's irreversible loss of her virginity.[6]

What Bettelheim and others do with few hesitations, reservations, or second thoughts is to turn a tale depicting the most brutal kind of serial murders into a story about idle female curiosity and duplicity. These critics invite us to view the heroine's quite legitimate curiosity as a perversion (or at least as a serious peccadillo), one that brings in its wake "serious regrets." The genuinely murderous rages of Bluebeard and his folkloric cousins would presumably never have been aroused had it not been for the (symbolic) infidelity of his wives. As horrifying as those multiple crimes may be, they still do not succeed in deflecting attention from the heroine's single transgression. That transgression, like the opening of Pandora's box, functions as the chief source of evil. Strangely, the chamber of horrors tucked away in Bluebeard's castle—with its mutilated corpses and pools of blood—is neatly converted from the locus of Bluebeard's crimes into the site of his wife's curiosity and infidelity.

We need look no further than the illustrations to Bluebeard's story to confirm this odd fact. One edition after another draws our attention to one of two "key" scenes in the tale. Either we witness the arousal of curiosity (as in Gustave Doré's illustration to Perrault's "Bluebeard" [figure 16]) or we see the satisfaction of that urge (as in

FIGURE 16. *Gustave Doré's masterful illustration for Perrault's "Blue-beard" is charged with obvious sexual overtones.*

Otto Brausewetter's pictorial narrative [figure 17]). It comes as no surprise that one illustrator after another perceived the handing over of the key as the central scene in the story. But it is odd that so many show us the heroine taking a peek behind the forbidden door or fleeing the forbidden chamber. Bluebeard's wife gets a good look at the roomful of corpses, but readers are generally spared the sight of the carnage. To be sure, illustrators of "children's literature" may not have been especially anxious to spotlight a scene of murder and

FIGURE 17. *Otto Brausewetter shows us the reaction of Bluebeard's wife to the scene of carnage behind the forbidden door.*

mutilation, but the persistence with which they focus on the heroine's curiosity and disobedience, while avoiding the depiction of Bluebeard's crimes, remains remarkable nonetheless.

That the folkloric and literary imagination would go to such lengths to create a cautionary tale warning women against curiosity (sexual or otherwise) seems odd. In "Bluebeard," there is a striking lack of congruity between the actual crime and its (near) punishment. Once the heroine commits what has been interpreted as the cardinal sin of curiosity, she becomes enmeshed in a sequence of events so dreadful that they bear virtually no relation to her original offense. To be sure, fairy tales tend to speak in hyperbolic terms, to inflate the hazards of a single false step, and to overstate the consequences of missed opportunities; but the heroine surely does not merit the monstrous fate that attends her act of opening the forbidden door. The bloodbath is simply too sensational a spectacle for so minor a transgression.

At this point, we need to step back to ask why Perrault, the Grimms, and virtually all other interpreters of the tale have gotten it so wrong. How is it that the stated lessons of "Bluebeard" so rarely square with the facts of the story? One of the observations that even the most casual reader of fairy tales soon makes concerns the moral dimensions of fairy-tale life. There are clearly plenty of times when virtue is rewarded just as evil is punished, and one is tempted to applaud Claude Brémond's definition of the fairy tale as a "morally edifying narrative which is governed by the optimistic requirement of a happy ending." But readers of almost any major collection of tales will discover that these stories also praise thievery, endorse gluttony, value cunning, and commend cheating. Lying and stealing are perfectly legitimate means for achieving social advancement. Yet over the centuries there has been no end to inscribing moral lessons on the tales by their rewriters and no end to decoding their hidden moral messages by their interpreters. In some cases, as with "Bluebeard," there is a clear consensus on what the tale seeks to impart. But often each recasting of a tale makes a different point, while every new interpretation seems to detect a hitherto undiscovered moral precept.

It can be amusing to observe the ways in which critics strain to find messages appropriate for children, especially when a text goes against the grain of conventional values. The hero of "The Golden Bird," for example, has no admirable qualities whatsoever. He kidnaps a princess against her will, steals his way to success, and repeatedly turns a deaf ear to sensible advice. Still, we learn from one critic that the story's "profound praise of placidity" teaches us "a calm acceptance of what ought to be astonishing." Another critic ventures the opinion that the tale extols the virtues of being "good-natured and agreeable," but only "at the appropriate time," since those qualities do not *always* stand the hero in good stead. There is more than a touch of sophistry to these attempts to tease meaning out of the tale.[7]

But what about "Bluebeard"? How is it that everyone seems to agree on the wrong message for that tale type? To begin with, the prohibitions enunciated in "Bluebeard" and "Fowler's Fowl" command the reader's attention. Both prohibitions set the plot in motion by presenting themselves in the form of temptations that lead directly to their violation. The desire to transgress is only quickened in each case by the very nature of the prohibition's formulation. Whatever is forbidden arouses curiosity; all else is deemed unworthy of attention. The many richly appointed rooms in Bluebeard's castle, for example, hold no delight for the young bride. They are overshadowed by the presence of the single, remote, forbidden chamber.

Prohibition/violation: these paired functions stand as one of the fairy tale's most fundamental plot sequences. As soon as we learn about the dire consequences that will attend the mere touching of a spindle, we know that Briar Rose will somehow search out and find the only spindle left in her father's kingdom. When the dying monarch in "Faithful Johannes" tells his servant to show his son every room save "the last room on a long corridor, where the portrait of the Princess of the Golden Roof is hidden," it is almost certain that that particular room will be the only one to pique the curiosity of the young prince. The mother of the Goose Girl has only one word of advice to give her daughter on her journey to a foreign kingdom: to guard with care a snippet of white cloth stained with three drops of her mother's blood. Needless to say, the first event of consequence on the girl's journey is the loss of the cloth. In fairy tales, violations of prohibitions are the order of the day.

Fairy tales represent interdictions in all manner of forms. The most basic simply takes the shape of an explicit prohibition directed at the protagonist. The Virgin Mary tells the heroine of "Mary's Child" that she may open twelve doors in the kingdom of heaven but that the thirteenth is forbidden to her. Often the prohibition

stands as a general, unwritten law in a kingdom. "The Gnome" recounts the misfortunes of three princesses who taste forbidden fruit
in their father's garden. At times interdictions take concrete form,
as in "Rapunzel," where the command not to stray is symbolized by
imprisonment in a tower. Occasionally, fairy tales even invert the
movement from interdiction to violation by substituting for it a
command and its fulfillment. As Vladimir Propp has pointed out:
"If children are urged to go out into the field or into the forest, the
fulfillment of this command has the same consequences as does the
violation of an interdiction not to go out into the forest or out into
the field." If we reflect on the ways in which an interdiction ("Don't
look into this one room") comes perilously close to a tantalizing proposal, then it quickly becomes clear just why the paired functions in-
terdiction/violation and command/fulfillment are interchangeable.[8]

It is easy to take fairy tales that rely on the prohibition/violation
sequence and turn them into cautionary tales. The prohibition is
simply translated from the specific to the general ("Don't look into
this room!" becomes "Don't be curious!"). What originally functioned as a motor of the plot and as a means of introducing villainy
becomes a general behavioral guideline. That many prohibitions
are issued by villains has not discouraged critics from revering them
as universal truths. Bluebeard's command (which stems from a
murderer's need to conceal the evidence of his crimes) is legiti-
mized; his wife's curiosity becomes an emblem of women's weakness
in the face of temptation. It is doubtful that anyone would, on careful reflection, advocate blind obedience to Bluebeard's command.
Yet his injunction not to look into the forbidden chamber remains
the most memorable part of the story and is repeatedly validated in
morals about the evils of curiosity. That prohibition takes hold of
our imaginations even more strongly than the visual horrors beyond the threshold of Bluebeard's door.

The prominence of the prohibition/violation sequence does not
fully explain why the curiosity of Bluebeard's wife is so widely assailed. The hero of "Faithful Johannes," for example, is not satisfied
with the many "treasures and magnificent rooms" of the palace he
has inherited; he must gain access to the one door forbidden to him.
As he tells his servant, "If I don't go in, I'm sure it will be the end of

me. Day and night I shall have no peace until I've seen it." This is suspiciously close to curiosity, though it is never labeled as such. Prince Ivan in the Russian tale "Marya Morévna" also finds himself unable to restrain his curiosity about a forbidden chamber. "You must not look into the room that is bolted fast and sealed with tar," he is warned. "If you disobey me, you will bring misfortune upon us all."[9] But for Prince Ivan, as for the prince in "Faithful Johannes," the violation of a prohibition does not lead to punishment, rather it launches him on the road to wealth and marriage. Clearly there is a double standard at work here in the moral order of the fairy-tale world.

There are those who would argue that "Bluebeard" sits uneasily beside such classic fairy tales as "Faithful Johannes" and "Marya Morévna." But attempts to trace Bluebeard's ancestry to such bloodthirsty historical figures as Gilles de Rais (a fifteenth-century mass murderer of children) or to assert Perrault's invention of the figure have repeatedly misfired.[10] For a source, or perhaps no more than a parallel, to "Bluebeard," we must look to the East even as we remain in the world of fiction and fairy tales. Keeping in mind that Bluebeard is repeatedly depicted as a saber-wielding tyrant dressed in Oriental robes and outfitted with a turban, we do not have to look long or hard to find his kindred spirit. King Schahriyar, as anyone who has read an unexpurgated version of *The Thousand and One Nights* will recall, disposes of one wife after another because of the discovery of his wife's sexual curiosity. After catching his first wife *in flagrante delicto*, he resolves to behead each successive wife after one night of pleasure. Women's sexual curiosity calls for death sentences. By contrast, the woman (like Scheherazade) who is capable of arousing male curiosity, rather than succumbing to female curiosity, lives happily ever after. Scheherazade satisfies her husband and curbs his murderous policies because she is capable of arousing his curiosity by telling stories every night. Cognitive curiosity becomes difficult to distinguish from sexual curiosity in this tale: the printed texts in *The Thousand and One Nights* along with the presence of three sons bear witness to the continual arousal and satisfaction of both.

Whether the frame story of *The Thousand and One Nights* inspired

"Bluebeard" or contaminated it, or whether it simply stands as its Oriental counterpart, is not clear. But the story of King Schahriyar and Scheherazade gives us a pronounced example of the way in which cognitive curiosity can be wedded to sexual curiosity. More important, it launches a tradition in which female curiosity is castigated as the death principle whereas male curiosity is celebrated as a liberating, life-giving force. In light of this Oriental legacy, it becomes all the less remarkable that examples of female curiosity are repeatedly accompanied by moral glosses in fairy tales, while instances of male curiosity stand as gateways to the world of high adventure.

The example of Bruno Bettelheim has shown us that many an interpreter is prepared to accuse Bluebeard's wife of sexual curiosity and to indict her for sexual infidelity. Yet she does nothing more than open a door and discover the victims of her husband's crimes. Just what does she discover beyond the door? Are we entitled to assign a symbolic value to it, or should we remain on a literal level? To begin with, it may be useful to look at another text that features curious heroines and a forbidden chamber. The Rumanian story known as "The Enchanted Pig" opens with a king's injunction to his three daughters. His formulation is strikingly similar to that of Bluebeard: "You may walk in the garden, and you may go into all the rooms in the palace except the room at the back in the right-hand corner."[11] With each passing day the daughters grow ever more restive until they can restrain themselves no longer. "Why should we not go into the room that our father forbade us to enter?" they protest in chorus. With some trepidation, they cross the threshold to discover a book that reveals the secrets of their prospective marriages. Time and again, the knowledge hidden behind the locked doors of fairy tales is carnal in the literal or figurative sense of the term. In light of these associations, Perrault's warning to children to defer curiosity does not seem quite so far off target.[12]

In "Bluebeard," the heroine is confronted with carnal knowledge in its most literal form. The visual horrors beyond the threshold are so terrifying that they defy pictorial depiction. The heroine's discovery of Bluebeard's dreadful secret might, as has been proposed, have something to do with a child's suspicions that adults have "terrible sexual secrets."[13] We do not have to reflect long and hard on the key ingredients to Perrault's story and to the Grimms' recasting of it to realize that intense curiosity, locked doors, and the perception of sadistic brutality set up a chain of interesting associations—associations linked to the primal scene. Bluebeard's chamber, with its terrifying display of carnality, could be said to give vivid shape to what children perceive as the nightmarish aspects of human sexuality. But the carnage that meets the heroine's eyes could just as well be viewed as a horrifying emblem of human mortality, in which case the story might give us the heroine's recognition of death.[14] Still, psychosexual readings of "Bluebeard" have the special advantage of motivating the weighty consequences of the heroine's curiosity: the punishment of beheading conforms perfectly to the psycho-logic of the text. Whether we read "Bluebeard" at a literal level as an encounter with death or at a symbolic level as a story concerned with the discovery of carnal knowledge, it displays a special capacity to magnify and dramatize the most profoundly disturbing facts and fantasies of a child's mental world.

The chain of associations linking carnage to carnality and to carnal knowledge is far less pronounced in the Grimms' variations on tales featuring chambers that serve as the site of matters both forbidding and forbidden. Only "Bluebeard," the story that the Grimms perceived as too close a cousin of Perrault's tale to include in their second edition of the *Nursery and Household Tales*, and (to a lesser extent) "Fowler's Fowl" elicit the same associations. "Mary's Child," by substituting the Virgin Mary for Bluebeard and the Trinity for the bloodbath behind the door, becomes a straightforward cautionary tale about the hazards of excessive curiosity. That the Virgin Mary could slip with ease into the functional slot occupied by Bluebeard is telling and does much to explain why it became easy for rewriters and critics of the tale type to let Bluebeard off the hook. In "Mary's Child," the heroine is too curious for her own good and escapes death only by admitting her "sin" and implicitly expressing remorse for it.

The Grimms' other stories of forbidden chambers and underground hiding places show us heroines whose curiosity enables them to realize that they must outwit the villainous bridegrooms who try to trap them into marriage. "The Castle of Murder," which appeared only in the first edition of the *Nursery and Household Tales*, shows us an intrepid heroine who ultimately defeats her wealthy, aristocratic husband. The heroine of "The Robber Bridegroom" shows the same kind of courage but is also wise enough to be suspicious of her prospective groom. What that tale recommends is perhaps best summed up in the advice given to the heroine of the British tale "Mr. Fox": "Be bold, be bold, but not too bold, / Lest that your heart's blood should run cold."[15] The rich ambiguities attending the curiosity of Bluebeard's wife in Perrault's tale are sorted out and funneled into two separate tale types by the Grimms. In the one, curiosity is self-defeating; in the other it is paired with intelligence to prove lifesaving.

The French Bluebeard is a bloodthirsty aristocrat; his German counterparts are a bandit in one tale, a wizard in another, and a rich gentleman in a third. Russian and Scandinavian variants of this particular tale type cast an animal in the role of villain.[16] As Andrew Lang has declared, the "metamorphosis of men into animals and animals into men is as common in household tales as a sprained ankle is in modern novels."[17] But despite the profusion of transformations and the ease with which men slip into the role of beasts, there surely is a deeper significance to these metamorphoses, to the seeming interchangeability of man and beast. To begin with, it is important to note that men such as Bluebeard and monsters such as Beast fulfill the same paradigmatic function and are virtually all bridegrooms. The central female figures of the tales in which they appear are, therefore, either newlyweds or girls about to enter the state of (in this case) unholy matrimony. Often they have been coerced into marriage by a father who has frivolously promised to hand over the first living thing that meets him on his arrival home or who seeks financial gain through the favorable marriage of his daughter.[18] Is it any wonder, then, that the heroines perceive their grooms and husbands as beasts and monsters? Fairy tales, after all, are notoriously "hero-centric": figures and events in the tale are all presented from the perspective of the central figure, in this case the heroine, who sees in her husband-to-be nothing but the incarnation of bestial impulses, a creature capable of violent mutilation and murder. Oddly enough, it is generally the human bridegrooms who indulge in shockingly uncivilized behavior and remain unrepentant to the bitter end. Their bestial counterparts, by contrast, are models of decorum and dignity. A ferocious or repugnant countenance can prove wholly misleading in fairy tales. Contrary to the conventional wisdom about fairy-tale appearances, physical ugliness is not necessarily a sign of moral deformity; it can throw moral beauty or other merits and distinctions into sharp relief.

If Bluebeard and his international clansmen show us that men can be like beasts, tales such as "The Frog King," "The Lilting, Leaping Lark," "Hans My Hedgehog," and "The Old Woman in the Forest" show us men as real beasts. What remains on a metaphorical level in one tale type takes on concrete reality in another. "Bluebeard," as we have seen, has repeatedly been read as a tale about curiosity and its consequences. But with its emphasis on forbidden chambers, its movement from curiosity to revulsion, its focus on the "spectacular" moment rather than on the actual act of violence and violation, it is more likely to be addressing fears about violence, death, and sexuality. The heroine's discovery that even the most exalted and noble personage can prove capable of beastlike behavior stands as the central horror of the tale.

Like "Bluebeard," stories about animal grooms have been provided with plentiful moral glosses. A girl makes the mistake of promising a frog anything he wants in return for a small favor, and her story turns into an object lesson on the importance of keeping promises. "When you make a promise, you must keep it," her father declares when she trembles at the prospect of letting the creature into the house. "He helped you when you were in trouble and you mustn't despise him now," he adds when she balks at the idea of letting the frog sleep in her bed. When a man allows himself to be persuaded to give to a lion the first creature he meets on his return home, his daughter (who rushes to greet him on his arrival) reminds *him*: "If you've made a promise you must keep it." In "Hans My

Hedgehog," deep humiliation and disgrace attend a girl's failure to keep her father's promise to marry the hero named in the story's title. The brides in stories of animal grooms often are further tested with prohibitions against looking at their husbands under certain conditions. Like the heroine of "Cupid and Psyche," they rarely can resist the temptation to shed light on the forbidden. Failure to heed the advice of an animal groom becomes the whetstone on which the tales' critics grind their moralizing axes. Here again, both those who have recorded the tales and those who interpret them have had no trouble reaching agreement on messages just as they all seem to conspire in disregarding the implications of what the heroine must face.[19] Tales such as "The Frog King," where the prospective marriage partner takes the shape of a beast, are more likely to be concerned with the anxiety and revulsion a child feels at the prospect of maturity and sexuality than to be offering meditations on the hazards of disobedience.

Tales in the animal-groom cycle often appear in truncated versions, but the full structure of the tale type appears virtually intact in Mme Leprince de Beaumont's "Beauty and the Beast" and in its German counterpart "The Lilting, Leaping Lark." In both stories, a father with three daughters plans a trip and, before leaving, takes requests from the girls for gifts. The youngest and most beautiful of the three makes the most modest request. In Mme de Beaumont's tale, Beauty asks for nothing more than a rose; in the Grimms' story, the heroine scorns pearls and diamonds for a "lilting, leaping lark." On the homeward leg of the journey, each father succeeds in acquiring the desired object, but only after inadvertently trespassing on the grounds of a prince imprisoned in the body of a beast. The two fathers narrowly escape death, and each ultimately surrenders his youngest daughter to the beast.

Up to this point in both stories, the plot focuses on the encounter between father and beast, between a figure who embodies paternal authority in its benevolent form and a figure who, despite the absence of epithets attached to him, must be seen as the very incarnation of coercive rage and violence. (In variant forms of this preliminary episode, the devil himself serves as a functional equivalent of

the beast.) Both Beast in the French version and the lion in the German are less than reasonable when they apprehend the paternal
poachers. "Ungrateful wretch," Beast roars when he catches Beauty's father in the act of plucking a rose. "You shall pay for this with
your life! I give you fifteen minutes to make your peace with
heaven."[20] The lion in the Grimms' tale flies into a rage when he
nabs the would-be thief of his lark. "Nothing can save you," he bel-
lows in his fury. The contrast between the civilized face of paternal
good will and the savage visage of beastly malice could not be more
strikingly marked than in this single dramatic encounter. In tales of
animal grooms, father figures invariably personify the sweet voice
of reason, wisdom, and prudence. Paternal authority is dressed in
the most favorable possible colors.

But things are not always what they seem in fairy tales, which have
a way of concealing their complexity on the very surface of things.
The "civilized" fathers of tales in the animal-groom cycle end by de-
livering their daughters up to a ferocious beast in order to save their
own lives. Beasts, in turn, are not quite so savage as they appear at
first blush. Mme de Beaumont's Beauty, whose views are admittedly
colored more by eighteenth-century cynicism about the nobility
than by folk wisdom, tells Beast: "There are many men who make
worse monsters than you, and I prefer you, notwithstanding your
looks, to those who under the semblance of men hide false, corrupt,
and ungrateful hearts."[21] The "fierce lion" of "The Lilting, Leaping
Lark" turns out to be the most well-bred and mild-mannered king
of beasts. Even the repulsive-looking frog-king comports himself in
a way that runs counter to his appearance. Except for his petulant
insistence on joining the princess in bed, he remains a perfect
gentleman.

If the first phase of animal-groom tales is marked by the opposition civilized/savage and the movement toward its inversion, the second phase of the action plots the heroine's response to the double
nature of the prince/beast figure. In many tales, the female protagonist quickly recognizes the humane qualities of her captor and
comes to value them more highly than external appearances.[22]
Love, with its power to civilize even the most barbaric monster, dis-

enchants the prince and restores him to his human condition. As folk wisdom tells us, love conquers all. Yet not all tales of bridegrooms bound by a spell unfold in so harmonious a fashion, with love proving stronger than curses and various forms of bewitchment. Kisses and tears (with their power to symbolize passion and compassion) often release a beast from his enchanted condition, but decapitation and other acts of violence can prove equally effective. In "The Three Little Birds," the young heroine and her two brothers encounter a large black dog: "When they struck it in the face, it turned into a handsome prince." The fairy-tale heroine who reacts with aversion, loathing, or anger to the beastly nature of her prospective spouse is no less likely to effect a magical transformation than her tenderly affectionate or compassionate counterpart.

That the two possible responses (tenderness/aggression) to animal grooms correspond to the dual nature of fairy-tale beasts (civilized/savage) does not explain why tenderness and aggression achieve exactly the same end. What child or adult has failed to register surprise when the faithless princess in "The Frog King" lives happily ever after with the young man whom she "dashed against the wall" in his enchanted state? "Now you'll get your rest, you nasty frog!" she shouts at him with seemingly irrepressible glee. Although some variant forms of this tale feature a princess who freely admits the frog to her chambers despite his repellent appearance and who thereby liberates him, others (and they are the most prominent) give us a princess who is perfectly capable of an act demanding cold-bloodedness even more chilling than the one depicted by the Grimms. In Scottish and Gallic versions of "The Frog King," the princess beheads her suitor. A Polish variant replaces the frog with a snake and recounts in lavish detail the princess's act of tearing the creature in two. A more tame, Lithuanian text requires the burning of the snake's skin before the prince is freed from his reptilian state.

From other folkloric sources it becomes evident that the reversal of a metamorphosis—the return from animal, vegetable, or mineral form to human shape—usually requires sacrifice. In some cases, as in the story of "Faithful Johannes," the hero must be prepared to sacrifice his son in order to release his servant from a state of petrifaction. In others, as in "The Golden Bird," the hero must summon up the courage to shoot a benevolent animal helper and to cut off its head and paws. The acts of violence embedded in various versions of "The Frog King" may, in their original form, have been motivated by compassion rather than hostility. The fairy-tale victim, or rather beneficiary, of an act of physical mutilation is forever indebted to the agent, who possesses the steely courage to carry out the forbidding deed. The very strength of the agent's passion or compassion endows him with the fortitude to execute the deed, however cruel it may seem. Tenderness and violence are virtually wedded in these tales. The princess in the Grimms' version of "The Frog King" may simply be displaying her spontaneous reaction to the unending importunities of a "disgusting frog" when she hurls him against the wall, but she may also have behind her act the weight of folkloric traditions that require an act of physical violence for love to flourish in its most human and humane form.²³

In many tales of animal grooms, neither an act of love nor a deed of violence suffices to reverse the spell cast on a prince by a wicked witch or evil fairy. The heroine of the tale may actually live for some time with her animal husband—though it is said (perhaps for the sake of propriety) that he returns to his human shape at night—before she is obliged to undertake a redemptive journey for the sake of her husband. The journey is motivated by the bride's violation of a prohibition. That prohibition, no matter what form it takes, comes to constitute the didactic core of the tale type. If the heroine is barred from looking at her husband or must avoid letting light fall on him, her story is read as a reminder to restrain curiosity and to avoid excessive intimacy with one's husband. If the heroine fails to return from home to her husband after a prescribed period of time, her tale is read as a lesson in the hazards of inordinately strong attachments to parents. There may be a kernel of psychological truth in these interpretations, but they tend to single out only one link in the long chain of the plot's events. Broken promises and violated prohibitions, moreover, have a positive function in the logic of the fairy-tale narrative. Even when it must have been obvious that a broken word or the violation of a prohibition took the heroine one step

further in the process of disenchanting her beloved, Wilhelm
Grimm still slipped in adages about the importance of keeping
promises. Rather than coming to terms with the absence of a moral
order and the presence of repetitive narrative segments (e.g., pro-
hibition/violation, command/fulfillment), he persisted in adding
moral pronouncements even where there was no moral.

The most challenging question raised by animal-groom tales still
remains to be answered. What accounts for the transformation of
dashing young princes into beasts? A quick survey of bewitched
husbands in the Grimms' collection reveals that they are predomi-
nantly ferocious beasts. Lions and bears are not uncommon con-
sorts for fairy-tale heroines. Reptiles are also popular forms assumed by enchanted princes, and many a fairy-tale couple begins its
courtship when a frog or snake accosts an unwary young girl. Other
equally revolting forms of animal life emerge as heroes in the international class of animal grooms: pigs, hedgehogs, and donkeys all
press themselves upon young, innocent girls. In sum, the menagerie
of animal grooms displays impressive diversity, even if it is domi-
nated by savage rather than tame beasts. Only rarely does the prince
metamorphose into anything other than an animal. Stories recounting the transformation of young men into heads of massive proportions, into trees, and even into ovens constitute little more than exceptions to a widespread and pervasive rule.[24]

Fairy tales tell us precious little about the circumstances leading to
the metamorphosis of men into animals. A "wicked fairy" of unspecified origin and motive weaves a spell over Perrault's Beast. In
the Grimms' "The Lilting, Leaping Lark," the prince is in an enchanted state from the start. The tale of Snow White and Rose Red
names a "wicked dwarf" as the culprit responsible for the transformation of a prince into a bear. In nearly every other tale recounting
the wedding of a woman to an enchanted prince, an "old witch," a
"wicked witch," or a "witch" plain and simple engineers the metamorphosis. Curiously, her motives remain unknown. The fairies,
witches, and gnomes who set the plots of these tales in motion function as disembodied agents of evil who choose innocent male by-
standers as targets for their magical spells.

It may well be that these sorceresses translate the metaphorical wisdom of old wives on sexuality ("men are beasts") into literal terms. Jan Öjvid Swahn has pointed out that "Beauty and the Beast" belongs to a tale type that developed "almost exclusively in a female milieu." That story and others like it may have been told by women to women in the context of covert reflections on maturity, marriage, and sexuality.[25] But it is also possible to see in these stories of beast marriages popular versions (what Hans Naumann has called "gesunkenes Kulturgut") of classical myths in which gods assume the form of beasts before displaying their amorous intentions. These myths in turn remind us that many primitive societies traced their origins to the union between a woman and a totem beast. In folktales as in myths, the humble female partner turns the head of the disguised deity or monarch through her physical attractiveness.

Stories like "Beauty and the Beast" may derive from classical myths and primitive beliefs, but they assuredly give us distinctly tame versions of them. The popular imagination succeeded in avoiding the theme of sodomy by transforming the mythical beast into an enchanted human. This process of civilization had gone so far by the time Charles Perrault appropriated the story for his collection that he could divest the transformation from beast to human of magic. Physical deformities may make Riquet à la Houppe (in the story of that title) look like a beast, but his other attributes are so winning that they inspire a love that transforms him from a hunchback into the handsomest of men. Here we are no longer in the realm of "fairy enchantment" (as Perrault makes clear), but in the sphere of psychological allegory.

If there is a secret message planted in fairy tales, it is inscribed in plain sight, right on the surface of each tale's events. Reading fairy tales requires us to set aside our preconceptions about the "lessons" imparted by specific tales. More often than not, these explicit lessons come from the pens of experts in the art of bowdlerizing fairy tales. Perrault, as we have seen, found Bluebeard's murders of less consequence than the curiosity of Bluebeard's wife about a forbidden chamber. He was perfectly prepared to read "Bluebeard" as a cautionary tale warning women against excessive curiosity. Those who trust the tale rather than its teller will quickly understand why Perrault and others were so anxious to single out curiosity as the principal subject of "Bluebeard." By highlighting the centrality of curiosity, Perrault succeeded in obscuring the connections between forbidden chambers and crimes of passion. It is hardly surprising that by the time the *Nursery and Household Tales* appeared, "Bluebeard" had branched off into two separate narratives: one a cautionary fairy tale about the hazards of curiosity, the other a folk tale depicting the triumph of a clever young woman over a bloodthirsty villain.

"Bluebeard," as we have seen, was easy to transform from a tale of high adventure charged with sexual meaning into a didactic story rehearsing the perils of curiosity or celebrating the power of craft. "Beauty and the Beast" may not have been converted into a cautionary tale by its many retellers, recorders, and rewriters, but it too has become domesticated over the centuries. Rather than taking a didactic turn, however, it has moved in the direction of sentimentalization. The theme of love's humanizing power has so overshadowed the link between sexuality and bestiality that few readers are shocked by the appearance of the animal groom. Still, the nervous insistence of various tellers on including mawkish speeches and on articulating banal messages does not drown out the deeper and more profound chords sounded by the tale's events. They resonate throughout the plot and can be silenced only through a stark reorchestration of the story line. Perrault, the Grimms, and others may have tampered with the tales they heard and failed to capture the authentic voice of the folk, but they only occasionally so distorted the plot of a tale that it was wholly deprived of its original meaning. Unintentionally perhaps, they preserved the deeper implications of the stories they recorded while making them suitable bedtime fare for children.

EPILOGUE

Getting Even

ONE OF THE most memorable fairy tales of all time is recited by a grandmother in Georg Büchner's powerful play *Woyzeck*.

> Once upon a time there was a poor little child with no father and no mother, everything was dead, and no one was left in the whole world. Everything was dead, and it went and searched day and night. And since nobody was left on earth, it wanted to go up to the heavens, and the moon was looking at it so friendly, and when it finally got to the moon, the moon was a piece of rotten wood and then it went to the sun and when it got there, the sun was a wilted sunflower and when it got to the stars, they were little golden flies stuck up there like the shrike sticks 'em on the blackthorn and when it wanted to go back down to the earth, the earth was an upset pot and it was all alone and it sat down and cried and there it sits to this day, all alone.[1]

Most fairy-tale characters have a hard time of it in their stories and histories, but at least they can console themselves with the prospect of living "happily ever after." In this classic anti–fairy tale (to use a term coined by the critic André Jolles), the cardinal law of a happy ending is violated: helplessness and isolation are so intensified in the course of the tale that the child-hero lives unhappily ever after. By ending his tale with a situation that usually marks the beginning of a fairy tale, Büchner succeeded in subverting the ground rules of the genre.

It did not take the genius of Georg Büchner to create the antipodal form of the fairy tale. In the *Nursery and Household Tales*, we can find numerous examples. "The Knapsack, the Hat, and the Horn" ends with the hero's decimation of entire towns and villages. Blowing on a magical horn, he destroys everything in sight until he alone is left to survey the devastation. "Then he was king all by himself,

[179]

and he blew on his horn until he died."[2] Here, however, it is not the hero's helplessness that is pushed to the limits, but rather his power. The two tales by Büchner and the Grimms, taken together, remind us of the extent to which fairy tales put on display the extremes of helplessness and omnipotence. A hero wallowing in self-pity is as common as a hero reveling in his power to take reprisals against enemies.

If we move from classical fairy tales to fables and other types of folk tales in the Grimms' collection, the picture can be equally lugubrious. "The Death of the Hen" not only gives us the graphic details of the episode named in its title, but also, after relating the drowning of the hen's entire funeral cortege, concludes with the death of Hen's husband: "He dug a grave for her, put her in, made a mound over her, sat down on the mound, and grieved until he too died. So then they were all dead." "The Mouse, the Bird, and the Sausage" begins with the description of a harmonious cooperative in which the three title figures have joined forces and live comfortably by sharing household chores. Each pulls his oar according to his abilities. "But when things go well, you start looking for something new." When the bird insists on reshuffling the household responsibilities so that he can stay at home, the sausage ends by falling victim to a hungry dog, the mouse perishes in a pot of soup, and the bird falls into a well and drowns.

"How Children Played Butcher with Each Other," the most ghastly tale in the Grimms' collection, happily never entered the pages of the second edition of the *Nursery and Household Tales*. In the first edition the Grimms went so far as to offer two different versions of it. The first describes the fatal consequences of a children's game, which takes a tragic turn when one boy "playing" butcher slaughters another "playing" swine. The second version offers a chain of events even more lurid. A boy who takes the butcher's role murders his brother; his mother, witnessing the event from a window, is so enraged and distraught that she plunges a knife into the heart of her son; she returns to the house to find that the child she had been bathing has drowned in her absence; in the end, she hangs herself, and her grief-stricken husband dies shortly thereafter.

After reading this account, it becomes clear that much of the material that came into the Grimms' hands was hardly suited for children.[3] The Grimms, however, eliminated violence only under protest. "How Children Played Butcher with Each Other" seemed to Wilhelm Grimm a perfectly acceptable children's story; he had heard the story in his youth and found that it had taught him an important lesson about caution and restraint.[4]

When it came to mounting scenes of revenge and retaliation, Wilhelm Grimm gave free play to his imagination. It never occurred to him to eliminate beheadings, stabbings, slashings, and other forms of bloodshed. "Darling Roland," for example, not only recounts a woman's decapitation of her daughter, but gives a vivid picture of the victim, "bathed in blood." More important, it gives us an elaborate description of the villain's punishment. Just as the mother/witch is about to pluck a flower, a fiddler strikes up a tune: "Like it or not she had to dance, for it was a magic tune. The faster he played the higher she had to jump. The brambles ripped the clothes from her body and scratched her until she was covered with blood. Since he wouldn't stop playing, she had to dance until she fell down on the ground dead."

As noted earlier, Wilhelm Grimm may have found allusions to pregnancy offensive, but he had no such scruples about violence. He rarely let slip the opportunity to have someone burned at the stake, drowned, forced to dance in red-hot shoes, torn to pieces, or stripped naked and put in a barrel studded with nails and harnessed to a horse. Even in the ten "Legends for Children" appended to the *Nursery and Household Tales*, one story ends in the following way after a wicked mother and her ill-tempered daughter head for the woods: "On the way so many lizards and snakes attacked the two of them that they couldn't get away. In the end they stung the wicked child to death. They stung the mother in the foot, because she had not raised her better." The punishment of villains is invariably described in greater detail than the good fortune of heroes. That villains die in the most painful possible way seems to be a precondition for the hero's happiness and in some tales even constitutes the "happy end." The description of Cinderella's wedding is almost wholly devoted to an elaborate account of how doves peck out the eyes of the stepsisters. Snow White's wedding really has only one central event: the death of the stepmother after she is forced to dance in red-hot iron shoes. The king, the queen, and her six brothers may all live happily ever after in "The Six Swans," but not until the queen's wicked mother-in-law is burned at the stake. Reward-and-punishment tales, with their two contrasting figures, invariably end with a tableau of humiliation and torture. In "Mother Holle," for example, a dutiful heroine's good fortune is put on display immediately; the remainder of the text is devoted to the trials of the heroine's lazy counterpart and ends with a bath of pitch that sticks to the lazy girl for the rest of her life. As another collector of fairy tales put it, in the coda to his version of "Snow White," "revenge can be as sweet as love."[5]

German fairy tales, as we have seen, repeatedly show us heroes in the role of victim. Hans Dumm is everyone's favorite whipping boy, and the youngest of three sons is always underprivileged and taken for a fool. The many female Cinderellas in the *Nursery and Household Tales* are subjected to all manner of abuse and humiliation, while proud princesses are outsmarted by their suitors and must slave away in kitchens, doing all the dirty work. A tableau of utter helplessness in the face of adversity brings down the curtain on the first act of one fairy tale after another. In stark contrast to the Grimms' heroes, the villains possess power, strength, and craft, along with murderous tenacity. Whether they take the form of fire-breathing dragons or cold-blooded witches, they are so pitiless that they fail to elicit pity once the tables are turned on them. We have seen that stepmothers, ogres, beasts, and other fairy-tale monsters are so demonized that they possess no redeeming features. It is impossible to forgive and forget them; hence the paucity of fairy tales that end with scenes of reconciliation. Instead, the humiliation and helplessness of the hero at the start are balanced by retaliation and revenge at the end.

The fairy tale's movement from victimization to retaliation possesses a classic balance and symmetry. In the end, old scores are settled and wrongs are redressed. The sufferings inflicted on the vic-

tim or intended for him are ultimately visited on the adversary. A
woman who throws her daughter-in-law into a river ends by drowning. The stepmother who proposes to abandon her stepdaughter in
the woods is torn to pieces by wild animals. There is no casual ca-
priciousness in the selection of appropriate punishments or in the
means of establishing justice. This is the Old Testament logic of an
eye for an eye. In fairy tales, getting even is the best revenge.[6]

Despite the best efforts of Wilhelm Grimm, there are several tales
in the *Nursery and Household Tales* that do not establish a clear justification (punishment) or motivation (revenge) for scenes of cruelty.
In these tales, violence is not placed in the service of reasserting order and establishing equilibrium; instead it is used to wreak havoc
and to create a vision of burlesque anarchy. We are once again in the
realm of the comic folk tale rather than the classic fairy tale. "Mr.
Korbis," one of the less well-known stories in the *Nursery and Household Tales*, shows us the extent to which the depiction of unrestrained violence and cruelty can produce comic effects. In that
story, a hen, rooster, cat, millstone, egg, duck, pin, and needle travel
together in style to the home of the unfortunate Mr. Korbis. They
invade his home and lie in wait for his return.

> When Mr. Korbis came home, he went to the hearth and wanted to
> make a fire, but the cat threw ashes into his face. He quickly ran to the
> kitchen and wanted to wash himself, but the duck squirted water in
> his face. He wanted to dry himself with the towel, but the egg came
> rolling toward him, broke, and glued his eyes shut. He wanted to sit
> down in a chair and rest, but the pin stuck him. That made him angry
> and he flung himself on the bed, but when he put his head on the pil-
> low, the sewing needle stuck him so sharply that he yelled out, flew
> into a rage, and wanted to run outside. But when he got to the door,
> the millstone jumped down and knocked him dead.

Not a very pleasant tale, but one that invariably elicits laughter.
Here we are far removed from the world of "The Juniper Tree,"
where a crushing blow from a millstone liberates an entire family
from the oppressive influence of a woman. When the sequence of
"gags" in "Mr. Korbis" takes a fatal turn at the end, the tale does not
veer off into the melodramatic or tragic mode. The unwitting victim

of the various pranks has done nothing to deserve the nasty turns done to him—this is not a tale of victimization and retaliation. What we have is slapstick, a sequence of pratfalls and humiliations that has no order or logic. Wilhelm Grimm must have found this account of unmotivated cruelty somewhat disconcerting, for the last edition of the *Nursery and Household Tales* contains the following final sentence: "Mr. Korbis must have been a very wicked man."

While fairy tales often show us children triumphing over wicked adults, folk tales enact the same victimization/retaliation drama between underdogs and top dogs. Indeed it might be tempting to read "Mr. Korbis" as a tale in which the servants of man rebel against their master and take revenge. But this seems to be missing the point of the tale. Many a story in the *Nursery and Household Tales* (and this is a fact that Wilhelm Grimm clearly did not want to face) depicts violence purely for the sake of violence. That scenes of wanton cruelty can take on the character of surreal comedy is an unpleasant fact to acknowledge. Take the case of "The Fires of Youth," a tale that ranks among the grisliest and yet silliest in the Grimms' collection. Saint Peter and the Lord take lodgings one night at the home of a blacksmith, where they meet a decrepit beggar whom they decide to rejuvenate. Using the tools of the blacksmith's trade, they transform the beggar into a vigorous, able-bodied young man. After Saint Peter and the Lord depart, the blacksmith proposes to repeat the process with his mother-in-law. Eager to recover her youth, she agrees.

> And so the blacksmith made a big fire and pushed the old woman into it, and she twisted and turned and yelled bloody murder. "Sit still," he said. "Why are you screaming and writhing about? Just wait until I work the bellows harder." So he worked the bellows until all her rags caught on fire. The old woman screamed relentlessly, and the blacksmith thought to himself: "I haven't got it quite right yet." So he pulled her out and threw her into a tub of water. At that she screamed so loud that the blacksmith's wife and daughter-in-law could hear her all the way to the house. They rushed down the stairs and saw the old woman lying doubled up in the tub of water, screaming and screeching, with her face all wrinkled and shriveled and shapeless. The two women, who were both with child, were so horrified that they gave

birth that very night to two boys. But their babies weren't human, they were apes. They ran off into the forest, and founded the race of apes.

Again the victimization/retaliation pattern of fairy tales is absent. The blacksmith is not getting even; he is simply getting the better of his mother-in-law. The blacksmith's clumsy imitation of his superiors and his mother-in-law's display of pain make for the comedy (however grim) of the scene.

Over the years, the Grimms' *Nursery and Household Tales* has come under heavy fire from educators, for the tales are generally held to be more gruesome and horrific than most other such stories. After World War II, the Allied occupying powers in some German cities went so far as to ban the *Nursery and Household Tales* from schoolrooms and to order the collection withdrawn from circulation.[7] The Grimms' stories came to be viewed as nourishers and reflectors of a cruel, perverse national mentality. The only question that remained open was whether to see them as causal contributors to the horrors of the Hitler regime or simply as early signs of what was to come. In the introduction to his volume of Italian folktales, Italo Calvino states with pride that "the continuous flow of blood" in the Grimms' "brutal" tales is not to be found in their Italian counterparts. "The Italian folktale," he adds, "seldom displays unbearable ferocity. . . . The narrative does not dwell on the torment of the victim, not even under pretense of pity, but moves swiftly to a healing solution." Calvino concedes that even in Italian tales we witness the misery of victims to some extent. This is surely an understatement if we consider "Olive," in which the heroine stands "handless in the middle of the woods and dying of hunger and thirst, with . . . two babies in her arms." Calvino admits that descriptions of revenge are by no means absent from Italian tales: witches are routinely tarred and thrown on a pyre or pushed from windows and burned to death. Without scenes of victimization and retaliation, it would be hard to tell a fairy tale; they are the very stuff of the narrative. Italian tales may be terse in their descriptions of violence, but they do not in the least bracket the victim's pain and the villain's suffering.[8]

Calvino also makes the point that "gory ferocity is never gratuitous" in Italian folktales, and indeed one looks in vain through his massive collection for a tale along the lines of the Grimms' "Mr. Korbis." That story seems to have remained within German-speaking borders. But "The Fires of Youth" has countless cousins scattered all over the Eurasian folkloric map, and one of its variants found its way into Calvino's collection under the title "The Three Crones." In that story, three fairies turn a ninety-four-year-old woman into a beautiful young maiden who becomes the bride of a handsome young king. When one of the queen's two sisters seeks advice on rejuvenating herself, she is told to have herself planed by a carpenter.

> The old woman went running to the carpenter's shop lickety-split. "Carpenter, will you give me a good planing?"
> "Oh, my goodness!" exclaimed the carpenter. "You're already deadwood, but if I plane you, you'll go to kingdom come."
> . . . "Don't worry, I tell you. Here's a thaler."
> When he heard "thaler," the carpenter changed his mind. He took the money and said, "Lie down here on my workbench, and I'll plane you all you like," and he proceeded to plane a jaw.
> The crone let out a scream.
> "Now, now! If you scream, we won't get anything done."
> She rolled over, and the carpenter planed the other jaw. The old crone screamed no more: she was dead as dead can be.
> Nothing more was ever heard of the other crone. Whether she drowned, had her throat slit, died in bed or elsewhere, no one knows.[9]

Once again the "joke" is at the expense of an undeserving victim. The old woman who dies at the hands of the carpenter never once acts as anything more than helper to her aged sister. Calvino's tale may offer a less protracted picture of the victim's sufferings than the Grimms' story, but it surely is not less muted in its use of cruelty and violence for comic purposes.

The Grimms clearly hold no monopoly on violence in fairy tales and folk tales. The horrors of the stories, to borrow a phrase from Poe, are not really of Germany, but of the soul. When the Grimms appropriated (sometimes unwittingly) a tale from Perrault, they invariably drafted a tamer version. Their Little Red Riding Hood is rescued by a hunter and liberated from the bowels of a wolf. Their

Sleeping Beauty never has to tangle with a woman who demands to have her grandchildren for supper. Their Thumbling may be a prankster, but he never goes so far as to trick a giant into beheading his seven daughters. When it comes to the depiction of violence in fairy tales, nothing rivals Gustave Doré's illustration for Perrault's "Petit Poucet" ("Tom Thumb") (figure 18).

The British Jack tales are also hardly as innocuous and whimsical as they are often made out to be. To be sure, the cannibalistic tendencies of the giants in those stories are described so matter-of-factly that the effect can be droll: " 'My man is an ogre,' one giant's wife tells Jack, 'and there's nothing he likes better than boys broiled on toast.' " When the giant chants his famous "Fee-fi-fo-fum" doggerel, his wife pacifies him by telling him that he must have caught a whiff of "the scraps of that little boy you liked so much for yesterday's dinner." The words of the giant, by contrast, are more pointedly chill-

FIGURE 18. *Gustave Doré's illustration for Perrault's "Tom Thumb" shows us the ogre about to slit the throats of his seven daughters.*

ing: "Art thou the villain who killed my kinsmen? Then I will tear thee with my teeth, suck thy blood, and grind thy bones to powder."[10] Jack's dispatching of the giant, the revenge he takes against his powerful adversary, is always described so graphically that it leaves nothing to the imagination.

Those who hold that German fairy tales are unique in the degree to which they indulge in morbid descriptions of cruelty and violence would do well to cast a glance at a few of the Russian tales of Baba Yagá. The hut of this cunning old hag lies in the darkest reaches of the forest. Propped up on hens' feet, it is enclosed by a fence of human bones crowned with skulls. The gateposts are human legs, the bolts are arms, and the lock is made of teeth. Every fairy-tale hero knows that this witch delights in eating young children and drinking their blood. The fiends and villains of Russian folklore are no less bloodthirsty than French ogres, British giants, and German witches. When Baba Yagá cackles, "Foo! Foo! I smell Russian flesh!" she strikes terror into the heart of the tale's hero. Here too, the helplessness of the hero is thrown into sharp relief by the overpowering coldbloodedness of his opponent. Yet helplessness and victimization are once again balanced by revenge and retaliation. Fair Vassilisa gets the chance to watch her stepmother (in league with Baba Yagá) and her two stepsisters burn to cinders when a glowing skull fixes its eyes on them. In another tale, an evil witch is tied to a horse's tail, and the horse is set loose across an open plain. The final tableaux of fairy tales do not differ radically as we move from east to west or from north to south.

Setting up generalizations about national or cultural differences by comparing episodes in different versions of one tale type is a hazardous business. It is, for example, easy to draw false conclusions by contrasting the end of Perrault's "Cendrillon" with that of the Grimms' "Aschenputtel." Perrault's Cinderella makes amends to her stepsisters after they throw themselves at her feet and beg her forgiveness. The Grimms tell it differently: "On the day of Aschenputtel's wedding, the two stepsisters came and tried to ingratiate themselves and share in her happiness." They join the wedding procession, but on the way to the church and back, doves peck out their eyes. The contrast between compassion and retribution could not be more pronounced, and it is tempting to begin constructing arguments about French charity and German cruelty. But is it really possible to compare a tale from Perrault's seventeenth-century collection of stories dedicated to the twenty-one-year-old Elisabeth Charlotte d'Orléans and a tale from the Grimms' nineteenth-century collection of stories designed for the folk? Perrault strained to please an aristocratic audience; the Grimms sought to capture the authentic voice of the common people. The manner inevitably affected the matter. Perrault's characters, for example, are intensely aware of fashions (the prince in "The Sleeping Beauty of the Wood" finds the princess's hundred-year-old gown hopelessly out of style); the Grimms' figures are more concerned with fundamentals (their prince focuses on the courtyard and the kitchen rather than on the apparel of his beloved). The graceful style and elegant plotting of Perrault's *Contes* stands in sharp contrast to the rough-hewn prose and often primitive story lines of the *Nursery and Household Tales*.

Comparing "Cendrillon" with "Aschenputtel" is problematic on grounds other than the differences between Perrault and the Grimms. Although the Grimms give us an uncharitable heroine in one version of the Cinderella story, they show us a compassionate heroine in another variant. Two-eyes in "One-eye, Two-eyes, and Three-eyes" also suffers at the hands of her sisters and mother, but in the end she lets bygones be bygones. When two poor women come to her castle begging for alms, she recognizes in them her sisters: "Two-eyes welcomed them and treated them well and took care of them, and with all their hearts they both regretted the evil they had done their sister in their youth." Most of the Grimms' Cinderellas are not so magnanimous, but the example of "One-eye, Two-eyes, and Three-eyes" shows us just how unsound it is to draw comparative conclusions on the basis of one French variant and one German variant. Making a case for the pronounced cruelty and brutality of the *Nursery and Household Tales* would require a full-scale comparative analysis of comparable collections.

The comparison of the Grimms' "Cinderella" with their "One-eye, Two-eyes, and Three-eyes" is also revealing in that it shows how a few minor changes can radically alter the values set down in a tale. With a few swift strokes of the pen it is easy to turn cruelty to compassion, violence to tenderness, or naiveté into craft. Hence the hazards of reading too deep a meaning into random details of one national version of one tale type. Although it is true that the profound resonance found by the *Nursery and Household Tales* in Germany over the years suggests that the brothers captured something of the spirit of a nation even if they did not succeed perfectly in capturing the voice of the folk, their final edition must constantly be checked against earlier editions and against national and international variants of each tale in it.

Determining national rankings for the degree of violence and cruelty in fairy tales is like one of those impossible tasks posed in the tales. It is clear, however, that violence and cruelty number among the hard facts of all fairy tales. The victimization/retaliation pattern that appears in one tale type after another invites the depiction of heartless behavior and merciless punishments. Pathetic helplessness and vulnerability give way to unlimited wealth and power. Given the power relationships in fairy tales, it is self-evident why these stories should prove attractive to children. A sense of forlorn weakness in the face of all-powerful guardians and adversaries replicates perfectly the feelings of young children toward adults. The fairy tale's movement from victimization to retaliation gives vivid but disguised shape to the dreams of revenge that inevitably drift into the mind of every child beset by a sense of powerlessness. That the hero's initial state of misery is exaggerated and inflated beyond the limits of realism makes the fantasy all the more satisfying. Both the hero's reward and his oppressor's sufferings are richly deserved.

The question of the merits of fairy tales as children's literature has been debated endlessly over the years.[11] As one critic frames the question: "Do children need horror in stories? If so, how much and how soon?"[12] One camp of educators and psychologists rallies to the side of censorship, perfectly prepared to remove the *Nursery and Household Tales*—even in its adulterated versions—from the shelves of libraries and nurseries. The other camp, whose most eloquent spokesman is Bruno Bettelheim, argues for the civilizing power of the Grimms' tales and sees in them instruments of enlightenment. *Children Need Fairy Tales*, the German title of Bettelheim's volume states. Even before the Grimms started collecting their tales, Samuel Johnson proclaimed that "babies do not want to hear about babies; they like to be told of giants and castles, and of somewhat [*sic*] which can stretch and stimulate their little minds." Whether he would have approved of man-eating giants and cannibalistic witches is another question. In any case, the response to his declaration came swiftly in Richard Edgeworth's defiant demand: "Supposing that they do prefer such tales, is this a reason why they should be indulged in reading them?"[13]

It is not easy to take sides in this debate. Fairy tales may constitute the childhood of fiction, but they are not necessarily the fiction of childhood. Although the stories often side with the child-hero in his struggle against powerful adversaries and culminate in the triumph of the young and weak, they put a good deal of pain and suffering on display along the way. The degree to which that pain and suffering dominate the tale varies greatly depending on cultural norms, pedagogical demands, and individual preferences. No fairy tale was ever meant to be written in granite. Like all oral narrative forms, the fairy tale has no "correct," definitive form. Instead it endlessly adjusts and adapts itself to every new culture as it takes root. With no firm rules dictating the degree of violence appropriate for a fairy tale, every time and place sets its own parameters.

In the Grimms' collection, the true horror stories are not so much tales based on the victimization/retaliation model as cautionary tales—texts that rely on a transgression/punishment model for their plotting. These stories end with the triumph of adult wisdom over childish disobedience, curiosity, or naughtiness. Often they go so far as to end with the deaths of the youthful protagonists. In "Frau Trude," the "stubborn and insolent" heroine disobeys her parents and leaves home to meet up with the witch named in the tale's title. Frau Trude welcomes her young guest, turns her into a block of wood, throws it into the fire, and warms herself by the blaze. Here both witch and parents win the contest between child and adult.

There is only one story in the *Nursery and Household Tales* that surpasses "Frau Trude" in its stark portrayal of the punishment of children. "The Naughty Child" tells of a youngster who refuses to be obedient. "God was displeased with it and made it sick." The child dies, is buried, but asserts a strong will even beyond the grave by thrusting an arm into the air. Only when the mother makes her way to the grave and whips the arm with a switch does the child find peace.

Both these stories preach straightforward lessons about the virtues of telling the truth, suppressing curiosity, and practicing obedience. They seem consciously designed to impart specific lessons framed by adults for children. As cautionary tales, they demonstrate how children with undesirable traits—deceitfulness, curiosity, insolence—come to a bad end. Power is invested solely in adults, who use their superior strength and intelligence to teach children a lesson. These stories, with their single-minded focus on the transgression/punishment pattern, their unique power relationships, their explicit morals, and their implicit call for conformity are the most horrifying stories in the Grimms' collection. By inverting the power structure and the underlying pattern of classic fairy tales, they are likely to instill fear rather than confidence in the children who hear them and read them.

Whether ferocity and violence take a tragic turn or lead to comic antics, the description of their effects exercises a powerful hold on the imagination of children. Adults also have not been immune to the charm of the fairy tale's horrors and the folk tale's cruelties. Few people look to fairy tales for models of humane, civilized behavior. The stories have taken hold for a far more important reason: the hard facts of fairy-tale life offer exaggerated visions of the grimmer realities and fantasies that touch and shape the lives of every child and adult.

APPENDIXES

A

Selected Tales from the First Edition of the
NURSERY & HOUSEHOLD TALES

SOME OF THE texts discussed extensively in this book have not been
translated into English. I offer here my own translations. With the
exception of "Rapunzel," none of these tales entered the pages of
the second edition.

VOLUME 1

8. *The Hand with the Knife*

There once was a girl who had three brothers. The boys meant
everything to their mother, and the girl was always put at a disadvantage and treated badly. Every day she had to go out to a barren
heath to dig peat, which was used for cooking and heating. A dull
old tool was all she had to do the nasty work.

The little girl had an admirer, an elf who lived in a hill near her
mother's house. Whenever she passed by that hill, the elf would
stretch his hand out of a boulder and hold out a very sharp knife
that had special powers and could cut through anything. She was
able to dig out the peat quickly with that knife, go home with the
required amount, and when she got to the boulder, she tapped on it
twice. Then the hand would reach out to take back the knife.

When the mother began to notice how quickly and effortlessly the
girl brought home the peat, she told the brothers that someone else
had to be helping her with the work, otherwise it wouldn't be possible. The brothers stealthily followed her and saw how she got the
magical knife, then caught up with her and forced her to give it to
them. They headed back, struck the rock as the girl had done, and
when the good elf stretched his hand out, they cut it off with his own

knife. The bloody arm pulled back, and because the elf believed that his beloved had betrayed him, he was never seen again.

12. *Rapunzel*

There once lived a man and a woman who had long wanted a child but who had never had one. Finally, however, the woman was with child. This couple had in the back of their house a small window from which they could look into the garden of a fairy. The garden was full of flowers and herbs of all kinds, but no one dared enter it. One day the woman was standing at a window looking down into the garden when she caught sight of a fabulous bed of rapunzel and was seized by a craving for it. Since she knew that she couldn't have any, she began to waste away in misery. Finally her husband got scared and asked what was wrong. "Oh, if I can't get to eat any of the rapunzel behind our house, I'll die." Her husband loved her very much and decided that he would try to get her some, no matter what. One evening he climbed over the high wall and hastily uprooted a handful of rapunzel, which he took home to his wife. His wife didn't lose a moment in making a salad of it and bolted it down greedily. It tasted so good, so very good, that the next day her craving was three times as great. When her husband realized that he wouldn't have a moment's peace, he went back into the garden, where he got a big fright when he saw the fairy standing right there in front of him and scolding him harshly for daring to enter her garden and steal from it. He tried as hard as possible to excuse himself with his wife's pregnancy and explained how dangerous it was to refuse her anything. The fairy replied: "I'll accept what you say and even let you take as much rapunzel as you want so long as you give me the child that your wife is now carrying."

The husband was so terrified that he agreed to everything, and when his wife gave birth, the fairy appeared right away, named the little girl *Rapunzel*, and went off with her.

Rapunzel became the most beautiful child on earth. When she turned twelve, the fairy locked her up in a tall tower that had neither a door nor a staircase, only a tiny window at the very top. When the fairy wanted to get in, she would just stand below and call out:

> "Rapunzel, Rapunzel!
> Let your hair down for me."

Rapunzel had splendid hair, as fine as spun gold, and whenever the fairy called to her, she would undo her hair and wrap it around a hook on the window. Her hair dropped some twenty ells and the fairy climbed up on it.

One day a prince made his way through the forest where the tower was. He saw beautiful Rapunzel standing at the window and heard her singing with so sweet a voice that he fell hopelessly in love with her. But since there was not a single door to the tower and no ladder that could reach that high, he became distraught. Still, every day he went into the forest until one day he saw the fairy come and say:

> "Rapunzel, Rapunzel!
> Let your hair down."

Then he understood just what kind of ladder he needed to get into the tower. He had taken care to remember the words that he had to repeat, and the next day, once it was dark, he went to the door and called up:

> "Rapunzel, Rapunzel!
> Let your hair down."

At that she unfastened her hair, and when it reached the ground, he took hold of it firmly and was pulled up.

At first Rapunzel was frightened, but soon she came to like the young king so much that she agreed to let him visit every day and to pull him up. The two lived joyfully for a time, and the fairy did not catch on at all until Rapunzel told her one day: "Tell me, Godmother, why my clothes are so tight and why they don't fit me any longer." "Wicked child!" shouted the fairy. "What are you telling me!" And she immediately saw how she had been betrayed and flew into a rage. Then and there she took Rapunzel's beautiful hair, wrapped it a few times around her left hand, grabbed a pair of scissors with her right and snip, snip, it was cut off. Then she sent her out into a desert, where things went very badly for her and where, after a time, she gave birth to twins, a boy and a girl.

On the very day she sent Rapunzel into exile, the fairy waited until evening and fastened the hair cut from Rapunzel's head to a hood. When the prince came and said:

> "Rapunzel, Rapunzel!
> Let your hair down!"

she let the hair down, but the prince was truly astonished when he found the fairy up there in place of his beloved Rapunzel. "Let me tell you something," said the enraged fairy. "Rapunzel is forever lost to a scoundrel like you."

The prince felt so wretched that he hurled himself from the tower. He managed to survive, but he lost both his eyes, ended up roaming in the forest, ate nothing but grass and roots, and did nothing but cry. A few years later he arrived in the very same desert where Rapunzel was living in such misery with her children. Her voice seemed familiar to him, and just at that moment she recognized him and fell into his arms. Two of her tears fall into his eyes, at that they become clear again, and he can see just as before.

22. *How Children Played Butcher with Each Other*
   (two versions)

In a city called Franecker located in West Friesland, it happened that young children aged five and six, both boys and girls, were playing with each other. And they told one boy that he should be the butcher, another boy that he should be the cook, and a third that he should be the pig. They decided that one little girl should play the cook, another was to be the assistant to the cook; the assistant was to catch the blood from the pig in a little basin so that they could make sausages from it. The butcher, as had been agreed, went at the boy who was playing the pig, pulled him down to the ground, and cut his throat with a little knife; the assistant to the cook caught the blood in her little basin. A councilor who happens to be passing by sees the whole miserable spectacle: he dashes off with the butcher, takes him up to the house of the mayor, who immediately calls a meeting of all councilors. They deliberated at length on the matter and had no idea what to do, for they realized that it had all been child's play. One of them, a wise old man, ventured the opinion that the chief judge should put a nice red apple in one hand and a gilder in the other, and that he call the child and stretch both hands out to him: if the child took the apple, he would be declared innocent; if he took the gilder, he would be killed. This was done: the child, laughing, reached out for the apple and was therefore not subjected to any kind of punishment.

A man once slaughtered a pig while his children were looking on. When they started playing in the afternoon, one child said to the other: "You be the little pig, and I'll be the butcher," whereupon he took an open blade and thrust it into his brother's neck. Their mother, who was upstairs in a room bathing the youngest child in a tub, heard the cries of her other child, quickly ran downstairs, and when she saw what had happened, drew the knife out of the child's neck and, in a rage, thrust it into the heart of the child who had been the butcher. She then rushed back to the house to see what her other child was doing in the tub, but in the meantime it had drowned in the bath. The woman was so horrified that she fell into a state of utter despair, refused to be consoled by the servants, and hanged herself. When her husband returned home from the fields and saw this, he was so distraught that he died shortly thereafter.

54. *Hans Dumm*

Once there was a king living happily with a daughter who was his only child. This princess unexpectedly gave birth to a child, and no one knew who the father was. The king had no idea what to do. Finally he ordered the princess to go to church with the child; there the child was to be given a lemon, and the person to whom it gave the lemon would be declared father of the child and husband of the princess. So it came to pass, but orders were given that no one but good-looking people should be admitted to the church. Now in this city there lived a short, misshapen, hunchbacked fellow who was not terribly bright and who was therefore called Hans Dumm. Somehow he pressed himself into the crowd and managed to make his way unseen into the church. When the child was supposed to give away the lemon, it handed it to Hans Dumm. The princess was in shock; the king was so outraged that he put her and the child along with Hans Dumm out to sea in a sealed cask. The cask floated into the waters and once they were all alone, the princess started complaining and said: "You think you're so clever, you disgusting hunchback, but you're to blame for my misfortune. Why did you force your way into the church? You can't possibly have anything to do with the child."

"Oh yes I do," Hans Dumm replied. "I sure do have something to do with it. After all I once wished that you would have a child, and whatever I wish for comes true."

"If that's true, then why don't you wish us something to eat?"

"Happy to oblige," Hans Dumm replied. But he ended up wishing for a bowl piled high with potatoes. The princess would have preferred something better, but she was so hungry that she helped him eat the potatoes. Once they had had their fill, Hans Dumm said: "Now I'm going to wish us a beautiful ship!" and hardly were the words out of his mouth than they found themselves in a fabulous ship. Everything they could want was there in abundance. The pilot steered straight for land and when they got out, Hans Dumm said: "Now I want a castle right over there." Suddenly a magnificent castle appeared, and servants came in golden uniforms and led the princess and her child into the castle. When they got to the middle of the hall, Hans Dumm said: "Now I'll wish that I were a smart young prince!" All at once he lost his hump, and he became handsome, tall, and amiable. He greatly pleased the princess and became her husband.

For a long time they lived happily. Then one day the old king rode out into the woods, lost his way, and arrived at the castle. He was quite astonished by it, for he had never seen it before and rode in. The princess recognized her father immediately, but he didn't recognize her. After all, he thought that she had perished at sea a long time ago. She was a fabulous hostess, and when he made plans to go home, she secretly put a goblet of gold in one of his bags. Once he had ridden off, she sent a couple of servants after him. They stopped him and searched him. When they found the goblet of gold in his bag, they took him back with them. He swore to the princess that he had not stolen it and that he had no idea how it had ended up in his bag. "As you can see," she said, "you shouldn't jump to hasty conclusions about a person's guilt." And she revealed that she was his daughter. The king was overjoyed, and they all lived happily together. After his death, Hans Dumm became king.

84. *The Mother-in-Law*

Once upon a time there lived a king and a queen, and that queen had a wickedly evil mother-in-law. When the king went off to war, the old queen had her daughter-in-law locked up in a musty room in the cellar, and her two little boys were also locked up with her. One day she thought to herself, I would love to eat one of the two children, whereupon she summoned the cook and had him go down to the cellar to get one of the little boys and slaughter him and prepare him for cooking.

"What kind of sauce should I prepare?" asked the cook. "A brown one," replied the old queen.

The cook went down to the cellar and said: "Oh my queen, the old queen wants me to slaughter and cook your son tonight." The young queen was deeply distressed and said: "Why can't we just take a baby pig instead? You can cook it just as she wanted and tell her that it's my child."

The cook did just that and presented the roasted suckling in a brown sauce: "Here's the child." And she ate it with a hearty appetite.

Soon the old woman thought to herself, the flesh of that child was so delicate and tasty, I'll just have to eat the other one too. She summoned the cook, sent him to the cellar, and had him slaughter the second son.

"In what kind of sauce should I cook him?" "A white one," replied the old queen.

The cook went down the stairs and said: "Now the old queen has ordered me to slaughter and cook your second little son." The young queen said: "Take a suckling pig and cook it the way she likes it."

The cook did just that and presented the suckling pig to the old woman in a white sauce, and she ate it with an even heartier appetite.

Finally, the old woman thought to herself: "Now the children are in my body, and I can eat the young queen herself." She summoned the cook and ordered him to cook the young queen. —

(Fragment: the third time the cook slaughters a young hind. But now the young queen has a lot of trouble keeping her children from crying, and the old woman will realize that they are still alive, etc.)

VOLUME 2

57. *The Starving Children*

There was once a woman who fell into such deep poverty with her two daughters that they didn't even have a crust of bread left to put in their mouths. When they finally became so famished that the mother was beside herself with despair, she said to the elder: "I will have to kill you so that I'll have something to eat." The daughter replied: "Oh no, dearest mother, spare me. I'll go out and see to it that I can get something to eat without begging for it." So she went out, came back, and brought with her a small piece of bread which they all ate, but it was too little to ease their hunger pangs. And so the mother said to the other daughter: "Now it's your turn." But she replied: "Oh no, dearest mother, spare me, I'll go out and get something to eat without anyone noticing it." So she went out, came back, and brought with her two small pieces of bread; they all ate them, but it was too little to ease their hunger pangs. And so, after a few hours, the mother said to them once again: "You will have to die, otherwise we'll all perish." They replied: "Dearest mother, we'll lie down and go to sleep, and we won't rise again until the Day of Judgment." And so they lay down and slept so soundly that no one could awaken them. The mother went off, and not a soul knows where she is.

B

Prefaces to the First and Second Editions of the
NURSERY & HOUSEHOLD TALES

THE *Nursery and Household Tales* appeared in two volumes, each published separately with its own preface. Wilhelm Grimm was responsible for the wording of the two prefaces; the spirit of what he had to say, however, reflects the shared sentiments of the two brothers on folklore and the art of collecting it. For the second edition of the tales, published in 1819, Wilhelm Grimm amalgamated the two prefaces, adding, revising, and deleting passages as he saw fit. I offer translations of all three, for they have never before been available in complete form in English. These documents tell us more about the genesis and authorial intention of the collection than any other statements drafted by the Grimms. Wilhelm Grimm's discursive style, florid images, and occasionally obscure literary references do not make for easy reading (even the Grimms' contemporaries complained about the prose of the prefaces). Yet these prefaces still reveal more precisely than any other source just what the Grimms had in mind when they set about putting together their collection of tales.

The Grimms' reverence for the folk and for its every creative expression is clearly reflected in these texts, as is their nostalgia for a past era that fueled the creative energies of the folk. The preface of the first edition (published in 1812) begins by extolling the virtues of what the Grimms called *Volkspoesie* and ends with the brothers' self-congratulations on their efforts in salvaging the remnants of that poetry, on their tact in collecting tales, and on their precision in recording them. "We tried to collect these tales in as pure [*rein*] a form as possible," they declared. "No details have been added or embellished and changed." The claim is probably an honest one, especially if one considers that such authors as Johann Karl August

Musäus were making similar statements about their ornate literary versions of "folk fairy tales"—some of which ran more than fifty pages. By 1819, the Grimms had changed their tune about their methods of collecting. They no longer insisted on fidelity to the letter (as it were) of the tales they had heard, but on fidelity to their spirit. They claimed to have resisted the temptation to add episodes or to improve on what they heard, but they also conceded that the "phrasing" of each text was mainly their own. More important, for the second edition of the *Nursery and Household Tales*, they freely admitted that they had taken care to eliminate "every phrase not appropriate for children." The brothers had originally set their sights on producing a contribution to the "history of poetry" and had no intention of publishing an "entertaining volume." Yet in the end Wilhelm Grimm found himself responding to popular demand and expectations rather than to scholarly needs. With each new edition, the tales veered more sharply away from the rough-hewn simplicity of their first versions to a sanitized and stylized literary form that proved attractive to both parents and children.

I. PREFACE TO VOLUME 1 OF THE FIRST EDITION

When a storm or some other mishap sent by heaven destroys an entire crop, it is reassuring to find that a small spot on a path lined by low hedges or bushes has been spared and that a few stalks remain standing. If the sun favors them with light, they continue to grow, alone and unobserved, and no scythe comes along to cut them prematurely for huge storage bins. But at the end of the summer, once they have ripened and become full, poor devout hands come to seek them out; ear upon ear, carefully bound and esteemed more highly than entire sheaves, they are carried home, and for the entire winter they provide nourishment, perhaps the only seed for the future. That is how it all seems to us when we review the riches of German poetry from olden times and discover that nothing of it has been kept alive, even the memory of it is lost—folk songs and these innocent household tales are all that remain. The places by the stove, the hearth in the kitchen, attic stairs, holidays still celebrated, meadows and forests in their solitude, and above all the untrammeled imagination have functioned as hedges preserving them and passing them on from one generation to the next. These are our thoughts after surveying this collection; at first we were convinced that much had been lost in this area too, and that the only tales still left were the ones we already knew, which are told by others in variant forms (as is always the case). But ever on the watch for everything that is really still *left* of this poetry, we also wanted to get to know these different versions, and much that was new thereby unexpectedly came to light. Even though we were not able to make broad inquiries, our collection so grew from year to year that now, after some six years have passed, it seems rich to us. We realize, of course, that we may still be lacking a great deal, but we are also gratified by the thought that we have the most and the best of the lot. Everything has been collected, with a few exceptions as noted, from oral traditions in Hesse and in the Main and Kinzig regions of the duchy of Hanau, from where we hail. For that reason, happy memories are associated with every single tale. Few books have been produced with so much pleasure, and we are delighted to thank publicly all those who had a part in it.

It is probably just the right time to collect these tales, since those who have been preserving them are becoming ever harder to find (to be sure, those who still know them know a great deal, because people may die, but the stories live on). The custom of telling tales is ever on the wane, just as all the cozy corners in homes and in gardens are giving way to an empty splendor that resembles the smile with which one speaks of these tales—a smile that looks elegant but costs so little. Where they still exist, the tales live on in such a way that no one thinks about whether they are good or bad, poetic or vulgar. We know them and we love them just because we happen to have heard them in a certain way, and we like them without reflecting why. Telling these tales is so extraordinary a custom—and this too the tales share with everything immortal—that one must like it no matter what others say. At any rate, one can quickly see that the custom persists only in places where one finds a warm receptivity to poetry or where there are imaginations not yet warped by the perversities of life. In that very spirit we do not intend to praise these tales or even to defend them against opposing views: their very *existence* suffices to protect them. Whatever has succeeded in bringing so much pleasure so often, and has at the same time moved and instructed, carries its own inner justification and must have issued from the eternal wellspring that bedews all life, even if it is only a single drop enclosed by a small protective leaf, yet shimmering in the rosy dawn.

These stories are suffused with the same purity that makes children appear so wondrous and blessed to us: they have the same bluish-white, flawless, shining eyes (that small children so love to grab at),[1] which are as big as they will ever get, even as other bodily parts remain delicate, weak, and awkward for use on earth. Most of the events in these stories are so basic that many readers will have encountered them in real life, but like all things true to life, they appear fresh and moving. Parents have no food left, and as a result, have to cast out their children, or a hard-hearted stepmother makes them suffer[2] and would even like to see them die. Or siblings find themselves all alone in the woods, the wind frightens them, they are afraid of wild animals, but they stand by each other with all due loyalty. Little Brother knows how to find his way back home again, or, if he has been bewitched, Little Sister leads him around in the form of a fawn and collects greens and mosses for his bed; or she sits silently and sews him a shirt of star flowers to break a magic spell. The entire range of this world is clearly defined: kings, princes, faithful servants and honest tradesmen, above all fishermen, millers, colliers, and herdsmen (those who have stayed closest to nature) make an appearance; everything else is alien and unknown to that world. As in myths that tell of a golden age, all of nature is alive; the sun, the moon, and the stars are approachable, give presents, and can

---

[1] Fischart, *Gargantua*, 129b. 131b.

[2] The situation appears here often and is probably the first cloud to rise on each child's horizon, evoking the first tears, which people fail to see, but angels count. Flowers have even acquired their names in this way; the Viola tricolor is called "little stepmother" because each of its yellow leaves has a slender green leaf beneath it that holds it up. Those are said to be the chairs given by a mother to her own happy children; the two stepchildren stand mournfully above in dark violet, and they have no chairs.

even be woven into gowns; dwarves mine metals in the mountains; mermaids sleep in the water; birds (doves are the most beloved and the most helpful), plants, and stones all speak and know just how to express their sympathy; even blood can call out and say things. This poetry exercises certain rights that later storytelling can only strive to express through metaphors. The easy, innocent familiarity between large and small is indescribably endearing, and we get more pleasure from a conversation between the stars and a poor child abandoned in the woods than from hearing the music of the spheres. Everything beautiful is golden and strewn with pearls; there are even golden people living there; misfortune, by contrast, is a dark power, a horrid cannibalistic giant who is, however, vanquished, since a good woman who knows just how to avert misfortune stands ready to help. These narratives always end by opening the prospect of boundless happiness. Evil is also neither inconsequential nor something close to home, and not something very bad, to which one could become accustomed, but something terrible, black, and wholly alien that you cannot even approach; the punishment of evil is equally terrifying: snakes and poisonous reptiles devour their victims, or the evil person dances to death in red-hot iron shoes. Many things have their own obvious meanings: a mother gets her real child back just when she succeeds in getting a laugh from the changeling that familiar spirits have substituted for her own child; the life of a child similarly begins with a smile and continues in joy, and when it smiles in its sleep, angels are talking with it. A quarter hour of each day is exempt from the power of magic, and then the human form steps forth freely, as if no power could envelop us completely. Every day offers moments when man can rid himself of everything that is false and can see clearly; on the other hand, the magic spell is never completely broken, and a swan's wing is left in place of an arm; or because a tear was shed, an eye is lost with it; or worldly cleverness is humbled, and the numbskull alone, ridiculed and despised by everyone, yet pure of heart, has good fortune. In these features we can see the basis for the moral precept or for the relevant object lesson that can be derived so readily from these tales; it was never their purpose to instruct, nor were they made up for that reason, but a moral grows out of them, just as good fruit develops from healthy blossoms without help from man. The proof of all authentic poetry is that it is never without some connection to real life and returns to it, just as clouds return to their place of birth once they have watered the earth.

The essence of these stories seems to us as follows: outwardly they resemble all folktales and legends; never fixed and always changing from one region to another, from one teller to another, they still preserve a stable core. They are, however, clearly distinguishable from *local folk legends*, which are attached to real places or to heroes of history, and of which we have not included any examples here, though we collected a good many and intend to publish them at a later date. We have often included several variants of one and the same tale owing to the pleasingly distinctive tone of the variations; the less significant we have put in an appendix; but all in all we have collected as faithfully as was possible for us. It is also clear that these tales were forever being created anew as time went on, but for just that reason their core must be very old. The age of some can be shown to be almost three centuries, for there are allusions to them in Fischart and Rollenhagen (which are noted where appropriate), but beyond doubt they are even older than that, even if lack of evidence makes direct proof impossible. There is only one sure piece of evidence, and it is built on the tales' connections with heroic epics and indigenous animal fables. But this is not the appropriate place to go into details. We have said something about this matter in the appendix.

The closeness of this poetry to the earliest and simplest forms of life accounts for its widespread diffusion; there is not a single culture that does without it. Even the Negroes of West Africa entertain their children with stories, and Strabo expressly says the same about the Greeks. (In the end, one will find similar attestations among others, which goes to show just how much these tales were esteemed by those who understood the value of a voice speaking directly to the heart.) This explains another most remarkable circumstance, and that concerns the widespread diffusion of the German tales. In that respect, they not only match the heroic stories of Siegfried the dragon slayer, but even surpass them, for we find these tales, and precisely these tales, throughout Europe, thus revealing a kinship among the noblest peoples. From the north, we know only the Danish heroic ballads, which contain much that is pertinent here, even if in the form of songs, which are not quite appropriate for children since they are meant to be sung. But here too the dividing line can hardly be drawn with greater precision than for the more serious historical legend, and there are actually areas of overlap. England has the Tabart collection, which is not very rich, but what treasures of oral narratives must still exist in Wales, Scotland, and Ireland! Wales has a real treasure just in its *Mabinogion* (now in print). Similarly, Norway, Sweden, and Denmark have retained their riches; the southern countries less so. We know of nothing from Spain, but a passage from Cervantes leaves no room for doubt about the existence and telling of tales.[3] France must surely have more than what was published by Perrault, who treated them as children's tales (not so his inferior imitators, Aulnoy, Murat); he gives us only nine, though these are the best known stories and also among the most beautiful. The merit of his work rests on his refusal to add things and on his decision to leave the stories unchanged, aside from minor details. His manner of presentation deserves special praise for being as simple as was possible for him. There is really nothing more difficult than using the French language to tell children's stories in a naive and simple manner, that is, without pretentiousness, for the language in its current state twists itself almost spontaneously into epigrammatic remarks and finely honed dialogue (just look at the conversation between Riquet à la houpe and the stupid princess, as well as the end of "Petit Poucet"); sometimes the tales are unnecessarily long and drawn out. A study about to be published holds that Perrault invented these tales and only through him (born 1633, died 1703) did they reach the people; it also maintains that an imitation of Homer appears in the story of Tom Thumb, which alleg-

---

[3] —y aquellas (cosas) que à ti te deven parecer profecias, no son sino palabras de consejas, ocuentos de viejas, como aquellos del cavallo sin cabeça, y de la varilla de virtudes, con que se entretienen al fuego las dilatadas noches del invierno. Colloq. entre cip. y Berg.

edly has the aim of making Ulysses' plight when confronted with Polyphemus understandable to children. Johanneau had a better view on this matter. The older Italian collections are richer than all the others: first and foremost the *Nights* of Straparola, which contains many good things, but especially *The Pentamerone* of Basile, as well known and beloved in Italy as it is rare and unknown in Germany. Written in the Neapolitan dialect, it is in every respect an excellent work. The content is almost entirely without gaps and without inauthentic additions; the style is replete with good turns of phrase and sayings. To translate it in a lively way requires a Fischart[4] and his age; we plan to make all this clear in the second volume of the present collection, in which everything furnished by foreign sources will find a place.

We have tried to collect these tales in as pure a form as possible. In many, the narrative flow is interrupted by rhymes and lines of verse which sometimes clearly alliterate but are never sung during the telling of a tale; precisely these are the oldest and the best tales. No details have been added or embellished or changed, for we would have been reluctant to expand stories already so rich by adding analogies and allusions; they cannot be invented. A collection of this kind has never existed in Germany. The tales have almost always been used as the stuff of longer stories, which have been expanded and edited at pleasure. To be sure, they had some value for that purpose, but what belonged to children was always torn out of their hands, and nothing was given them in return. Even those who kept children in mind could not resist mixing in mannerisms of contemporary writing; there was hardly ever enough diligence in collecting so that only a few tales, picked up by chance, were published.[5] Had we been fortunate enough to be able to tell the stories

---

[4] With the language of his day and with his admirable memory, what a much better book of tales he could have produced, had he recognized the value of a true, unadulterated recording.

[5] *Musäus* and *Naubert* used as material what we have called local legends; the far more admirable *Otmar* used only those; an *Erfurt* collection of 1787 is weak, a *Leipzig* collection of 1799 hardly belongs here, even though it is not all bad; a collection from *Braunschweig* of 1801 is the richest of these, although in a very different tone. There was nothing for us to take from the latest *Büsching* collection, and it should be ex-

in a specific dialect, then they would no doubt have gained much; here we have one of those cases where a high degree of development, refinement, and artistry in language misfires, and where one feels that a purified literary language, as effective as it may be for other purposes, has become brighter and more transparent, but also more insipid and would have failed to capture the essentials.

We bequeath this book to well-meaning hands and cannot help but think of the powerful blessing that dwells in them. We hope that the book will remain completely unknown to those who begrudge poor and modest souls these small morsels of poetry.

KASSEL, *October* 18, 1812

II. PREFACE TO VOLUME 2 OF THE FIRST EDITION

Even with the heavy pressures of time, this second collection of household tales moved along substantially more quickly and easily than the first. This was in part because it had earned itself friends who supported it, in part because those who would have liked to support it earlier now clearly perceived the what and how of it; also we were favored by the kind of luck that looks to be chance but that generally accompanies the efforts of diligent, persevering collectors. Once you become accustomed to looking out for something, you find it far more frequently than can be imagined, and that is the case in general with folk customs and manners, as with folk sayings and anecdotes.

---

pressly noted that a collection published a few years ago by our namesake *A. L. Grimm* in Heidelberg under the title *Children's Tales* was not done very well and has absolutely nothing to do with us and with our work.

The recently published *Winter Tales* by Father *Johann* (Jena at Voigt 1813) only has a new title and actually appeared ten years ago.

They have the same author as the Leipzig collection. Peter Kling is his name, and he has written both books in the same manner. Only the sixth and part of the fifth tale are of value; the others have no substance and, apart from a few details, are hollow inventions.

We ask those who have the opportunity and the desire to help us to improve the details of this book, to complete its fragments, and especially to collect new and unusual animal fables. We would be most grateful for such information, which is best sent to the publisher or to bookstores in Göttingen, Kassel, and Marburg.

We owe the lovely Low German tales from the principalities of Paderborn and Münster to a deed of special good will and friendship; the intimate tone of the dialect in them is especially auspicious in light of their internal integrity. Out in the celebrated regions of German freedom, the tales have continued to serve as an almost regular Sunday pastime in many places; in the mountains the shepherds tell a story that is also known in the Harz region and probably indigenous to every mountainous region: the story of Kaiser Rotbart, who lives there with his treasures, and also of the race of giants known as the Hühnen and how they threw their hammers to each other from mountain peaks hours apart; there are many things there that we plan to publish elsewhere. The region remains rich in ancient customs and songs.

One of those happy pieces of luck was the acquaintance with a peasant woman from the village of Zwehrn near Kassel. Through her we acquired a good part of the tales published here along with a number of additions to the first volume. They can therefore be counted as genuinely Hessian. This woman, still vigorous and not much over fifty, is called Viehmann. She has a firmly set, pleasant face with bright, clear eyes and was probably beautiful when she was young. She has these old stories clearly in mind, a gift which she says is not given to everyone; many persons cannot remember anything at all. She narrates carefully, confidently, and in an unusually lively manner, taking pleasure in it. At first, she speaks spontaneously, then, if one asks, she repeats what she has said slowly so that, with a little practice, it can be transcribed. In this way, much was taken down verbatim and no one will fail to recognize its authenticity. Those who believe that oral narratives are routinely falsified, that they are not carefully preserved, and that long recitations are, as a rule, impossible, should have the chance to hear how precisely she stays with each story and how keen she is to narrate correctly; when she retells something, she never changes its substance and corrects an error as soon as she notices it, even if it means interrupting herself. Devotion to tradition is far stronger among people who always adhere to the same way of life than we (who tend to want change) can understand. For that very reason, oral narratives, which have stood the test of time, have a certain intimacy and inner effectiveness that other things, which may on the surface seem far more dazzling, rarely attain. The epic basis of folk poetry resembles the color green as one finds it throughout nature in various shades: each satisfies and soothes without ever becoming tiresome.

The true value of these tales must really be set quite high; they put our ancient heroic poetry in a new light that could not have been produced in any other way. Briar Rose, who is put to sleep after being pricked by a spindle, is really Brynhild, put to sleep after being pricked by a thorn—not the Brynhild of the *Nibelungenlied*, but the Old Norse one herself. Snow White sleeps peacefully with the same glowing red colors of life on her cheeks as Snæfrid, the most beautiful woman of all, at whose coffin sits Harald Fair-Hair. Like the faithful dwarves, he keeps watch over and guards the maiden in suspended animation. The piece of apple stuck in her throat is a special fruit with soporific powers. The story of the golden feather that is dropped by a bird and for which a king sends out search parties the world over is the tale of King Mark in "Tristan," to whom a bird brings the golden hair of a princess, for whom he then develops a longing. We have a better understanding of why Loki sticks fast to a huge eagle once we have read the tale of the golden goose that both men and women stick to when they touch it; who does not recognize Sigurd's own story in the evil goldsmith, the talking bird, and the episode recounting the eating of a heart? This volume offers other towering and overpowering tales (to some extent they are already in the poem) of Sigurd and his youth—tales that bring welcome assistance to the difficult task of interpreting the treasure that is to be divided up. Nothing is more reliable or more secure than what flows from two sources that were separated at an early date and later joined in a single river bed; these folktales have kept intact German myths that were thought to be lost, and we are firmly convinced that if a search were conducted in all the hallowed regions of our fatherland, long neglected treasures would transform themselves into fabulous treasures and help to found the study of the origins of our poetry. It works the same way with the many dialects of our language; in them a large part of the words and peculiarities that we had long held to be defunct live on unrecognized.

The aim of our collection was not just to serve the cause of the history of poetry: it was also our intention that the poetry living in it be effective, bring pleasure wherever it could, and that it therefore become a manual of manners. In this context, it has been noted that this or that might prove embarrassing and would be unsuitable for children or offensive (such as the naming of certain situations and relations—there are those who do not even want them to hear bad things about the devil) and that parents might not want to put the book right into the hands of their children. That concern might well be appropriate in certain cases, and then one can easily make selections; on the whole it is really unnecessary. Nature itself is our best witness, for she has let these flowers and leaves grow in these colors and shapes; whoever fails to find them right for certain needs, unknown to nature, can pass right by them, but ought not to demand that they therefore be colored and cut in a different fashion. To put it another way: rain and dew benefit everything on earth; whoever is afraid to put plants outside because they are too delicate and could be injured and instead prefers to moisten them indoors can hardly demand an end to rain and dew. Everything that is natural can also be healthy, and that is what we should be after. Incidentally, we do not know of a single healthy and powerful book used to educate the people (and that includes the Bible) in which such delicate matters do not actually appear to an even greater extent; proper usage sees no evil here, but finds, as an attractive saying has it, a document of our hearts. Children can read the stars without fear, while others, so superstition has it, insult angels by doing the same thing.

We have published variant forms, along with relevant notes, in the appendix; those who feel indifferent to such things will find it easier to skip over them than we would have found it to omit them; they belong to the book, since it is a contribution to the history of German folk poetry. These different versions seem more noteworthy to us than they do to those who see in them nothing more than variants or corrupt forms of a once extant archetypal form. For us they are more likely to be attempts to capture through numerous approaches an inexhaustibly rich ideal type. The repetition of single sentences, episodes, and introductory phrases should be viewed as epic lines that occur again and again as soon as the tone that starts them off is heard. They should not be interpreted in any other way. Everything that has been collected here from oral traditions is (with the exception of "Puss in Boots" perhaps) purely German in its origins as well as in its development and has not been borrowed from any sources, as can easily be proved on the basis of externals if one wanted to dispute that fact for individual tales. The evidence usually marshaled for reliance on Italian, French, or Oriental books, which are not read by the people (especially if they live in the country), reminds us of attempts to prove the recent vintage of tales by pointing to the presence of soldiers, apprentices, or of cannons, pipes, and other new things in them. But these things, like the words of our spoken language, are just what was refashioned by the lips of each storyteller, and you can be sure that sixteenth-century story-tellers spoke of mercenaries and muskets rather than of soldiers and cannons, just as the hat that makes its wearer invisible was in the age of knights a magic helmet.

The translation of *The Pentamerone* initially promised for this volume had to make way for the native tales, as did the selection of those from the *Gesta Romanorum*.

KASSEL, *September* 30, 1814

III. PREFACE TO THE SECOND EDITION

When an entire crop is destroyed by a storm or some other mishap sent by heaven, it is reassuring to find that a small spot on a path lined by low hedges or bushes has been spared and that a few stalks remain standing. If the sun favors them with light, they continue to grow, alone and unobserved, and no scythe comes along to cut them prematurely for huge storage bins. But at the end of the summer, once they have ripened and become full, poor devout hands come to seek them out: ear upon ear, carefully bound and esteemed more highly than entire sheaves, they are carried home, and for the entire winter they provide nourishment, perhaps even the only seed for the future.

That is how it seemed to us when we discovered that nothing was left of all those things that had flourished in earlier times; even the memory of them was nearly gone except for some songs, a few books, legends, and these innocent household tales. The places by the stove, the hearth in the kitchen, attic stairs, holidays still celebrated, meadows and forests in their solitude, and above all the untrammeled imagination have functioned as hedges preserving them and passing them on from one generation to the next.

It is probably just the right time to collect these tales, since those who have been preserving them are becoming ever harder to find. To be sure, those who still know them know a great deal, because people may die, but stories live on: still, the custom of telling the tales is ever on the wane, just as all the cozy corners in homes and in gardens, which have lasted from grandfather to grandson, are now giving way to the constant changes of an empty splendor that resembles the smile with which one speaks of these household tales—a smile that looks elegant but costs so little. Where they still exist, they live on in such a way that no one thinks about whether they are good or bad, poetic or (for intelligent people) vulgar. We know them and we love them just because we happen to have heard them in a certain way, and we like them without reflecting why. Telling these tales is so extraordinary a living custom—and this too the tales share with all that is immortal—that one must like it no matter what others say. At any rate, one can quickly see that the custom persists only in places where one finds a warm receptivity to poetry or where there are imaginations not yet warped by the perversities of life. In that very spirit we do not intend to praise these tales or even to defend them against opposing views: their very existence suffices to protect them. Whatever has succeeded in bringing so much pleasure so often, and has at the same time moved and instructed, has its own inner justification and must have flowed from the eternal wellspring that bedews all life; even if it is only a single drop enclosed by a small leaf, still it shimmers in the rosy dawn.

For that reason these stories are suffused with the same purity that makes children appear so wondrous and blessed to us; they have the same bluish-white, flawless, shining eyes,[1] which are as big as they will ever get, even as other body parts remain delicate, weak, and awkward for use on earth. That is the reason that we wanted, through our collection, first of all to serve the cause of the history of poetry and mythology, but it was also our intention that the poetry living in it be effective and bring pleasure wherever it could, and also that the book serve as a manual of manners. To that end we are not aiming at the kind of innocence achieved by timidly excising whatever refers to certain situations and relations that take place every day and that simply cannot be kept hidden. In doing that you can fool yourself into thinking that what can be removed from a book can also be removed from real life. We are looking for innocence in the truth of a straightforward narrative that does not conceal anything wrong by holding back on it. Nonetheless, in this new edition, we have carefully eliminated every phrase not appropriate for children. If there is still a strong feeling that one thing or another might embarrass parents or seem offensive to them and that they therefore might not want to put this book directly into the hands of their children, that concern might well be justified in certain cases, and the parents can then simply make selections: on the whole, that is to say for a healthy situation, it is certainly not necessary. Nature itself is our best witness, for she has let those flowers and leaves grow in these colors and shapes; whoever fails to find them right for certain needs cannot demand that they therefore be colored and cut in a different fashion. To put it another way, rain and dew benefit everything on earth; whoever is afraid to put plants outside because they are too delicate and could be injured and instead prefers to moisten them indoors with lukewarm water can hardly demand an end to rain and dew. Everything that is natural can also be healthy, and that is what we should be after. Incidentally, we do not know of a single healthy and powerful book used to educate the people (and that includes the Bible) in which such delicate matters do not appear to an even greater extent: proper usage sees

---

[1] that small children so like to grab at (Fischart's *Gargantua*, 129b. 131b.), and that they would like to have.

no evil here, but finds, as an attractive saying has it, a document of our hearts. Children can read the stars without fear, while others, so superstition has it, insult angels by doing the same thing.

We have been collecting these tales for some thirteen years. The first volume, which appeared in 1812, contained mainly what we had collected from oral traditions in Hesse, in the Main and Kinzig regions of the duchy of Hanau, from where we hail. The second volume was completed in 1814 and was produced more quickly, in part because the book had earned itself friends who supported it when they perceived its what and how, in part because we were favored by the kind of luck that looks to be chance but that usually accompanies the efforts of diligent, persevering collectors. Once you become accustomed to looking out for something, you find it far more frequently than can be imagined, and that is the case in general with folk customs and manners, as with folk sayings and anecdotes. We owe the lovely Low German tales from the principalities of Münster and Paderborn to a deed of special good will and friendship: the intimate tone of the dialect in them is especially auspicious in light of their internal integrity. Out in the celebrated realms of German freedom, stories and tales continue to serve as a regular holiday pastime in many areas, and the region remains rich in ancient customs and songs. In those places where the written language has not yet been spoiled by the introduction of foreign things or weighed down by too much freight, and where it ensures that memory is not allowed to become careless—in general among people whose literary culture is of no great consequence—oral traditions are stronger and more vigorous. Lower Saxony seems to have preserved far more than most areas. How much fuller and richer a collection would have been possible in the fifteenth century, or in the sixteenth century when Hans Sachs and Fischart were in Germany!

It was one of those happy pieces of luck that we met a peasant woman from the village of Niederzwehrn near Kassel. She told us most of the tales—and also the best—in the second volume. Frau Viehmann was still quite vigorous and not much over fifty. Her features were firm, intelligent, and pleasant; her eyes were bright and clear.[2] She had the old stories clearly in mind, and she herself said

[2] Our brother Ludwig Grimm made a remarkably accurate and natural etching of

that not everyone had this gift and that most people could not keep
things in the right order. She narrated carefully, confidently, and in
an unusually lively manner, taking pleasure in it. At first she spoke
spontaneously, then, if one asked, she repeated what she had said
slowly so that, with a little practice, it could be transcribed. In this
way, much was taken down verbatim and no one will fail to recognize its authenticity. Those who believe that oral narratives are routinely falsified, that they are not carefully preserved, and that long
recitations are, as a rule, impossible should have had the chance to
hear how precisely she stayed with each story and how keen she was
to narrate correctly; when she retold something, she never changed
its substance and corrected an error as soon as she noticed it, even if
it meant interrupting herself. Devotion to tradition is far stronger
among people who always adhere to the same way of life than we
(who tend to want change) can imagine. For that very reason, oral
narratives, which have stood the test of time, have a certain intimacy
and inner effectiveness that other things, which may on the surface
seem more dazzling, rarely attain. The epic basis of folk poetry resembles the color green as one finds it throughout nature in various
shades: each satisfies and soothes without ever becoming tiresome.

In addition to the tales in the second volume, we also received numerous contributions to the first, including many superior renditions of tales included in it, from the same or similar sources. Hesse,
being a mountainous region off the major thoroughfares and prin-
cipally oriented toward agriculture, has the advantage of preserving
old traditions and customs more carefully. A certain seriousness, a
healthy, sturdy, and stalwart character, which is sure to go down in
history, even the tall, handsome physique of the men in those regions that were once the home of the Chatti have been preserved in
this way, and they all make the lack of comfort and elegance, which
one notices quickly by contrast to other states (coming from Saxony,
for example) appear as an advantage. One begins to feel that the
rather rough-hewn but often truly splendid regions are, like the

---

her, which can be found in a collection of his works (published by Weigel in Leipzig).
During the war this good woman was beset by misery and misfortune, which benevolent friends sought to relieve, but did not succeed in lifting. The father of her numerous grandchildren died of a fever, the orphans brought illness and dire poverty
to her already wretched hut. She became ill and died on Nov. 7, 1816.

stern and stoic way of life, part of a whole. The Hessians in general must be counted among the people in our fatherland who have, through the changing times, held fast to their original homelands as well as to their own special character.

For this second edition, we wanted to incorporate into our book everything that we have been collecting. For that reason, the first volume has been almost completely reworked; fragments have been completed, many stories have been told more directly and simply, and there are very few tales that do not appear in an improved form. We have reviewed everything that seemed suspicious, namely what might have been of foreign origin or that could have been adulterated by additions, and we deleted it if that was the case. In their place we put new pieces, among them contributions from Austria and Bohemia, with the result that there is much here that was hitherto unknown. We had only a small amount of space for annotations before; now that the book has been expanded we have been able to reserve a third volume for them. It has thereby become possible not only to publish what we were obliged to hold back before, but also to supply new material that belongs here and that we hope will make even clearer the scholarly value of these traditions.

So far as the manner in which we collected is concerned, accuracy and truth were what counted for us above all. We did not add anything from our own resources, nor did we embellish any events and features of the story itself. Instead we tried to relate the content just as we had heard it; we hardly need emphasize that the phrasing and filling in of details were mainly our work, but we did try to preserve every particularity that we noticed so that in this respect the collection would reflect the diversity of nature. Anyone who has undertaken a similar venture will understand that collecting this material is by no means a carefree and careless business. On the contrary, only with time does one acquire the kind of attentiveness and tact required to sort out what is pure, simple, and yet intact from what is inauthentic. Various stories that complemented each other and that could be conjoined without the need to delete conflicting passages have been published as a single story. When stories deviated from each other, each then having its own peculiar features, we gave preference to the best one and saved the others for the notes. These different versions are more noteworthy to us than they are to those who see in them nothing more than variants or corrupt forms of a once extant archetypal form. For us they are more likely to be attempts to capture through numerous approaches an inexhaustibly rich ideal type. The repetition of single sentences, episodes, and introductory phrases should be viewed as epic lines that occur again and again as soon as the tone that starts them off is heard. They should not be interpreted in any other way.

We were happy to keep distinctive dialects. Had we been able to do that throughout, each story would no doubt have been improved. Here we have one of those cases where a high degree of development, refinement, and artistry in language misfires, and where one feels that a purified literary language, as effective as it may be for other purposes, has become brighter and more transparent, but also more insipid and would have failed to capture the essentials. Unfortunately the Low Hessian dialect in the vicinity of Kassel and in the border areas of the former Saxon and Franconian districts of Hesse is an indistinct mixture of Low Saxon and High German that is difficult to take down.

As far as we know, there are no collections of tales like this one in Germany. Others have either published a small number of tales that were preserved by chance or they viewed the tales as raw materials for creating larger narratives. We are firmly opposed to such reworkings. It is, to be sure, indisputable that a part of every lively feeling for a work of art includes some poetic creativity and re-creativity; without them oral traditions would be barren and moribund. That is in fact one of the reasons that every region tells a story in its own way and that every teller narrates differently. But there is quite a difference between the kind of half-unconscious development that resembles the quiet growth of plants watered by the source of life itself and a deliberate reshaping that arbitrarily binds things together, or even glues them together. We just cannot give our approval to that. The sole guide would then be a poet's momentary whim, which itself would depend on his own background. In the more natural creative process, the spirit of the folk reigns supreme in every detail and does not leave room for individual desires. If one concedes the scholarly value of these oral narratives, that is, if one admits that they have preserved ideas and forms from the past, then it is obvious that their value is almost always lost once they have been reworked. Poetry has nothing to gain from it, for where else does it live than where it touches the soul, cooling and refreshing it, or heating and fortifying it? Every reworking of these tales that compromises their simplicity, innocence, and artless purity tears them out of the circle in which they belong, where they are constantly in demand and no one tires of them. It may be, and this is the best possible case, that they can be given a certain delicacy, charm, a wittiness that plays upon the foibles of the times, a dainty portrait of feelings, all of which is not too difficult for an educated mind steeped in the poetry of all nations; but this gift is more decorative than useful. It is directed toward the single performance or reading (to which we have grown accustomed), and it works its charms and sharpens them to that end. But wittiness becomes dull through repetition, and what lasts is peaceful, quiet, and pure. The hand skilled in such reworkings resembles the one that had the unfortunate gift of turning everything it touched, including food, into gold. For all its wealth, it cannot satisfy our hunger or quench our thirst. Especially when the power of imagination alone must create a mythological world with all its images, how barren, wholly empty, and formless everything appears despite the best and most forceful language! These remarks are, it should be added, directed only at those reworkings that aim to make these tales more beautiful and more poetic, and not at the spontaneous efforts to capture them that belong to the spirit of the times. Who would, after all, want to delimit the borders of poetry?

   We bequeath this book to well-meaning hands and cannot help but think of the powerful blessing that dwells in them. We hope that the book will remain completely unknown to those who begrudge poor and modest souls these small morsels of poetry.

KASSEL, *July* 3, 1819

C

English Titles, Tale Numbers, and German Titles of Stories Cited

FOR THE convenience of those who wish to consult the German originals of the tales discussed, I list the English titles in alphabetical order, the tale numbers, and the German titles. In most cases, the English titles conform to the designations formulated by Ralph Manheim in *Grimms' Tales for Young and Old*. Where I deviate from Manheim's usage, I cite my title in parentheses.

Ashputtle (Cinderella), 21   *Aschenputtel*

Bearskin, 101   *Der Bärenhäuter*

Blue Light, The, 116   *Das blaue Licht*

Boy Who Left Home to Find out about the Shivers, The (The Fairy Tale of One Who Went Forth to Learn Fear), 4   *Märchen von einem, der auszog, das Fürchten zu lernen*

Brave Little Tailor, The, 20   *Das tapfere Schneiderlein*

Brier Rose (Briar Rose), 50   *Dornröschen*

Carnation, The, 76   *Die Nelke*

Cast-iron Stove, The, 127   *Der Eisenofen*

Cinderella, *see* Ashputtle

Clever Else, 34   *Die kluge Else*

Clever Gretel, 77   *Das kluge Gretel*

Clever Hans, 32   *Der gescheite Hans*

Clever Little Tailor, The, 114   *Das kluge Schneiderlein*

Crystal Ball, The, 197   *Die Kristallkugel*

Darling Roland, 56   *Der Liebste Roland*

Death of the Hen, The, 80   *Von dem Tode des Hühnchens*

Devil's Grimy Brother, The, 100   *Des Teufels rüßiger Bruder*

D

Bibliographical Note

LISTED below are the principal available German editions of the *Kinder- und Hausmärchen*. My citations are from these editions. Quotations from the first edition refer to Friedrich Panzer's volume rather than to Heinz Rölleke's 1986 reprint of that edition, since the latter appeared when my manuscript was already complete.

Die älteste Märchensammlung der Brüder Grimm: Synopse der handschriftlichen Urfassung von 1810 und der Erstdrucke von 1812. Ed. Heinz Rölleke. Cologny-Genève: Fondation Martin Bodmer, 1975 (manuscript versions of the tales).

Die Kinder- und Hausmärchen der Brüder Grimm: Vollständige Ausgabe in der Urfassung. Ed. Friedrich Panzer. Wiesbaden: Emil Vollmer, 1953 (1st edition).

Kinder- und Hausmärchen. Gesammelt durch die Brüder Grimm. Ed. Heinz Rölleke. 2 vols. Göttingen: Vandenhoeck & Ruprecht, 1986 (1st edition).

Brüder Grimm. Kinder- und Hausmärchen. Ed. Heinz Rölleke. 2 vols. Cologne: Eugen Diederichs, 1982 (2d edition).

Kinder- und Hausmärchen gesammelt durch die Brüder Grimm. Ed. Heinz Rölleke. Frankfurt a.M.: Deutscher Klassiker Verlag, 1985 (3rd edition).

Brüder Grimm. Kinder- und Hausmärchen. Ed. Heinz Rölleke. 3 vols. Stuttgart: Reclam, 1982 (7th edition).

The number of comprehensive studies in English on the Grimms and on their collection is surprisingly small. The two biographies of the brothers by Murray B. Peppard and by Ruth Michaelis-Jena are useful, though dated. Peppard's *Paths Through the Forest: A Biography of the Brothers Grimm* (New York: Holt, Rinehart and Winston, 1971) is somewhat more informative on the tales than Michaelis-Jena's *The Brothers Grimm* (London: Routledge & Kegan Paul, 1970). Bruno Bettelheim's *The Uses of Enchantment: The Meaning and Importance of Fairy Tales* (New York: Random House, Vintage Books, 1977) stands as the classic psychoanalytic study of the Grimms' tales. Jack Zipes, by contrast, explores the process of socialization and politicization set in motion by tale telling in his essays on the Grimms' tales in *Breaking the Magic Spell: Radical Theories of Folk and Fairy Tales* (Austin: University of Texas Press, 1979), and *Fairy Tales and the Art of Subversion: The Classical Genre for Children and the Process of Civilization* (New York: Wildman Press, 1983). John Ellis's concerns turn on the genesis of the collection and on the Grimms' alleged misrepresentation of their source material: *One Fairy Story Too Many: The Brothers Grimm and Their Tales* (Chicago: Univ. of Chicago Press, 1983). The most concise yet comprehensive discussion of the Grimms' collection is still Linda Dégh's "Grimm's *Household Tales* and Its Place in the Household: The Social Relevance of a Controversial Classic," *Western Folklore*, 38 (1979), 83–103. Interpretive essays by the renowned Swiss folklorist Max Lüthi are now available in English translation: *Once upon a Time: On the Nature of Fairy Tales* (New York: Ungar, 1970), and *The European Folktale: Form and Nature*, trans. John D. Niles (Philadelphia: Institute for the Study of Human Issues, 1982).

Critical studies in German of the Grimms and their collection are legion. Two vital reference works for studying the *Nursery and Household Tales* are the *Anmerkungen zu den Kinder- und Hausmärchen* compiled by Johannes Bolte and Georg Polívka (Leipzig: Dieterich, 1913–32) and the (not yet complete) *Enzyklopädie des Märchens*, ed. Kurt Ranke et al. (Berlin: Walter de Gruyter, 1977–). A recently published biography of the brothers is rich in detail and broad in its coverage: Jürgen Weishaupt, *Die Märchenbrüder: Jacob und Wilhelm Grimm—ihr Leben und Wirken* (Kassel: Thiele & Schwarz, 1985). Ludwig Denecke's bibliographical efforts are indispensable reading matter for scholars in the field: *Jacob Grimm und sein Bruder Wilhelm* (Stuttgart: Metzler, 1971). Gunhild Ginschel's chapter on the genesis and development of the *Nursery and Household Tales* has stood the test of time: *Der junge Jacob Grimm, 1805–1819* (Berlin: Akademie, 1967). The best introduction to the brothers and their collection is Heinz Rölleke's recently published *Die Märchen der Brüder Grimm* (Munich: Artemis, 1985). His collection of essays on the Grimms' tales also makes for fascinating reading: *"Wo das Wünschen noch geholfen hat": Gesammelte Aufsätze zu den "Kinder- und Hausmärchen" der Brüder Grimm* (Bonn: Bouvier, 1985). Folkloristic studies by Lutz Röhrich are always rewarding, but his *Märchen und Wirklichkeit: Eine volkskundliche Untersuchung* (Wiesbaden: Franz Steiner, 1956) is especially valuable. Finally, on violence in folk tales and fairy tales, Carl-Heinz Mallet is especially illuminating: *Kopf ab! Gewalt im Märchen* (Hamburg: Rasch und Röhring, 1985).

NOTES

PREFACE

1. Shaw's remarks on "Grimm" appear in a 1910 essay entitled "What I owe to German Culture," which was published for the first time in its original English version in *Adam* 35 (1970): 5–16. For C. S. Lewis's account of his reading of fairy tales, see "On Three Ways of Writing for Children," in *Of Other Worlds: Essays and Stories*, ed. Walter Hooper (London: Geoffrey Bles, 1966), p. 25. Jack Zipes states that the Grimms' collection ranks as "the second most popular and widely circulated book in Germany . . . , second only to the Bible" (*Fairy Tales and the Art of Subversion: The Classical Genre for Children and the Process of Civilization* [New York: Wildman Press, 1983], pp. 53–54).

2. Anonymous review of *Fairy Tales, or the Lilliputian Cabinet containing Twenty-four choice pieces of Fancy and Fiction*, collected by Benjamin Tabart, *The Quarterly Review* 21 (1819): 95. Thomas Mann, "He Was Mankind's Friend," in *George Bernard Shaw: A Critical Survey*, ed. Louis Kronenberger (Cleveland: World Publishing Co., 1953), p. 251.

3. Reinhold Steig, *Achim von Arnim und die ihm nahe standen*, vol. 3 (Stuttgart and Berlin: Cotta, 1904), pp. 251–52. For further details of the book's reception, see T. F. Crane, "The External History of the *Kinder- und Hausmärchen* of the Brothers Grimm," *Modern Philology* 14 (1917): 557–610.

4. On changing concepts of childhood through the ages, see Philippe Ariès, *Centuries of Childhood* (New York: Knopf, 1962). It is interesting to note the observations of one critic on the consequences of a childhood without fairy tales for children in Dickens' works: "In one novel after another, children deprived of fairy tales are morally, emotionally, sometimes even physically stunted, whereas those who have grown up with them are virtuous and full of life—or at least are intended to seem that way." See Michael C. Kotzkin, *Dickens and the Fairy Tale* (Bowling Green, Ohio: Bowling Green University Popular Press, 1972), p. 41.

5. Charles Dickens, "A Christmas Tree," in *Christmas Stories* (London: Chapman and Hall, 1898), p. 8.

6. The anecdote is recounted by Lutz Röhrich, "Argumente für und gegen das Märchen," in *Sage und Märchen: Erzählforschung heute* (Freiburg: Herder, 1976), p. 23.

7. Bruno Bettelheim, *The Uses of Enchantment: The Meaning and Impor-*

tance of Fairy Tales (New York: Random House, Vintage Books, 1977), p. 25.

8. In his essay "The Storyteller: Reflections on the Works of Nikolai Leskov," Walter Benjamin notes that the fairy tale is "the first tutor of children because it was once the first tutor of mankind" (*Illuminations*, trans. Harry Zohn [New York: Harcourt, Brace & World, 1968], p. 102).

9. Roger Sale, *Fairy Tales and After: From Snow White to E. B. White* (Cambridge, Mass.: Harvard University Press, 1978), p. 29.

10. Vladimir Propp, *Morphology of the Folktale*, trans. Laurence Scott (Austin: University of Texas Press, 1968). Propp's study was completed in 1928 but was translated into English only some thirty years later.

11. Propp himself points out that analysis of the compositional elements of folktales was only the first phase of a larger project that was ultimately to encompass historical, sociological, and religious matters. See "The Structural and Historical Study of the Wondertale," in Propp's *Theory and History of Folklore*, trans. Ariadna Y. Martin and Richard P. Martin, ed. Anatoly Liberman (Minneapolis: University of Minnesota Press, 1984), pp. 67–81.

12. Propp, *Morphology of the Folktale*, p. 16.

13. Robert Darnton, "Peasants Tell Tales: The Meaning of Mother Goose," in *The Great Cat Massacre and Other Episodes in French Cultural History* (New York: Basic Books, 1984), p. 13. Other scholars, whose work I discuss in chapter 2, have made similar arguments, but none more convincingly or eloquently than Darnton.

14. The seventh and last edition of the Grimms' *Nursery and Household Tales* contains 200 stories and 10 children's legends (*Kinderlegenden*). Since there are two entries under tale 151 (variants of one tale type), there are, strictly speaking, 211 texts in the collection.

15. Translator's preface, *Grimms' Tales for Young and Old*, p. 2. Manheim based his translation on *Kinder- und Hausmärchen gesammelt durch die Brüder Grimm* (Munich: Winkler, 1949).

CHAPTER 1

1. On violence in fairy tales, see Lutz Röhrich, "Die Grausamkeit im deutschen Märchen," *Rheinisches Jahrbuch für Volkskunde* 6 (1955): 176–224, and Christa Federspiel, *Vom Volksmärchen zum Kindermärchen* (Vienna: Notring, 1968), pp. 304–13.

2. Jost Hermand mistakenly claims that the Grimms deleted violent episodes from the tales ("Biedermeier Kids: Eine Mini-Polemik," *Mo-*

natshefte 67 [1975]: 59–66). John Ellis, by contrast, finds that the Grimms actually "*increased* the level of violence and brutality when, for example, those in the tales who suffered it deserved it according to their moral outlook." See his *One Fairy Story Too Many: The Brothers Grimm and Their Tales* (Chicago: University of Chicago Press, 1983), p. 79.

3.   *Die Kinder- und Hausmärchen der Brüder Grimm: Vollständige Ausgabe in der Urfassung,* ed. Friedrich Panzer (Wiesbaden: Emil Vollmer, 1953), p. 155.

4.   Dorothea Viehmann's tale is printed in volume 3 of Heinz Rölleke's edition of the 1856 version of the Grimms' collection: *Brüder Grimm: Kinder- und Hausmärchen* (Stuttgart: Reclam, 1980), pp. 192–93.

5.   For the original manuscript version of "The Frog King or Iron Heinrich," see *Die älteste Märchensammlung der Brüder Grimm: Synopse der handschriftlichen Urfassung von 1810 und der Erstdrucke von 1812,* ed. Heinz Rölleke (Cologny-Genève: Fondation Martin Bodmer, 1975), pp. 144–46.

6.   For a summary of the Grimms' editing of this tale, see their *Anmerkungen zu den einzelnen Märchen,* in Rölleke, ed., *Brüder Grimm: Kinder- und Hausmärchen,* vol. 3, pp. 69–72. John Ellis also discusses these changes (*One Fairy Story Too Many,* pp. 77–78).

7.   The Grimms' declaration of the principles guiding their project appeared in their "Aufforderung an die gesammten Freunde deutscher Poesie und Geschichte erlassen," in Heinz Rölleke, *Die Märchen der Brüder Grimm* (Munich: Artemis, 1985), pp. 63–69. For Jacob's remarks on the main purpose of the collection, see *Achim von Arnim und Jacob und Wilhelm Grimm,* ed. Reinhold Steig (Stuttgart: Cotta, 1904), p. 206.

8.   Ferdinand Grimm, who was working for the Grimms' publisher Reimer, reported sales figures to his brother Wilhelm. See Wilhelm's letter of 4 May 1815 in *Der Briefwechsel zwischen Jacob und Wilhelm Grimm aus der Jugendzeit,* ed. Herman Grimm and Gustav Hinrichs, 2d ed., ed. Wilhelm Schoof (Weimar: Hermann Böhlaus Nachfolger, 1963), p. 435. On figures for *Struwwelpeter,* see Rolf Engelsing, *Analphabetentum und Lektüre: Zur Sozialgeschichte des Lesens in Deutschland zwischen feudaler und industrieller Gesellschaft* (Stuttgart: Metzler, 1973), p. 92. Wilhelm's calculations are recorded in a letter of 13 June 1816 to Jacob in *Unbekannte Briefe der Brüder Grimm,* ed. Wilhelm Schoof (Bonn: Athenäum, 1960), pp. 143–44.

9.   For Jacob and Wilhelm's complaints about their straitened financial

circumstances, see *Der Briefwechsel zwischen Jacob und Wilhelm Grimm aus der Jugendzeit*, pp. 388, 396. Wilhelm's hopes about royalties are reflected in a letter of 2 June 1815, printed in the same volume of correspondence, p. 440. For further details on the Grimms' finances, see Jürgen Weishaupt, *Die Märchenbrüder: Jacob und Wilhelm Grimm–ihr Leben und Wirken* (Kassel: Thiele & Schwarz, 1985).

10.   Jacob's letter to Wilhelm appears in the *Briefwechsel zwischen Jacob und Wilhelm Grimm aus der Jugendzeit*, p. 438.

11.   The available correspondence between Reimer and the Grimms constitutes an interesting chapter in the history of the *Nursery and Household Tales*. The nineteen letters in the Staatsbibliothek Preussischer Kulturbesitz (on which this account is in part based) have been published by Wilhelm Schoof, "Neue Beiträge zur Entstehungsgeschichte der Grimmschen Märchen," *Zeitschrift für Volkskunde* 52 (1955): 112–43. Two additional letters in the Brüder Grimm-Museum in Kassel appear in Jutta Rissmann's "Zum Briefwechsel der Brüder Grimm mit dem Verleger Reimer," *Brüder Grimm Gedenken*, ed. Ludwig Denecke (Marburg: N. G. Elwert, 1984), 114–19.

12.   References to the reviews of both Büsching and Rühs are noted in Wilhelm Grimm's copy of the first edition of the *Nursery and Household Tales* in the Brüder Grimm-Museum in Kassel. Both reviews are reprinted in Wilhelm Schoof's "150 Jahre 'Kinder- und Hausmärchen': Die Grimmschen Märchen im Urteil der Zeitgenossen," *Wirkendes Wort* 12 (1962): 331–35. Rühs' essay denouncing the Grimms appeared under the title "Ankündigung," in *Die Musen* 1 (1812): 200–203. For Wilhelm Grimm's comments on Büsching's review, see *Achim von Arnim und Jacob und Wilhelm Grimm*, p. 297. For Jacob Grimm's views on Büsching's incompetence as a reviewer, see *Der Briefwechsel der Brüder Jacob und Wilhelm Grimm mit Karl Lachmann*, ed. Albert Leitzmann (Jena: Frommann, 1927), p. 81.

13.   *Der Briefwechsel der Brüder Jacob und Wilhelm Grimm mit Karl Lachmann*, p. 144.

14.   For the comments of Schlegel and Brentano, see August Wilhelm von Schlegel, *Sämtliche Werke*, ed. Eduard Böcking (Leipzig: Weidman, 1847), vol. 12, p. 391, and *Achim von Arnim und Clemens Brentano*, ed. Reinhold Steig (Stuttgart: Cotta, 1894), vol. 1, p. 309. Arnim's advice appears in *Achim von Arnim und Jacob und Wilhelm Grimm*, p. 263. For Voß's letter, see *Briefe von Heinrich Voß an Christian von Truchseß*, in *Briefe von Heinrich Voß*, ed. Abraham Voß (Heidelberg: C. F. Winter, 1834), vol. 2, p. 37.

15.   For A. L. Grimm's criticisms, see his preface to *Lina's Mährchenbuch: Eine Weynachtsgabe* (Frankfurt: Wilmans, 1816).

16.   A. L. Grimm, "Das Märchen von Brunnenhold und Brunnenstark," *Lina's Mährchenbuch*, pp. 191–216.

17.   For a discussion of Albert Ludwig Grimm's criticisms, see Heinz Rölleke's essay in volume 3 of *Brüder Grimm: Kinder- und Hausmärchen*, p. 605. The clash between A. L. Grimm and the Grimm brothers is also recounted by Gabriele Seitz, *Die Brüder Grimm: Leben – Werk – Zeit* (Munich: Winkler, 1984), p. 58. To Achim von Arnim, Jacob Grimm declared that the *Nursery and Household Tales* "had not been written for children." See *Achim von Arnim und Jacob und Wilhelm Grimm*, p. 269. Finally, Ferdinand Grimm's advice appears in a letter of 4 March 1816 to Wilhelm, cited by Heinz Rölleke, ed., *Kinder- und Hausmärchen: Brüder Grimm* (Cologne: Diederichs, 1982), vol. 2, p. 573.

18.   *Die Kinder- und Hausmärchen der Brüder Grimm*, ed. Friedrich Panzer, p. 85.

19.   Herman Grimm's observation appears in his *Beiträge zur deutschen Culturgeschichte* (Berlin: Wilhelm Hertz, 1897), p. 244. In a letter of 10 February 1815, Achim von Arnim congratulated Wilhelm Grimm on the collection and praised his editing procedures. Arnim recognized that Jacob did not approve of these procedures, but encouraged Wilhelm to continue on the same track. (*Achim von Arnim und Jacob und Wilhelm Grimm*, p. 319.) Gunhild Ginschel, on the other hand, argues that Arnim intentionally exaggerated the intensity of the editorial disagreements between Jacob and Wilhelm. In her view the brothers were more or less of one mind when it came to revisions. See *Der junge Jacob Grimm, 1805–1819* (East Berlin: Akademie Verlag, 1967), pp. 212–21, 237–38. Jacob Grimm's statement about his editorial efforts appeared in a letter of 19 February 1860 to Franz Pfeiffer, published in *Germania* 11 (1866): 248–49. It is possible, of course, that Jacob Grimm meant the first two volumes when he referred to the "first editions." Still, sweeping changes were also made from the manuscript to the first edition. In a letter of 28 February 1851, Wilhelm Grimm states that from the second edition onward, he alone took on editorial responsibility. See *Briefe der Brüder Grimm*, ed. Hans Gürtler and Albert Leitzmann (Jena: Frommann, 1923), p. 235.

20.   For further details on the *Kleine Ausgabe*, see Heinz Rölleke's "Zur Biographie der Grimmschen Märchen," in his edition of the 1819 version of the *Kinder- und Hausmärchen*, vol. 2, pp. 547–56. The *Kleine Ausgabe* was recently reissued as *Kinder- und Hausmärchen gesammelt durch die*

Brüder Grimm, ed. Heinz Rölleke (Frankfurt a.M.: Insel, 1985). On the first English translation, see Ruth Michaelis-Jena, "Edgar und John Edward Taylor, die ersten englischen Übersetzer der Kinder- und Hausmärchen," *Hessische Blätter für Volkskunde* 64/65 (1974): 183–202.

21.   Vilma Mönckeberg, *Das Märchen und unsere Welt: Erfahrungen und Einsichten* (Düsseldorf: Diederichs, 1972), pp. 14–15. Louis L. Snyder writes about children's reactions to "The Jew in the Brambles." See his *Roots of German Nationalism* (Bloomington: Indiana University Press, 1978), p. 49.

22.   C. S. Lewis's words appear in his essay "Sometimes Fairy Stories May Say What's Best to Be Said," in *Of Other Worlds: Essays and Stories*, ed. Walter Hooper (London: Geoffrey Bles, 1966), p. 37. On the title *Kinder- und Hausmärchen*, see Wilhelm Grimm, "Über das Wesen der Märchen," in *Kleinere Schriften*, ed. Gustav Hinrichs (Berlin: Ferd. Dümmler, 1881), vol. 1, p. 333. Jacob Grimm's remarks on the title appear in *Achim von Arnim und Jacob und Wilhelm Grimm*, p. 239. Finally, Ralph Manheim is the translator of *Grimm's Tales for Young and Old: The Complete Stories* (New York: Doubleday, 1977).

23.   *Perrault's Complete Fairy Tales*, trans. A. E. Johnson et al. (New York: Dodd, Mead, 1961), p. 68.

24.   *Perrault's Complete Fairy Tales*, p. 88. I have taken the liberty of making the translation somewhat more readable.

25.   J.R.R. Tolkien, "On Fairy-Stories," in *The Tolkien Reader* (New York: Ballantine Books, 1966), pp. 3–84.

26.   Robert Darnton discusses in detail the social function of fairy tales for French peasants and bases his remarks in part on du Fail's account. See "Peasants Tell Tales: The Meaning of Mother Goose," in *The Great Cat Massacre and Other Episodes in French Cultural History* (New York: Basic Books, 1984), pp. 9–72, and Noël du Fail, *Propos rustiques, baliverneries, contes et discours d'eutrapel* (Paris: Charles Gosselin, 1842). Angela Merkelbach-Pinck discusses the vitality of oral narrative traditions in one German-speaking region in the introduction to her edition of *Lothringer Volksmärchen* (Kassel: Im Bärenreiter, 1940), pp. 7–18. On the decline of narration with the rise of industrialization, see Leza Uffer, *Rätoromanische Märchen und ihre Erzähler*, Schriften der Schweizerischen Gesellschaft für Volkskunde, no. 29 (Basel: G. Krebs, 1945), p. 21.

27.   See Darnton, "Peasants Tell Tales," pp. 9–10, for the French version. Italo Calvino describes the Italian version in his notes to *Italian Folktales*, trans. George Martin (New York: Pantheon Books, 1980), p. 720.

28. Richard Schickel notes that Disney's solution to the "multitude of grisly problems" raised by the Grimms' version of "Snow White" was to devote as much footage as possible to the dwarves (unnamed in the Grimms' tale) and to minimize the role of the wicked queen. Still, after Disney's animated film was released, debates raged throughout this country about the appropriateness of the film for children. See *The Disney Version: The Life, Times, Art and Commerce of Walt Disney* (New York: Simon and Schuster, 1968), pp. 216, 220.

29. John Ellis's charge that the Grimms consciously deceived the German public about their sources and editing procedures has been rebutted by Heinz Rölleke, review of *One Fairy Story Too Many, Fabula* 25 (1984): 330–32, and by Jack Zipes, "Mountains out of Mole Hills, a Fairy Tale," *Children's Literature* 13 (1985): 215–19.

30. John Ellis argues that the source material collected by the Grimms was "completely recast and rewritten" and that it was already far removed from the "folk" (*One Fairy Story Too Many*, p. 70). But Ellis's narrow definition of the authentic sources of folk culture as "older, untainted, and untutored German peasant transmitters of an indigenous oral tradition" (p. 35) is problematic, since it presumes that elderly, illiterate peasants have a monopoly on folktales. As Vladimir Propp contends, folklore existed long before the emergence of a distinct peasantry. Propp finds that all classes but the "ruling class" number among the purveyors of folk culture. See "The Nature of Folklore," in *Theory and History of Folklore*, trans. Ariadna Y. Martin and Richard Martin, ed. Anatoly Liberman, Theory and History of Literature, no. 5 (Minneapolis: University of Minnesota Press, 1984), pp. 3–15. For another interesting counterargument to Ellis's views, see Alan Dundes, "Who Are the Folk?" in *Interpreting Folklore* (Bloomington: Indiana University Press, 1980), pp. 1–19. Finally, a number of experts in folkloristic fieldwork emphasize that their informants were generally workers and tradesmen, only rarely peasants. See Erich Sielaff, "Bemerkungen zur kritischen Aneignung der deutschen Volksmärchen," *Wissenschaftliche Zeitschrift der Universität Rostock* 2 (1952/53): 241–301.

31. On the role of the audience in shaping the content of fairy tales, see Linda Dégh, *Folktales and Society: Story-Telling in a Hungarian Peasant Community*, trans. Emily M. Schossberger (Bloomington: Indiana University Press, 1969), and Max Lüthi, "Goal-Orientation in Story-telling," in *Folklore Today*, ed. Linda Dégh, Henry Glassie, and Felix Oinas (Bloomington: Indiana University Press, 1976), pp. 357–68.

32. In an essay on the ways in which context influences folkloric texts,

Alan Dundes offers striking examples of how audience behavior, more specifically facial expression, can affect the telling of a story ("Texture, Text, and Context," in *Interpreting Folklore*, pp. 20–32). Peter Taylor and Hermann Rebel note that some peasant storytellers did not wish to practice their craft in the presence of the Grimms. See "Hessian Peasant Women, Their Families, and the Draft: A Social-Historical Interpretation of Four Tales from the Grimm Collection," *Journal of Family History* 6 (1981): 347–78. Heinz Rölleke points out that the content of the tales must have been colored by the fact that many of the storytellers were young unmarried women: "Die Frau in den Märchen der Brüder Grimm," in *"Wo das Wünschen noch geholfen hat": Gesammelte Aufsätze zu den Kinder- und Hausmärchen der Brüder Grimm* (Bonn: Bouvier, 1985), pp. 220–35. Leza Uffer discusses the practical difficulties of remaining a neutral presence while listening to folk narrators (*Rätoromanische Märchen und ihre Erzähler*, pp. 7–8). Finally, Elizabeth Fine proposes that folklorists strive to record both verbal and contextual features of folkloric performances, thus assuring us that we have printed texts that tell a tale, describe the way in which it was told, and document the specific situation in which the performance was enacted. See *The Folkloric Text: From Performance to Print* (Bloomington: Indiana University Press, 1984).

33. Rölleke, *Die älteste Märchensammlung der Brüder Grimm*, pp. 154–56. John Ellis views this passage as "characteristic of oral peasant storytelling" and as a "real example of the natural speech of the people." He is quick to charge the Grimms with rewriting the text in a literary language "that no peasant would ever have uttered," although he does not add that the "peasant version" was cast in a language that few literate people would have the patience to read (*One Fairy Story Too Many*, p. 69).

34. John Ellis summarizes the scholarly discussion on the stylization of texts by the Grimms (*One Fairy Story Too Many*, pp. 41–42). He argues that most critics have glossed over the many substantial changes made from one edition to the next by the Grimms and, instead, have emphasized less substantive stylistic changes. Giuseppe Cocchiara, by contrast, finds that the Grimms produced an authentic work of art precisely because they did not remain faithful to the letter but adhered to the spirit of the tales they heard. See *The History of Folklore in Europe*, trans. John N. McDaniel (Philadelphia: Institute for the Study of Human Issues, 1981), pp. 227–29. The best and most even-handed discussion of the Grimms' stylistic changes remains Gunhild Gin-

schel's chapter on the *Kinder- und Hausmärchen* in *Der junge Jacob Grimm, 1805–1819*, pp. 212–78. Wieland's statement appears in his introduction to *Dschinnistan* in *Gesammelte Schriften* (Berlin: Weidmann, 1938), vol. 18, p. 9. On translation from oral source to written document as a distorting process, see Heda Jason, "Content Analysis of Oral Literature: A Discussion," in *Patterns in Oral Literature*, ed. Heda Jason and Dimitri Segal (The Hague: Mouton, 1977), pp. 261–310.

35. Rölleke, *Die älteste Märchensammlung der Brüder Grimm*, p. 106.

36. Max Lüthi, *Once upon a Time: On the Nature of Fairy Tales*, trans. Lee Chadeayne and Paul Gottwald (Bloomington: Indiana University Press, 1976), pp. 26–28.

37. *Die Kinder- und Hausmärchen der Brüder Grimm*, ed. Friedrich Panzer, p. 122.

38. Cited by Rudolf Schenda, *Volk ohne Buch: Studien zur Sozialgeschichte der populären Lesestoffe, 1770–1910* (Frankfurt a.M.: Klostermann, 1970), pp. 43–44.

39. *Die Kinder- und Hausmärchen der Brüder Grimm*, ed. Friedrich Panzer, p. 198. On the Grimms and their role in the socialization process, see Otto Gmelin, *Böses kommt aus Kinderbüchern: Die verpaßten Möglichkeiten kindlicher Bewußtseinsbildung* (Munich: Kindler, 1972), pp. 40–52, and Jack Zipes, *Fairy Tales and the Art of Subversion: The Classical Genre for Children and the Process of Civilization* (New York: Wildman, 1983), pp. 45–70.

40. *Die Kinder- und Hausmärchen der Brüder Grimm*, p. 76.

41. These lines are from the conclusion to the tale "The Twelve Brothers." On proverbs in the collection, see Wolfgang Mieder, *"Findet so werdet ihr suchen!" Die Brüder Grimm und das Sprichwort* (Bern: Lang, 1986).

42. On the history of the Grimms' "Rapunzel," see Max Lüthi, "Die Herkunft des Grimmschen Rapunzelmärchens," *Fabula* 3 (1959): 95–119.

43. Stith Thompson, *The Folktale* (1946; reprint ed., Berkeley: University of California Press, 1977), p. 5.

44. On the problem of nomenclature, see William Bascom, "The Forms of Folklore Prose Narratives," *Journal of American Folklore* 78 (1965): 3–20, and Linda Dégh, "Folk Narrative," in *Folklore and Folklife*, ed. Richard M. Dorson (Chicago: University of Chicago Press, 1972), pp. 53–84.

45. On that tale's genesis and history, see the highly informative essay by Heinz Rölleke, "Schneeweißchen und Rosenroth: Rätsel um ein

Grimmsches Märchen," in *"Wo das Wünschen noch geholfen hat,"* pp. 191–206.

46. Louis L. Snyder argues that the Grimms viewed their collection as "a reflection of true German folkish culture" and that the tales themselves reveal "a special combination of German characteristics" (*Roots of German Nationalism*, p. 54). Ellis represents the view at the other end of the spectrum, believing that any analysis of the stories in the *Nursery and Household Tales* "tells us more about the attitudes of the Grimms than of the German people" (*One Fairy Story Too Many*, p. 102).

47. Ellis, *One Fairy Story Too Many*, pp. 64–66.

48. Rölleke, *Die älteste Märchensammlung der Brüder Grimm*, p. 70.

49. Peter Dettmering, afterword to *Die Kinder- und Hausmärchen der Brüder Grimm in ihrer Urgestalt* (Lindau: Antiqua, 1985), p. xvii.

50. As Ginschel points out, however, the Grimms did not put into print every single tale version available to them. Hence the changes made from the original manuscript to the first printed edition often incorporated elements from unrecorded oral performances and did not necessarily represent the Grimms' own arbitrary thinking about how a tale should read. See Ginschel, *Der junge Jacob Grimm, 1805–1819*, pp. 215–16.

CHAPTER 2

1. *Perrault's Complete Fairy Tales*, trans. A. E. Johnson (New York: Dodd, Mead, 1961), p. 77. I have modified the last line of the verse in order to capture fully Perrault's meaning.

2. Marianne Rumpf advances the view that "Little Red Riding Hood" is based on historical fact (*Ursprung und Entstehung von Warn- und Schreckmärchen* [Helsinki: Academia Scientiarum Fennica, 1955]). Erich Fromm and Bruno Bettelheim offer depth-psychology readings. See Fromm's *The Forgotten Language: An Introduction to the Understanding of Dreams, Fairy Tales and Myths* (New York: Rinehart, 1951), p. 241, and Bettelheim's *The Uses of Enchantment: The Meaning and Importance of Fairy Tales* (New York: Random House, Vintage Books, 1975), pp. 177, 182. For the National Socialist line, see Linda Dégh, "Grimm's *Household Tales* and Its Place in the Household: The Social Relevance of a Controversial Classic," *Western Folklore* 38 (1979): 83–103, and Christa Kamenetsky, "Folktale and Ideology in the Third Reich," *Journal of American Folklore* 90 (1977): 168–78. The view that the story represents a parable of rape is put forward by Susan Brownmiller, in *Against Our Will: Men, Women, and Rape* (New York: Simon and Schus-

ter, 1975), pp. 309–10. For fascinating anthologies containing variant forms of this classic fairy tale, see Hans Ritz, *Die Geschichte vom Rotkäppchen: Ursprünge, Analysen, Parodien eines Märchens* (Emstal: Muriverlag, 1981), and Jack Zipes, *The Trials and Tribulations of Little Red Riding Hood: Versions of the Tale in Sociocultural Context* (South Hadley, Mass.: Bergin & Garvey, 1983). And for a discussion of key illustrations of the story, see Jack Zipes, "A Second Gaze at Little Red Riding Hood's Trials and Tribulations," *The Lion and the Unicorn* 7/8 (1985): 78–109.

3. On P'teejah, see Alan Dundes, "The Study of Folklore in Literature and Culture: Identification and Interpretation," *Journal of American Folklore* 78 (1965): 136–42. For Bettelheim's view, see *The Uses of Enchantment*, p. 290. Ernest Jones's remarks appear in "Psycho-analysis and Folklore," in *Essays in Applied Psychoanalysis* (London: Hogarth, 1951), p. 12. Erich Fromm's further comments on "Little Red Riding Hood" are in *The Forgotten Language*, p. 240.

4. Antti Aarne, *Verzeichnis der Märchentypen*, FF Communications, no. 3 (1910; rpt. Helsinki: Academia Scientiarum Fennica, 1959); Antti Aarne, *The Types of the Folktale: A Classification and Bibliography*, trans. and enlarged by Stith Thompson, 2d revision (Helsinki: Academia Scientiarum Fennica, 1981). For incisive criticisms of Aarne's system of classification, see Vladimir Propp, "The Principles of Classifying Folklore Genres," in *Theory and History of Folklore*, pp. 39–47, and Robert Plant Armstrong, "Content Analysis in Folkloristics," in *Trends in Content Analysis*, ed. Ithiel de Sola Pool (Urbana: University of Illinois Press, 1959), pp. 153–55.

5. Kurt Ranke, *Die zwei Brüder: Eine Studie zur vergleichenden Märchenforschung*, FF Communications, no. 114 (Helsinki: Academia Scientiarum Fennica, 1934); Archer Taylor, *The Black Ox: A Study in the History of a Folk-tale*, FF Communications, no. 70 (Helsinki: Academia Scientiarum Fennica, 1927); and Warren E. Roberts, *The Tale of the Kind and Unkind Girls* (Berlin: de Gruyter, 1958).

6. See Dan Ben-Amos, introduction to *Folklore Genres*, ed. Dan Ben-Amos (Austin: University of Texas Press, 1976), p. xvii. Max Lüthi correctly points out that the ideal type is nothing more than an artificial construct. See *The European Folktale: Form and Nature* (Philadelphia: Institute for the Study of Human Issues, 1982), p. 101. Gyula Ortutay's "Principles of Oral Transmission in Folk Culture" discusses the relationship between the ideal type and its variants. See his *Hun-*

garian Folklore: Essays (Budapest: Akadémiai Kiadó, 1972), pp. 132–73.

7. *Anmerkungen zu den Kinder- und Hausmärchen der Brüder Grimm,* 5 vols. (Leipzig: Dieterich'sche Verlagsbuchhandlung, 1913–32). Volumes 4 and 5 are devoted to definitions of the *Märchen* and to analysis of various collections. On the genesis of these volumes, see Joseph Campbell, "Folkloristic Commentary," *Grimm's Fairy Tales,* trans. Margaret Hunt (New York: Pantheon Books, 1944), p. 855.

8. Mlle de la Force, "Persinette," in *Le Cabinet des Fées* (Geneva: Barde, Manget, 1785), pp. 43–57.

9. Giambattista Basile, "Petrosinella," in *The Pentamerone,* ed. N. M. Penzer (London: John Lane, 1932), vol. 1, pp. 135–39.

10. Italo Calvino, introduction to *Italian Folktales,* trans. George Martin (New York: Pantheon Books, 1980), p. xxi.

11. August Nitschke discusses characteristic traits of German folk heroes in *Stabile Verhaltensweisen der Völker,* vol. 2 of *Soziale Ordnungen im Spiegel der Märchen* (Stuttgart: Formmann-Holzboog, 1977), pp. 27–31. On heroines in French folktales, see Paul Delarue and Marie-Louise Tenèze, *Le Conte populaire français* (Paris: G.-P. Maisonneuve et Larose, 1976), vol. 1, pp. 44–45; and Lutz Röhrich, *Märchen und Wirklichkeit: Eine volkskundliche Untersuchung* (Wiesbaden: Franz Steiner, 1956), p. 143. The progressive tendency westward toward demystification of events is observed both by August von Löwis of Menar, *Der Held im deutschen und russischen Märchen* (Jena: Eugen Diederichs, 1912), and by Elisabeth Köchlin, *Wesenszüge des deutschen und des französischen Volksmärchens: Eine vergleichende Studie zum Märchentypus von "Amor und Psyche" und vom Tierbräutigam* (Basel: Benno Schwab, 1945). Finally, on the ways in which folktales assimilate the outlook of a community, see Margarethe Wilma Sparing, *The Perception of Reality in the Volksmärchen of Schleswig-Holstein: A Study in Interpersonal Relationships and World View* (Lanham, Maryland: University Press of America, 1984).

12. For Peter Taylor and Hermann Rebel, many of the tales from the Grimms' collection figure as "historical sources whose applicability is limited to late eighteenth-century Hesse-Cassel, whose largely feminine origins make them especially relevant to the history of Hessian peasant women" ("Hessian Peasant Women, Their Families, and the Draft: A Social-Historical Interpretation of Four Tales from the Grimm Collection," *Journal of Family History* 6 [1981], p. 349). John M. Ellis emphasizes that the two most renowned storytellers to serve as

sources for the Grimms' tales were not German, but of French Huguenot stock (*One Fairy Story Too Many: The Brothers Grimm and Their Tales* [Chicago: University of Chicago Press, 1983], pp. 25–36). His findings are based in part on Heinz Rölleke's "Die 'stockhessischen' Märchen der 'alten Marie': Das Ende eines Mythos um die frühesten Märchenaufzeichnungen der Brüder Grimm," in *Nebeninschriften* (Bonn: Bouvier, 1980), pp. 1–11. On Perrault and the Grimms, see H. V. Velten, "The Influence of Charles Perrault's *Contes de ma mère l'oie* on German Folklore," *Germanic Review* 5 (1930): 4–18. And Eugen Weber seems to believe that the "realistic substance" of fairy tales matched the real-life experiences of European peasants up to the mid-nineteenth century. See "Fairies and Hard Facts: The Reality of Folktales," *Journal of the History of Ideas* 42 (1981): 93–113.

13. Linda Dégh discusses the nature of the social institutions depicted in European folktales. See *Folktales and Society: Story-Telling in a Hungarian Peasant Community* (Bloomington: Indiana University Press, 1969), p. 65. Jack Zipes defines folktales as a "pre-capitalist art form" in *Breaking the Magic Spell: Radical Theories of Folk and Fairy Tales* (Austin: University of Texas Press, 1979), p. 29. Ruth Benedict makes the important point that "a conservatism that perpetuates long-discarded customs . . . is characteristic of a dead lore rather than a living one" (*Zuni Mythology* [New York: Columbia University Press, 1935], vol. 1, p. xiii). August Nitschke sees in "Cinderella" signs that date the tale back 10,000 years to the Mediterranean area. See his "Aschenputtel aus der Sicht der historischen Verhaltensforschung," in *Und wenn sie nicht gestorben sind. . . . Perspektiven auf das Märchen*, ed. Helmut Brackert (Frankfurt a.M.: Suhrkamp, 1980), p. 83.

14. Eugen Weber makes the point about realism in "Fairies and Hard Facts: The Reality of Folktales." The Grimms' comments can be found in their preface to the first edition of the *Nursery and Household Tales*, reprinted in Wilhelm Grimm's *Kleinere Schriften* (Berlin: Ferd. Dümmler, 1881), vol. 1, p. 322. William L. Langer notes that what was once "commonplace" with respect to children now seems "intolerable cruelty." See "Checks on Population Growth: 1750–1850," *Scientific American*, Feb. 1972: 93–99. On the persistence of infanticide in the nineteenth century (30 percent of all live births became victims of one form or another of the practice), see Langer's *Political and Social Upheaval, 1832–1852* (New York: Harper & Row, 1969), pp. 195–96.

15. Weber, "Fairies and Hard Facts: The Reality of Folktales," p. 96. Hans Traxler, *Die Wahrheit über Hänsel und Gretel: Die Dokumentation des*

Märchens der Brüder Grimm (Frankfurt a.M.: Bärmeier und Nikel, 1963).

16. George William Cox was the comparative mythologist who saw in fairy-tale heroes nothing more than the incarnation of solar deities. See his *Mythology of the Aryan Nations* (London: Spottiswoode, 1870), vol. 1, pp. 132n, 165n. Andrew Lang's critique of Cox appeared in his introduction to *Grimm's Household Tales*, vol. 1, trans. Margaret Hunt (London: George Bell and Sons, 1884), pp. xi–lxxv. Richard Dorson's "The Eclipse of Solar Mythology" appeared in the *Journal of American Folklore* 68 (1955): 393–416.

17. Max Müller, *Essays* (Leipzig: Wilhelm Engelmann, 1869), vol. 2, p. 143. For an incisive critique of the comparative mythologists, see Otto Rank, *The Myth of the Birth of the Hero*, trans. F. Robbins and Smith Ely Jelliffe, ed. Philip Freund (New York: Random House, 1932), pp. 9–13.

18. Friedrich von der Leyen, "Traum und Märchen," in *Märchenforschung und Tiefenpsychologie*, ed. Wilhelm Laiblin (Darmstadt: Wissenschaftliche Buchgesellschaft, 1969), pp. 1–12. Géza Róheim, "Fairy Tale and Dream," in *The Psychoanalytic Study of the Child*, ed. Ruth S. Eissler et al. (New York: International Universities Press, 1953), pp. 394–403.

19. Ernest Jones, "Psycho-analysis and Folklore," p. 12. On applications of psychoanalytic insights to folklore, see especially Paulo de Carvalho-Neto, *Folklore and Psychoanalysis*, trans. Jacques M.-P. Wilson (Coral Gables, Florida: University of Miami Press, 1972).

20. On various psychoanalytic readings of the dwarves in "Snow White," see Ingrid Spörk, *Studien zu ausgewählten Märchen der Brüder Grimm: Frauenproblematik – Struktur – Rollentheorie – Psychoanalyse – Überlieferung – Rezeption* (Königstein/Ts.: Anton Hain, 1985), pp. 176–78, and Otto F. Gmelin, *Böses kommt aus Kinderbüchern: Die verpaßten Möglichkeiten kindlicher Bewußtseinsbildung* (Munich: Kindler, 1972), p. 41.

21. Karl Abraham, "Zwei Beiträge zur Symbolforschung," *Imago* 9 (1923): 122–26. That psychoanalytic critics tend to translate one myth into another rather than to interpret is an observation made by Marie-Louise von Franz, "Zur Methode der Jungschen Märchendeutung," in Frederik Hetmann, *Traumgesicht und Zauberspur: Märchenforschung, Märchenkunde, Märchendiskussion* (Frankfurt a.M.: Fischer, 1982), pp. 66–72.

22. Vladimir Propp cites the statement from Lenin in "Folklore and Reality," in *Theory and History of Folklore*, p. 17. In the same essay, Propp discusses the antirealistic nature of Russian folktales. For W. H. Au-

den's comment, see "Grimm and Andersen," in *Forewords and Afterwords*, selected by Edward Mendelson (New York: Random House, 1973), p. 200.

CHAPTER 3

1. In a persuasive critique of Bruno Bettelheim's study of fairy tales, James W. Heisig points out that identifying with characters in the Grimms' collection "produces less often a sense of heroic strength in adversity than one of victimization, at first in adversity and then often in victory as well." See "Bruno Bettelheim and Fairy Tales," *Children's Literature* 6 (1977): 107. Or, as Linda Dégh puts it, readers of the Grimms' tales will "find no end to child abuse." See "Grimm's *Household Tales* and Its Place in the Household: The Social Relevance of a Controversial Classic," *Western Folklore* 38 (1979): 94. Finally, Marthe Robert claims that fairy tales always depict the child as victim, generally as the victim of an accident at birth. "It is the parents," she adds, "to whom must be imputed the unfortunate circumstances surrounding procreation and child-bearing." See *Origins of the Novel*, trans. Sacha Rabinovitch (Bloomington: Indiana University Press, 1980), p. 50.

2. Statistics on infanticide and abandonment of infants are more readily available than statistics on abandonment of children. See William L. Langer, *Political and Social Upheaval, 1832–1852* (New York: Harper & Row, 1969), pp. 195–96, and "Europe's Initial Population Explosion," *American Historical Review* 69 (1963): 1–17. For Ruth Benedict's observations, see *Zuni Mythology* (New York: Columbia University Press, 1935), vol. 1, p. xix.

3. In the Aarne/Thompson index of tale types, numbers 300–749 are taken up by "tales of magic."

4. Kurt Ranke, "Betrachtungen zum Wesen und zur Funktion des Märchens," *Studium Generale* 11 (1958): 656.

5. In the context of an intemperate attack on Lévi-Strauss's critique of his *Morphology of the Folktale*, Propp observed that his study had originally been entitled *Morphology of the Wondertale*. "To make the book more attractive," he added, "the editor replaced the word *wondertale* and in this way led everybody . . . to believe that the book would concern itself with the general laws of the folktale" ("The Structural and Historical Study of the Wondertale," in Vladimir Propp, *Theory and History of Folklore*, ed. Anatoly Liberman, trans. Ariadna Y. Martin and Richard P. Martin [Minneapolis: University of Minnesota Press,

1984], p. 70). Propp's definition of the wondertale appears in the same volume in the chapter "Historical Roots of the Wondertale" (p. 102).

6. For Propp's discussion of victim-heroes and seeker-heroes, see his *Morphology of the Folktale*, trans. Laurence Scott, 2d ed. (Austin: University of Texas Press, 1968), p. 39. Katalin Horn observes that victimization naturally motivates departure, which in turn leads to a life of adventure. See "Motivationen und Funktionen der tödlichen Bedrohung in den Kinder- und Hausmärchen der Brüder Grimm," *Schweizerisches Archiv für Volkskunde* 74 (1978): 20–40.

7. I borrow the phrase from Julius Braun, who claimed to find the source of all religious ideas and myths in ancient Egypt. See his *Naturgeschichte der Sage* (Leipzig: Alexander Danz, 1864), vol. 1, p. 8. The first and staunchest advocate of the theory that folktales originated in one region and spread from there over the entire globe was Theodor Benfey. India figured for him as the breeding ground of tales. See Theodor Benfey, introduction to *Pantschatantra: Fünf Bücher indischer Fabeln, Märchen und Erzählungen* (Leipzig: Brockhaus, 1859), vol. 1, pp. xxii–xxvii.

8. *The Letters of Sir Walter Scott, 1821–23*, ed. H.J.C. Grierson (London: Constable, 1934), p. 312. Similar sentiments are expressed by Scott in notes to his "Lady of the Lake"; these sentiments stand as one of the epigraphs to the first edition of the *Nursery and Household Tales*.

9. Propp, *Morphology*, p. 16.

10. Stith Thompson makes the argument about the "limitations of human life" in *The Folktale* (1946; rpt. Berkeley: University of California Press, 1977), p. 7. For Wilhelm Grimm's remarks, see his introduction to the first edition of the *Kinder- und Hausmärchen*, in his *Kleinere Schriften*, ed. Gustav Hinrichs (Berlin: Ferd. Dümmler, 1881), vol. 1, p. 322.

11. Jakobson's analysis of the contrast between folklore and literature appeared in an essay coauthored with Petr Bogatyrev, "Die Folklore als eine besondere Form des Schaffens," in Jakobson's *Selected Writings* (The Hague: Mouton, 1966), vol. 4, pp. 1–15. Other observations on the two fields can be found in Jakobson's essay "On Russian Fairy Tales," also in his *Selected Writings*, vol. 4, p. 91. For a dissenting view, one that argues for a common ground shared by folklore and literature, see Donald Ward, "The Performance and Perception of Folklore and Literature," *Fabula* 20 (1979): 256–64.

12. Propp's declaration concerning the uniform structure of fairy tales

appears in the *Morphology*, p. 23. His definition of functions appears on p. 21 of the *Morphology*.

13. For the source of those remarks, see Anatoly Liberman's introduction to Propp's *Theory and History of Folklore*, p. xiv. On Propp's scholarly career in general, see Isidor Levin, "Vladimir Propp: An Evaluation on His Seventieth Birthday," *Journal of the Folklore Institute* 4 (1967): 32–49.

14. Claude Lévi-Strauss, "La Structure et la Forme: Réflexions sur un ouvrage de Vladimir Propp," *Cahiers de l'Institut de Science économique appliquée* 99 (1960): 3–36. Reprinted as "L'Analyse morphologique des contes russes," *International Journal of Slavic Linguistics and Poetics* 3 (1960): 122–49. For an English translation of Lévi-Strauss's article and for Propp's irate and somewhat mean-spirited rebuttal (Lévi-Strauss called it an "offended harangue"), see Vladimir Propp, *Theory and History of Folklore*, pp. 67–81, 167–88. Eleazar Meletinsky offers interesting observations on Lévi-Strauss and Propp in his "Zur strukturell-typologischen Erforschung des Volksmärchens," *Deutsches Jahrbuch für Volkskunde* 15 (1969): 1–30.

15. A.-J. Greimas, *Sémantique structurale: Recherche de méthode* (Paris: Larousse, 1966). The diagram of the "actantial model" appears on p. 180.

16. Jonathan Culler, *Structuralist Poetics: Structuralism, Linguistics, and the Study of Literature* (Ithaca, N.Y.: Cornell University Press, 1975), p. 234.

17. E. Meletinsky et al., "Problems of the Structural Analysis of Fairytales," in *Soviet Structuralist Folkloristics*, ed. P. Maranda (The Hague: Mouton, 1974), pp. 73–189. The figure is taken from Meletinsky et al., p. 118. On overlapping roles, see also Max Lüthi's "Rumpelstilzchen: Thematik, Struktur- und Stiltendenzen innerhalb eines Märchentypus," *Antaios* 12 (1971): 419–36.

18. Susan Reid, "Myth as Metastructure of the Fairytale," in *Soviet Structuralist Folkloristics*, p. 152; Elli Köngäs Maranda and Pierre Maranda, *Structural Models in Folklore and Transformational Essays* (The Hague: Mouton, 1971), p. 33; and J. L. Fischer, "The Sociopsychological Analysis of Folktales," *Current Anthropology* 4 (1963): 254.

19. The point concerning the two sets of characters in fairy tales was made in the preface to the first edition of the Grimms' tales (Wilhelm Grimm, *Kleinere Schriften*, vol. 1, p. 322). The class structure of the fairy tale has been most recently investigated by Jack Zipes in *Breaking the Magic Spell: Radical Theories of Folk and Fairy Tales* (Austin: Univer-

sity of Texas Press, 1979). Family constellations in fairy tales are discussed in Meletinsky's "Problems of the Structural Analysis of Fairytales" (pp. 130–31) and are touched upon also by Alan Dundes
(introduction to *Morphology of the Folktale*, by Vladimir Propp, pp. xi–
xvii). Finally, on fairy tales as nothing more than the fulfillment of
wishes, J. L. Fischer notes that "if a fairy tale consisted purely of wish
fulfillment, there would be no conflict and no development, and it
would end as soon as it began" ("The Sociopsychological Analysis of
Folktales," p. 239).

20. As Max Lüthi emphasizes: "While nature—in the form of animals,
plants, and stars—generally responds in friendly fashion to the hero,
he is imperiled in the realm of his own family." See "Familie und Na-
tur im Märchen," *Volksüberlieferung: Festschrift für Kurt Ranke*, ed. Fritz
Harkort, Karel C. Peeters, and Robert Wildhaber (Göttingen: Otto
Schwartz, 1968), pp. 181–95.

21. Marthe Robert, "Un modèle romanesque: le conte de Grimm,"
Preuves 185 (1966): 33.

22. Sigmund Freud, "Family Romances," in the *Standard Edition of the
Complete Psychological Works of Sigmund Freud*, trans. James Strachey,
ed. Anna Freud et al. (London: Hogarth, 1959), vol. 9, pp. 237–41.

23. Freud, "Family Romances," p. 238.

24. On analogies between the hero of myths and the hero of the family
romance, see Otto Rank, *The Myth of the Birth of the Hero and Other Writings*, ed. Philip Freund (New York: Random House, 1932), p. 78.
Marthe Robert discusses similarities between fairy-tale plots and the
family romance ("Un modèle romanesque," pp. 24–34). Finally
Archer Taylor makes some observations about the universal hero patterns identified by J. G. von Hahn, Lord Raglan, Joseph Campbell,
Otto Rank, and Vladimir Propp. See "The Biographical Pattern in
Traditional Narrative," *Journal of the Folklore Institute* 1 (1964): 114–29.

25. On the role of parents in fairy tales, see Derek Brewer, *Symbolic Stories:
Traditional Narratives of the Family Drama in English Literature* (Cambridge: D. S. Brewer, 1980), pp. 15–53.

26. Otto Rank, *The Myth of the Birth of the Hero*, p. 78.

27. On the mechanism of projection in myth and folktale, see Alan
Dundes, " 'To Love My Father All,' " in *Interpreting Folklore* (Bloomington: Indiana University Press, 1980), pp. 211–22. Otto Rank's remarks appear in *The Myth of the Birth of the Hero*, p. 84.

28. On this point, see Max Lüthi, "Das Märchen," in *Volksmärchen und
Volkssage: Zwei Grundformen erzählender Dichtung* (Bern: Francke,

1961), pp. 9–21, and Volker Klotz, "Weltordnung im Märchen," *Neue Rundschau* 81 (1970): 73–91.

29. Tzvetan Todorov, "Narrative-Men," in *The Poetics of Prose*, trans. Richard Howard (Ithaca, N.Y.: Cornell University Press, 1977), pp. 66–79. In a now classic essay, Axel Olrik notes that in folkloric art "each attribute of a person and thing must be expressed in actions." See "Epic Laws of Folk Narrative," in *The Study of Folklore*, ed. Alan Dundes (Englewood Cliffs, N.J.: Prentice-Hall, 1965), p. 137.

30. Wallace Stevens, *Opus Posthumous*, ed. Samuel French Morris (New York: Alfred Knopf, 1971), p. 179.

31. *Die älteste Märchensammlung der Brüder Grimm: Synopse der handschriftlichen Urfassung von 1810 und der Erstdrucke von 1812*, ed. Heinz Rölleke (Cologny-Genève: Fondation Martin Bodmer, 1975), pp. 226–27.

32. Sigmund Freud, *Standard Edition*, vol. 5, p. 353.

33. The phrase is from Alan Dundes. See "The Crowing Hen and the Easter Bunny: Male Chauvinism in American Folklore," in *Interpreting Folklore* (Bloomington: Indiana University Press, 1980), p. 164.

34. C. G. Jung, "The Phenomenology of the Trickster in Fairytales," in his *Collected Works*, trans. R.F.C. Hull (London: Routledge & Kegan Paul, 1959), vol. 9, pt. 1, p. 217.

35. J.R.R. Tolkien, "On Fairy-Stories," in *Essays Presented to Charles Williams* (London: Oxford University Press, 1947), p. 47.

CHAPTER 4

1. Max Lüthi asserts that the disproportionately large number of female heroines in fairy tales can be traced to the prominent role women played in shaping the plots. See "The Fairy-Tale Hero," in *Once upon a Time: On the Nature of Fairy Tales*, trans. Lee Chadeayne and Paul Gottwald (Bloomington: Indiana University Press, 1976), pp. 135–46. By contrast Ralph S. Boggs asserts that 80 percent of German tales have a hero and that only 20 percent have a heroine ("The Hero in the Folk Tales of Spain, Germany and Russia," *Journal of American Folklore* 44 [1931]: 27–42). Neither Lüthi nor Boggs identifies his statistical sample.

2. Simone de Beauvoir's characterization appears in *The Second Sex*, trans. H. M. Parshley (New York: Bantam, 1952), pp. 271–72. For the list of heroic attributes, see Jack Zipes, *Fairy Tales and the Art of Subversion: The Classical Genre for Children and the Process of Civilization* (New York: Wildman Press, 1983), p. 57.

3. The first edition is reprinted in *Die Kinder- und Hausmärchen der Brüder*

Grimm: Vollständige Ausgabe in der Urfassung, ed. Friedrich Panzer (Wiesbaden: Emil Vollmer, 1953).

4. On the various types of heroes, see Katalin Horn, *Der aktive und der passive Märchenheld* (Basel: Schweizerische Gesellschaft für Volkskunde, 1983); August von Löwis of Menar, *Der Held im deutschen und russischen Märchen* (Jena: Eugen Diederichs, 1912); Ralph S. Boggs, "The Hero in the Folk Tales of Spain, Germany and Russia," pp. 27–42; Vincent Brun, "The German Fairy Tale," *Menorah Journal* 27 (1939): 147–55; and Louis L. Snyder, "Cultural Nationalism: The Grimm Brothers' Fairy Tales," in *Roots of German Nationalism* (Bloomington: Indiana University Press, 1978), pp. 35–54.

5. Constance Spender makes this point. See "Grimms' Fairy Tales," *The Contemporary Review* 102 (1912): 673–79.

6. These are the words of the fox in the Grimms' version of "The Golden Bird."

7. *Tales from the Thousand and One Nights*, trans. N. J. Dawood (Harmondsworth, Middlesex: Penguin Books, 1973), p. 165. Robert Crossley makes the point about Aladdin's lack of merit ("Pure and Applied Fantasy, or From Faerie to Utopia," in *The Aesthetics of Fantasy Literature and Art*, ed. Roger C. Schlobin [Notre Dame, Indiana: University of Notre Dame Press, 1982], pp. 176–91). On Aladdin's fortunes in Germany, see Erich Sielaff, "Bemerkungen zur kritischen Aneignung der deutschen Volksmärchen," *Wissenschaftliche Zeitschrift der Universität Rostock* 2 (1952/53): 241–301.

8. On the ethnographic significance of animals in fairy tales, see Lutz Röhrich, "Mensch und Tier im Märchen," *Schweizerisches Archiv für Volkskunde* 49 (1953): 165–93.

9. Eugen Weber finds that the celebration of compassion in fairy tales reflects the rareness of that virtue during the age in which the tales flourished: "Kindness, selflessness is the greatest virtue (perhaps because there is so little to give, perhaps precisely because it is so rare)." See "Fairies and Hard Facts: The Reality of Folktales," *Journal of the History of Ideas* 42 (1981): 93–113.

10. On the three phases of action in classical fairy tales, see E. Meletinsky, S. Nekludov, E. Novik, and D. Segal, "Problems of the Structural Analysis of Fairytales," in *Soviet Structural Folkloristics*, ed. P. Maranda (The Hague: Mouton, 1974), pp. 73–139. The authors divide the action of fairy tales into a preliminary test, a basic test, and an additional, final test.

11. Note the use in the tale of such heavy-handed transitions as "But now

I must tell you more about the king and the queen, who had left with the count." On the presence of only one single sharply defined plot in classical fairy tales, see Max Lüthi, *The European Folktale: Form and Nature*, trans. John D. Niles (Philadelphia: Institute for the Study of Human Issues, 1982), p. 34. Lüthi uses the term *Einsträngigkeit* (single-strandedness) to designate the absence of digressive plot lines in fairy tales. *Einsträngigkeit* is the term that Walter A. Berendsohn also uses to characterize the fairy tale's one-track plot structure in *Grundformen volkstümlicher Erzählkunst in den Kinder- und Hausmärchen der Brüder Grimm: Ein stilkritischer Versuch* (Hamburg: W. Gente, 1921), p. 33. The term has its origins in Axel Olrik's essay of 1919, which has been translated as "Epic Laws of Folk Narrative," in *The Study of Folklore*, ed. Alan Dundes (Englewood Cliffs, N.J.: Prentice-Hall, 1965), pp. 129–41.

12. On abasement as "a prelude to and precondition of *affiliation*" in "Cinderella," see Madonna Kolbenschlag, *Kiss Sleeping Beauty Good-bye: Breaking the Spell of Feminine Myths and Models* (New York: Doubleday, 1979), p. 72.

13. Friedrich Nietzsche, "Morgenröte," bk. 4, in *Friedrich Nietzsche: Werke in drei Bänden*, ed. Karl Schlechta (Munich: Hanser, 1954), vol. 1, p. 1172.

14. Bruno Bettelheim, *The Uses of Enchantment: The Meaning and Importance of Fairy Tales* (New York: Random House, Vintage Books, 1977), p. 281.

15. Stith Thompson emphasizes the ambiguous nature of the trickster's intellect: "The adventures of the Trickster, even when considered by themselves, are inconsistent. Part are the result of his stupidity, and about an equal number show him overcoming his enemies through cleverness." See *The Folktale* (1946; rpt. Berkeley: University of California Press, 1977), p. 319. In *World Folktales: A Scribner Resource Collection* (New York: Charles Scribner's Sons, 1980), Atelia Clarkson and Gilbert B. Cross confirm the ambiguity when they point out that "the most incongruous feature of the American Indian trickster is his tendency to become a dupe or play the buffoon even though he was the wily, clever trickster in a story told the day before" (p. 285).

16. Variants of the tale of the courageous tailor demonstrate that a single core theme can lend itself to two types of narratives: a biographical tale that focuses on the life of a hero and on his attempt to win the hand of a princess and an episodic tale that focuses on the various pranks played by a trickster. See the seven variants of "Das tapfere

Schneiderlein," in Leander Petzoldt, *Volksmärchen mit Materialien* (Stuttgart: Ernst Klett, 1982), pp. 42–72.

17. Max Lüthi, *The European Folktale*, pp. 34–35.

18. For a reading of the story along similar lines, see Roderick McGillis, "Criticism in the Woods: Fairy Tales as Poetry," *Children's Literature Association Quarterly* 7 (1982): 2–8.

19. As Vladimir Propp puts it, "when a helper is absent from a tale, this quality is transferred to the hero." See *Morphology of the Folktale*, trans. Laurence Scott (Austin: University of Texas Press, 1968), p. 83.

20. Robert Darnton, "Peasants Tell Tales: The Meaning of Mother Goose," in *The Great Cat Massacre and Other Episodes in French Cultural History* (New York: Basic Books, 1984), pp. 9–72. The quoted phrase appears on p. 44.

21. The retort is in Wagner's first version of *Siegfried* (Richard Wagner, *Skizzen und Entwürfe zur Ring-Dichtung*, ed. Otto Strobel [Munich: F. Bruckmann, 1930], p. 113).

22. The letter, dated 10 May 1851, appears in Richard Wagner, *Sämtliche Briefe*, ed. Gertrud Strobel and Werner Wolf (Leipzig: VEB Deutscher Verlag für Musik, 1979), vol. 4, pp. 42–44. Heinz Rölleke discusses Wagner's dependence on the Grimms' fairy tale in "Märchen von einem, der auszog, das Fürchten zu lernen: Zu Überlieferung und Bedeutung des *KHM* 4," *Fabula* 20 (1979): 193–204.

23. Thomas Mann, *The Magic Mountain*, trans. H. T. Lowe-Porter (New York: Knopf, 1964), pp. 719–29. Castorp is described, in German, as a "Schalk"; he is "verschmitzt" and "verschlagen." Mann's remarks on the fairy-tale quality of Castorp's story appear on p. v. Unfortunately Helen Lowe-Porter translated Mann's term *Märchen* (fairy tale) as "legend."

CHAPTER 5

1. The early reference to Mother Goose is cited in *The Oxford Dictionary of Nursery Rhymes*, ed. Iona and Peter Opie (Oxford: Clarendon Press, 1951), p. 39. Jacques Barchilon and Henry Pettit advance the view that Mother Gooses got their name from tending geese (*The Authentic Mother Goose Fairy Tales and Nursery Rhymes* [Denver: Alan Swallow, 1960], p. 10). Robert Darnton makes the connection between Mother Goose and the cackling sound made by geese. See "Peasants Tell Tales: The Meaning of Mother Goose," in *The Great Cat Massacre and Other Episodes in French Cultural History* (New York: Basic Books, 1984), p. 62. On Elizabeth Goose of Boston, see *The Oxford Dictionary of Nurs-*

ery Rhymes, pp. 37–38, and Jacques Barchilon and Henry Pettit, *The Authentic Mother Goose Fairy Tales and Nursery Rhymes*, pp. 8–9.

2. References to the animal fable featuring a goose are in Theodor Pletscher, *Die Märchen Charles Perrault's: Eine literarhistorische und literaturvergleichende Studie* (Berlin: Mayer & Müller, 1906), pp. 10–11, and J. R. Planché in the appendix to *Fairy Tales* (London: George Routledge, 1867), p. 510. On Queen Berthe and the associations around her, see Planché's appendix, pp. 510–12; Katherine Elwes Thomas, *The Real Personages of Mother Goose* (Boston: Lothrop, Lee & Shephard, 1930); Marianne Rumpf, "Berta," in *Enzyklopädie des Märchens: Handwörterbuch zur historischen und vergleichenden Erzählforschung*, ed. Kurt Ranke et al. (Berlin: de Gruyter, 1979); and Karl Simrock, *Bertha die Spinnerin* (Frankfurt a.M.: Heinrich Ludwig Brönner, 1853). P. Saintyves makes it clear that he hears no historical or mythological resonances in the name Mother Goose. See "Des contes de ma Mère l'Oye et des rapports supposés de cette expression avec les fables où figurent la Reine Pédauque, la Reine Berthe et la Fée Berchta," *Revue d'ethnographie et des traditions populaires* 5 (1924): 62–79.

3. On the German Berchta, see Jacob Grimm, *Deutsche Mythologie* (Berlin: Ferd. Dümmler, 1875), vol. 1, pp. 226–34.

4. *German Fairy Tales and Popular Stories as Told by Gammer Gretel*, trans. Edgar Taylor (London: Joseph Cundall, 1846), p. xi.

5. J. R. Planché, appendix to *Fairy Tales*, p. 510.

6. Walter Benjamin, "The Storyteller: Reflections on the Works of Nikolai Leskov," in *Illuminations*, trans. Harry Zohn (New York: Harcourt, Brace & World, 1968), p. 91.

7. Ruth B. Bottigheimer points out that nearly all variants of "Briar Rose" depict the heroine pricking her finger on a fiber, a spindle, or a needle. Spinning in those tales, she argues, represents a "neutral value"—it is nothing more than "a hinge on which the tale turns." See "Tale Spinners: Submerged Voices in Grimms' Fairy Tales," *New German Critique* 27 (1982): 141–50. That the fairy's curse obliges the king to order the destruction of all spinning tools might, however, be construed as wishful thinking on the part of some tale tellers.

8. For variants of "The Three Spinners," see Johannes Bolte and Georg Polívka, *Anmerkungen zu den Kinder- und Hausmärchen der Brüder Grimm* (Leipzig: Dieterichsche Verlagsbuchhandlung, 1913), vol. 1, pp. 109–15. "The Horrid Spinning of Flax," one version of "The Three Spinners," appears only in the first version of the *Nursery and Household Tales*. See *Die Kinder- und Hausmärchen der Brüder Grimm: Vollständige*

Ausgabe in der Urfassung, ed. Friedrich Panzer (Wiesbaden: Emil Vollmer, 1953), p. 89.

9. Jack Zipes argues that the Grimms "contributed to the literary 'bourgeoisification' of oral tales which had belonged to the peasantry and lower classes and had been informed by the interests and aspirations of these groups." See "Who's Afraid of the Brothers Grimm? Socialization and Politicization through Fairy Tales," in *Fairy Tales and the Art of Subversion: The Classical Genre for Children and the Process of Civilization* (New York: Wildman Press, 1983), pp. 45–70.

10. On social criticism in the Grimms' collection, see Lutz Röhrich, *Märchen und Wirklichkeit: Eine volkskundliche Untersuchung* (Wiesbaden: Franz Steiner, 1956), pp. 167–79. Ulrike Bastien finds that the Grimms toned down social criticism in successive versions of the tales, though clearly not systematically. See *Die "Kinder- und Hausmärchen" der Brüder Grimm in der literaturpädagogischen Diskussion des 19. und 20. Jahrhunderts* (Frankfurt a.M.: Haag und Herchen, 1981).

11. For a concise summary of the events surrounding the protesting professors, see Ruth Michaelis-Jena, *The Brothers Grimm* (London: Routledge & Kegan Paul, 1970), pp. 111–18.

12. On this point, see C. G. Jung, "On the Psychology of the Trickster Figure," in *Collected Works*, trans. R.F.C. Hull (London: Routledge & Kegan Paul, 1959), vol. 9, pt. 1, pp. 255–72.

13. Otto Kahn cites some of the king's motives in "Rumpelstilz hat wirklich gelebt: Textvergleichende Studie über das Märchen von Rumpelstilzchen (ATh 500) und eine Erklärung mit Hilfe der Rechtsgeschichte," *Rheinisches Jahrbuch für Volkskunde* 17/18 (1966/67): 143–84.

14. For discussions of variants of "Rumpelstiltskin," see Georg Polívka, "Tom Tit Tot: Ein Beitrag zur vergleichenden Märchenkunde," *Zeitschrift des Vereins für Volkskunde* 10 (1900): 254–72, 325, 382–96; Bolte and Polívka, *Anmerkungen zu den Kinder- und Hausmärchen der Brüder Grimm*, vol. 1, pp. 490–98; and Edward Clodd, *Tom Tit Tot: An Essay on Savage Philosophy in Folk-Tale* (London: Duckworth, 1898).

15. I have not sought to smooth the tale's rough edges. It is published in *Die älteste Märchensammlung der Brüder Grimm: Synopse der handschriftlichen Urfassung von 1810 und der Erstdrucke von 1812*, ed. Heinz Rölleke (Cologny-Genève: Fondation Martin Bodmer, 1975), pp. 238–40.

16. The heroine's line is cited by J. C. Cooper, *Fairy Tales: Allegories of the Inner Life* (Wellingborough, Northamptonshire: Aquarian Press, 1983), p. 70. The entire tale "Duffy and the Devil" (the Cornish version of "Rumpelstiltskin") is reprinted in Edward Clodd's "The Phi-

losophy of Rumpelstiltskin," *Folklore Journal* 7 (1889): 135–65. There the heroine cries out: "Curse the spinning and knitting! The devil may spin and knit for the squire, for what I care."

17. Roger Sale complains about how unfairly Rumpelstiltskin has been treated in *Fairy Tales and After: From Snow White to E. B. White* (Cambridge, Mass.: Harvard University Press, 1978), p. 44. Jack Zipes discusses a number of interesting rewritings of "Rumpelstiltskin" by authors whose sympathies are decidedly with the figure named in the tale's title. See *Fairy Tales and the Art of Subversion*, pp. 64–66. Lutz Röhrich points out that dishonesty and deceit triumph in the end in this particular tale. See "Rumpelstilzchen: Vom Methodenpluralismus in der Erzählforschung," in *Sage und Märchen: Erzählforschung heute* (Freiburg: Herder, 1976), pp. 272–91.

18. Max Lüthi makes this point in his splendid essay "Rumpelstilzchen: Thematik, Struktur- und Stiltendenzen innerhalb eines Märchentypus," in *Antaios* 12 (1971): 419–36.

19. Kaarle Krohn makes it clear that the two tales, despite superficial resemblances, are separate stories. He notes that the introductory episode about the lazy daughter regularly occurs in "The Three Spinners" but is found in only about half of all tale variants of "Rumpelstilzchen." In his view, that episode is an integral part of "The Three Spinners" alone.

20. Vladimir Propp notes that in the folktale "action is primary, not the reason for it." See "The Nature of Folklore," in *Theory and History of Folklore*, trans. Ariadna Y. Martin and Richard P. Martin, ed. Anatoly Liberman (Minneapolis: University of Minnesota Press, 1984), p. 26.

21. The tendency to provide realistic motivations for the pact is discussed by Gonthier-Louis Fink, "Les Avatars de Rumpelstilzchen: La Vie d'un Conte Populaire," in *Deutsch-Französisches Gespräch im Lichte der Märchen*, ed. Ernst Kracht (Münster: Aschendorff, 1964), pp. 46–72.

22. *Die goldene Spindel: Spinnstuben und Webermärchen aus vielen Jahrhunderten*, ed. Josef Lukas (Münsingen: Fischer Druck, 1978).

23. Volker Klotz makes this point. See "Weltordnung im Märchen," *Neue Rundschau* 81 (1970): 78. Ruth B. Bottigheimer concludes that, in the Grimms' tales, "spinning emerges as highly undesirable despite the surface message that it will lead to riches" ("Tale Spinners: Submerged Voices in Grimms' Fairy Tales," p. 150).

CHAPTER 6

1. Sir James Frazer, *The Golden Bough*, 3d ed. (New York: St. Martin's Press, 1966), vol. 3, p. 84.

2. "The Mother-in-Law" ("Die Schwiegermutter") is published in *Die Kinder- und Hausmärchen der Brüder Grimm: Vollständige Ausgabe in der Urfassung*, ed. Friedrich Panzer (Wiesbaden: Emil Vollmer, 1953), p. 277, and appears under the rubric *Bruchstücke* in the volume of annotations.

3. "The Sleeping Beauty in the Wood," in *Perrault's Complete Fairy Tales*, trans. A. E. Johnson (New York: Dodd, Mead, 1961), pp. 1–15.

4. "Sun, Moon and Talia," in *The Pentamerone of Giambattista Basile*, ed. N. M. Penzer (New York: E. P. Dutton, 1932), vol. 2, pp. 129–32.

5. For the text of "The Starving Children" ("Die Kinder in Hungersnot"), see *Die Kinder- und Hausmärchen der Brüder Grimm*, ed. Friedrich Panzer, p. 505. In *Trials and Tribulations of Little Red Riding Hood: Versions of the Tale in Sociocultural Context* (South Hadley, Mass.: Bergin & Garvey, 1983), Jack Zipes makes the point that many fairy tales featuring cannibalistic themes were based on superstitious fears about werewolves and witches.

6. *Die Kinder- und Hausmärchen der Brüder Grimm*, ed. Friedrich Panzer, p. 277. On cannibalism in fairy tales, see Macleod Yearsley, *The Folklore of Fairy-Tale* (London: Watt, 1924), pp. 38–49.

7. The exception that proves the rule can be found in an Icelandic fairy tale entitled "The Tale of Hildur, the Good Stepmother." It is worth noting, however, that Hildur does not become a stepmother until the end of the tale and that she protects her prospective stepdaughter from the posthumous curse of her biological mother. See *Adventures, Outlaws and Past Events: Icelandic Folktales III* (Reykjavík: Icelandic Review Library, 1977), pp. 19–28. (I am grateful to my colleague Stephen A. Mitchell for calling this tale to my attention.) On the role of stepmothers in general in fairy tales, see especially Werner Lincke, *Das Stiefmuttermotiv im Märchen der germanischen Völker* (Berlin: Emil Ebering, 1933), pp. 90–140; Ingeborg Weber-Kellermann, *Die deutsche Familie: Versuch einer Sozialgeschichte* (Frankfurt a.M.: Suhrkamp, 1974), pp. 32–37; and Eleazar Meletinsky, "Marriage: Its Function and Position in the Structure of Folktales," in *Soviet Structural Folkloristics*, ed. P. Maranda (The Hague: Mouton, 1974), pp. 61–72. Hannah Kühn draws on folkloric material for her analysis of the role of stepmothers in family life (*Psychologische Untersuchungen über das Stiefmutterproblem*, Beihefte zur Zeitschrift für angewandte Psychologie, no. 45 [Leipzig: Johann Ambrosius Barth, 1929]).

8. Therese Poser, among others, makes this point. See *Das Volksmärchen: Theorie – Analyse – Didaktik* (München: Oldenbourg, 1980), p. 89.

Karin Struck succinctly states the rationale behind the changes: "The stepmother is always the biological mother, even in the fairy tale about the juniper tree, but who would ever dare to blame his own mother for those things?" See "Erinnerungen an Hänsel und Gretel," in *Grimms Märchen—modern*, ed. Wolfgang Mieder (Stuttgart: Reclam, 1979), p. 23.

9. Ludwig Bechstein, introduction to his *Neues Deutsches Märchenbuch*, reprinted in Ludwig Bechstein, *Märchen* (Stuttgart: Parkland, 1985), pp. 498–99. The introduction was originally published in 1856.

10. Johannes Bolte and Georg Polívka, *Anmerkungen zu den Kinder- und Hausmärchen der Brüder Grimm* (Leipzig: Dieterich, 1913), vol. 1, pp. 412–23.

11. Werner Lincke notes this inconsistency in "Twelve Brothers." See *Das Stiefmuttermotif im Märchen der germanischen Völker*, p. 69.

12. Hedwig von Beit suggests that the two figures (stepmother and witch) are identical. Her argument draws on primitive beliefs that equate the murder of a witch's spiritual essence, whatever form it may take, with the destruction of her physical body. See *Symbolik des Märchens: Versuch einer Deutung*, 2d ed. (Bern: Francke, 1960), pp. 133–35.

13. Bruno Bettelheim, *The Uses of Enchantment: The Meaning and Importance of Fairy Tales* (New York: Random House, Vintage Books, 1977), p. 69. For Marthe Robert's remarks, see "Un modèle romanesque: le conte de Grimm," *Preuves* 185 (1966): 24–34.

14. The passage about the evil stepmother comes from "Little Brother and Little Sister." On royalty as an emblem of paternity and the consequent noble status of other family members, see Marthe Robert, "Un modèle romanesque," p. 26.

15. "Since our mothers—or nurses—were our earliest educators, it is likely that they first tabooed sex in some fashion; hence it is a female who turns the future groom into an animal" (Bruno Bettelheim, *The Uses of Enchantment*, p. 283). Sandra M. Gilbert and Susan Gubar argue that Snow White in the coffin has become the "eternally beautiful, inanimate *objet d'art* patriarchal aesthetics want a girl to be." See *The Madwoman in the Attic: The Woman Writer and the Nineteenth-Century Literary Imagination* (New Haven, Conn.: Yale University Press, 1979), p. 40. On the ways in which the fairy tale's vision of marriage and the ideal bride perpetuate certain cultural norms, see Karen E. Rowe, "Feminism and Fairy Tales," in *Don't Bet on the Prince: Contemporary Feminist Fairy Tales in North America and England*, ed. Jack Zipes (New York: Methuen, 1986), pp. 209–26.

16. Sandra M. Gilbert and Susan Gubar note, in another context, that Snow White is doomed from the start. Like her stepmother, she too is destined to become "a murderess bent on the self-slaughter implicit in her murderous attempts against the life of her own child." See *The Madwoman in the Attic*, p. 42. By contrast, Sibylle Birkhäuser-Oeri argues that Snow White's marriage represents a harmonious resolution to inner conflicts. See *Die Mutter im Märchen: Deutung der Problematik des Mütterlichen und Mutterkomplexes am Beispiel bekannter Märchen*, ed. Marie-Luise von Franz (Stuttgart: Adolf Bonz, 1976), pp. 75–76. On the "false bride" in fairy tales, see Paul Arfert, "Das Motiv von der unterschobenen Braut in der internationalen Erzählungsliteratur," Dissertation, Rostock 1897.

17. "The Three Little Men in the Woods" gives us a tale in which a daughter plants the seed of remarriage in her father's mind. Some versions of "Snow White" also show us a heroine conspiring with her future stepmother to persuade her father to remarry. Marthe Robert's observation that evil stepmothers far outnumber evil fathers can be backed by statistics. "In the Grimm collection," she writes, "only two or three wicked fathers are to be found, such as in *The Goose Girl at the Well* and in *The Twelve Brothers*, whereas the cruel stepmothers can scarcely be counted." See "The Grimm Brothers," *Yale French Studies* 43 (1969): 44–56. Actually, the number of cruel stepmothers can be counted without great effort; in the final edition of the tales there are thirteen.

18. Antti Aarne, *The Types of the Folktale*, trans. and enlarged by Stith Thompson, 2d rev. ed. (Helsinki: Academia Scientiarum Fennica, 1981), pp. 177–78. Heinrich Däumling discusses variants of "The Girl without Hands" in "Studie über den Typus des 'Mädchens ohne Hände' innerhalb des Konstanze-Zyklus," Dissertation, Munich 1912.

19. "Donkey-Skin," in *Perrault's Complete Fairy Tales*, pp. 92–99.

20. Ruth B. Bottigheimer argues that, in fairy tales, "the female's original access to power through her association with nature became perverted and denied, so that more recent versions of fairy tales relegate power held by females to the old, the ugly, and/or wicked." See "The Transformed Queen: A Search for the Origins of Negative Female Archetypes in Grimms' Fairy Tales," *Amsterdamer Beiträge zur neueren Germanistik* 10 (1980): pp. 1–12. On the association of power with repulsive female figures, see also Marcia R. Lieberman, " 'Some Day My Prince Will Come': Female Acculturation through the Fairy Tale," *College English* 34 (1972): pp. 383–95.

21. The version of "Snow White" with a father-rescuer appears in *Die älteste Märchensammlung der Brüder Grimm*, ed. Heinz Rölleke (Cologny-Genève: Fondation Martin Bodmer, 1975), p. 250. Erich Wulffen comments on "Thousandfurs" in "Das Kriminelle im deutschen Volksmärchen," *Archiv für Kriminalistik* 38 (1910): 355. On incest in fairy tales, see also Otto Rank, *Das Inzest-Motiv in Dichtung und Sage: Grundzüge einer Psychologie des dichterischen Schaffens*, 2d ed. (Leipzig: Franz Deuticke, 1926), pp. 337–86. A fine example of a tale in which a heroine has her cake and eats it too is "Erdkühlein," a German folktale not included in the Grimms' collection. There, the heroine rides off with her father to the kingdom of her beloved. For one version of the tale, see *Dornröschen und der Rosenbey: Motivgleiche Märchen*, ed. Barbara Stamer (Frankfurt a.M.: Fischer, 1985), pp. 99–105.

22. Roman Jakobson and P. Bogatyrev, "Die Folklore als eine besondere Form des Schaffens," in Roman Jakobson, *Selected Writings* (The Hague: Mouton, 1966), vol. 4, pp. 1-15.

23. Kay Stone states that tale type 510B (*The Dress of Gold, of Silver, and of Stars*) is usually omitted from anthologies "since the heroine is forced to leave home to avoid her father's threat of incestuous marriage." See "Things Walt Disney Never Told Us," in *Women and Folklore*, ed. Claire R. Farrer (Austin: University of Texas Press, 1975), pp. 42–50. In another essay, Stone argues that the conflict between two women in "Snow White," "Cinderella," and "Sleeping Beauty" is "not a Freudian conflict between mother and daughter because fathers play no great roles in these three tales." See "Fairy Tales of Adults: Walt Disney's Americanization of the Märchen," in *Folklore on Two Continents: Essays in Honor of Linda Dégh*, ed. Nikolai Burlakoff and Carl Lindahl (Bloomington, Ind.: Trickster Press, 1980), pp. 40–48.

24. Marian Roalfe Cox, *Cinderella: Three Hundred and Forty-Five Variants of Cinderella, Catskin, and Cap o' Rushes* (1892; rpt. Nendeln, Liechtenstein: Kraus, 1967). For a more recent close analysis of the tale type, see Anna Birgitta Rooth, *The Cinderella Cycle* (Lund: Gleerup, 1951). An invaluable modern resource for studying the tale is Alan Dundes' *Cinderella: A Folklore Casebook* (New York: Garland, 1982).

25. Johannes Bolte and Georg Polívka, *Anmerkungen zu den Kinder- und Hausmärchen der Brüder Grimm*, vol. 1, p. 461; Ernst Böklen, *Sneewittchenstudien: Fünfundsiebzig Varianten im engern Sinn* (Leipzig: J. C. Hinrichs, 1910), p. 9.

26. Gilbert and Gubar, *The Madwoman in the Attic*, p. 38.

27. Böklen, *Sneewittchenstudien*, pp. 68–69.

28. Bettelheim, *The Uses of Enchantment*, p. 206.

29. Louise Bernikow, however, advances the view that "Thousandfurs" may reflect "something of how it was in the world out of which the stories came." That Cinderella's male antagonists are replaced by female persecutors "must have to do with what is congenial to the mind that tells the story." See *Among Women* (New York: Harper and Row, Colophon Books, 1980), pp. 18–38. Marian Ury, by contrast, notes that in Japan "real-life situations that exposed a child to the possible malice of a stepmother must in fact have been comparatively rare." Nevertheless, the stepmother makes frequent folkloric appearances. See "Stepmother Tales in Japan," *Children's Literature* 9 (1981): 61–72.

30. As Vladimir Propp points out, the folk tale (in contrast to anecdotes, fables, and novellas) rarely draws on real life for its substance. See "Les Transformations des contes fantastiques," in *Théorie de la littérature*, ed. Tzvetan Todorov (Paris: Editions du Seuil, 1968), pp. 234–62.

CHAPTER 7

1. J. A. MacCulloch reflects on the irrationality of tales with animal grooms. See *Childhood of Fiction: A Study of Folk Tales and Primitive Thought* (New York: E. P. Dutton, 1905), p. 253. For the comment on tales of paternal persecution, see E. Sidney Hartland, "Notes on Cinderella," in *Cinderella: A Folklore Casebook*, ed. Alan Dundes (New York: Garland, 1982), p. 68.

2. For comparisons of various national versions of "Bluebeard," see Robert Darnton, "Peasants Tell Tales: The Meaning of Mother Goose," in *The Great Cat Massacre and Other Episodes in French Cultural History* (New York: Basic Books, 1984), pp. 44–47, and Felix Karlinger, *Das Motiv des "Blaubart" im europäischen Märchen* (Abruzzi: Edizioni Accademiche, 1973).

3. *Perrault's Complete Fairy Tales*, trans. A. E. Johnson et al. (New York: Dodd, Mead, 1961), p. 88.

4. Ludwig Bechstein, "Das Märchen vom Ritter Blaubart," *Deutsches Märchenbuch* (1857), reprinted in Ludwig Bechstein, *Märchen* (Stuttgart: Parkland, 1985), p. 349. Ludwig Tieck, *Werke*, ed. Richard Plett (Hamburg: Hoffmann und Campe, 1967), pp. 226, 238. Charles Dickens, *The Pickwick Papers* (Harmondsworth, Middlesex: Penguin Books, 1972), p. 355. On the role of curiosity in folkloric and literary variants of "Bluebeard," see Hartwig Suhrbier's introduction to his

anthology *Blaubarts Geheimnis: Märchen und Erzählungen, Gedichte und Stücke* (Cologne: Eugen Diederichs, 1984), pp. 21–26.

5. For the statement on Eve's sin, see J. C. Cooper, *Fairy Tales: Allegories of the Inner Life* (Wellingborough, Northamptonshire: Aquarian Press, 1983), pp. 72-73. On Pandora and Eve as literary antecedents of Bluebeard's wife, see the discussion of the Greek myth and the biblical episode in H. R. Hays, *The Dangerous Sex: The Myth of Feminine Evil* (New York: Putnam, 1964), pp. 79–95. The phrase "charade of innocence and vice" appears in Angela Carter's recasting of the Bluebeard tale. See the title story of her collection *The Bloody Chamber and Other Stories* (Harmondsworth, Middlesex: Penguin Books, 1981), pp. 7–41. Of the many commentators drawn to this text, only Emil Heckmann has questioned the logic of the test of obedience to which the heroine is subjected. See "Blaubart: Ein Beitrag zur vergleichenden Märchenforschung," Diss. Heidelberg 1930. The Scottish version of "Bluebeard" is cited by Humphrey Carpenter and Mari Prichard, *The Oxford Companion to Children's Literature* (London: Oxford University Press, 1984), p. 57.

6. Bruno Bettelheim, *The Uses of Enchantment: The Meaning and Importance of Fairy Tales* (New York: Random House, Vintage Books, 1977), p. 302. Alan Dundes sees the bloody key as a symbol of defloration: "Projection in Folklore: A Plea for Psychoanalytic Semiotics," in *Interpreting Folklore* (Bloomington: Indiana University Press, 1980), p. 46. For Carl-Heinz Mallet, the blood on the egg in "Fowler's Fowl" symbolizes the heroine's irreversible loss of virginity. See *Kopf ab! Gewalt im Märchen* (Hamburg: Rasch und Röhring, 1985), p. 201. Even the heroine of a "feminist" short story sees the egg as a "symbol of virginity, . . . that is why the wizard requires it unbloodied." See Margaret Atwood, "Bluebeard's Egg," in *Don't Bet on the Prince: Contemporary Feminist Fairy Tales in North America and England*, ed. Jack Zipes (New York: Methuen, 1986), p. 178.

7. Claude Brémond's definition appears in "The Morphology of the French Fairy Tale: The Ethical Model," in *Patterns in Oral Literature*, ed. Heda Jason and Dimitri Segal (The Hague: Mouton, 1977), p. 49. Perry M. Nodelman sees in "The Golden Bird" a "profound praise of placidity." See "What Makes a Fairy Tale Good: The Queer Kindness of 'The Golden Bird,' " in *Signposts to Criticism of Children's Literature*, ed. Robert Bator (Chicago: American Library Assn., 1983), pp. 184–91. Bernhard Paukstadt discusses the tale's celebration of good humor

in *Paradigmen der Erzähltheorie* (Freiburg: Hochschulverlag, 1980), p. 388.

8. Vladimir Propp, *Morphology of the Folktale*, trans. Laurence Scott (Austin: University of Texas Press, 1968), p. 53.

9. James Riordan, *Tales from Central Russia* (Harmondsworth, Middlesex: Kestrel Books, 1976), p. 151.

10. On this point, see Paul Delarue, *Le Conte populaire français* (Paris: Editions Erasme, 1957), vol. 1, pp. 198-99.

11. "The Enchanted Pig," in *The Red Fairy Book*, ed. Andrew Lang (New York: Longmans, Green, 1909), p. 104.

12. Jacques Barchilon argues that "Beauty and the Beast" reinforces "the taboo against infantile sexuality" by making sex appear to be beastlike. See "Beauty and the Beast: From Myth to Fairy Tale," *Psychoanalysis and the Psychoanalytic Review* 46 (1959): 19-29.

13. Bruno Bettelheim, *The Uses of Enchantment*, p. 302.

14. On the motif of the forbidden chamber, see E. Sidney Hartland, "The Forbidden Chamber," *Folk-Lore Journal* 3 (1885): 193-242. An interesting analysis of the intense curiosity aroused by another fictional genre appears in Geraldine Pederson-Krag's "Detective Stories and the Primal Scene," in *The Poetics of Murder: Detective Fiction and Literary Theory*, ed. Glen W. Most and William W. Stowe (San Diego: Harcourt Brace Jovanovich, 1983), pp. 13-20. On "Bluebeard" as the story of an encounter with death, see Derek Brewer, *Symbolic Stories: Traditional Narratives of the Family Drama in English Literature* (Cambridge: D. S. Brewer, 1980), pp. 15-53.

15. Joseph Jacobs, *English Fairy Tales* (London: The Bodley Head, 1968), p. 93.

16. On international variants of "Fowler's Fowl," see Johannes Bolte and Georg Polívka, *Anmerkungen zu den Kinder- und Hausmärchen der Brüder Grimm* (Leipzig: Dieterich, 1913), vol. 1, pp. 398-412.

17. Andrew Lang, introduction to *Grimm's Household Tales*, trans. Margaret Hunt (London: George Bell and Sons, 1884), vol. 1, p. xxxviii.

18. On the biblical provenance of the theme, see Renate Meyer zur Capellen, "Das schöne Mädchen: Psychoanalytische Betrachtungen zur 'Formwerdung der Seele' des Mädchens," in Helmut Brackert, ed., *Und wenn sie nicht gestorben sind. . . . Perspektiven auf das Märchen* (Frankfurt a.M.: Suhrkamp, 1980), pp. 89-119.

19. As J. A. MacCulloch points out, these tales are generally recognized as emphasizing a heroine's "forgetfulness and disobedience in staying too long at home" (*The Childhood of Fiction*, p. 254).

20. "Beauty and the Beast," by Mme Leprince de Beaumont, anthologized in *Perrault's Complete Fairy Tales*, p. 122.

21. "Beauty and the Beast," p. 128.

22. See, for example, the tale "The Dragon," in *Die älteste Märchensammlung der Brüder Grimm: Synopse der handschriftlichen Urfassung von 1810 und der Erstdrucke von 1812*, ed. Heinz Rölleke (Cologny-Genève: Fondation Martin Bodmer, 1975), pp. 112–14.

23. On this point, see Max Lüthi, *So leben sie noch heute: Betrachtungen zum Volksmärchen* (Göttingen: Vandenhoeck & Ruprecht, 1976), pp. 126–27.

24. For a listing of the kinds of transformations possible in this tale type, see Antti Aarne and Stith Thompson, *The Types of the Folktale: A Classification and Bibliography* (Helsinki: Academia Scientiarum Fennica, 1981), pp. 149–53, and Ernst Tegethoff, *Studien zum Märchentypus von Amor und Psyche* (Bonn: Kurt Schroeder, 1922). Elisabeth Koechlin notes that animal grooms in French tales tend to be more domesticated and civilized than their German counterparts. See *Wesenszüge des deutschen und des französischen Volksmärchens: Eine vergleichende Studie zum Märchentypus von "Amor und Psyche" und vom "Tierbräutigam"* (Basel: Benno Schwabe, 1945).

25. Jan Öjvid Swahn, *The Tale of Cupid and Psyche (AaTh 425 + 428)* (Lund: C.W.K. Gleerup, 1955), pp. 437–38.

EPILOGUE

1. *Georg Büchner: The Complete Collected Works*, trans. Henry J. Schmidt (New York: Avon Books, 1977), p. 199.

2. *Die Kinder- und Hausmärchen der Brüder Grimm. Vollständige Ausgabe in der Urfassung*, ed. Friedrich Panzer (Wiesbaden: Emil Vollmer, 1953), p. 160. In the final version of the tale, the hero blows so hard on his horn that everything around him collapses. The king and his daughter are crushed to death. But the hero puts down his horn before the entire city is leveled and thus gains a kingdom over which he can rule.

3. For further examples, see *Märchen aus dem Nachlaß der Brüder Grimm*, ed. Heinz Rölleke (Bonn: Bouvier, 1977).

4. *Achim von Arnim und Jacob und Wilhelm Grimm*, ed. Reinhold Steig (Stuttgart: J. G. Cotta, 1904), vol. 3, p. 266.

5. On reward-and-punishment tales, see Rina Drory, "Ali Baba and the Forty Thieves: An Attempt at a Model for the Narrative Structure of the Reward-and-Punishment Fairy Tale," in *Patterns in Oral Literature*, ed. Heda Jason and Dimitri Segal (The Hague: Mouton, 1977), pp.

31–48. J.K.A. Musäus made the remark on revenge in his *Volksmärchen der Deutschen* (Munich: Winkler, 1976), p. 115.

6. On the concept of justice in fairy tales, see André Jolles, *Einfache Formen* (Halle: Niemeyer, 1929), pp. 238–46, and Volker Klotz, "Weltordnung im Märchen," *Neue Rundschau* 81 (1970): pp. 73–91.

7. Linda Dégh, "Grimm's *Household Tales* and Its Place in the Household: The Social Relevance of a Controversial Classic," *Western Folklore* 38 (1979): 96, and Walter Nissen, *Die Brüder Grimm und ihre Märchen* (Göttingen: Vandenhoeck & Ruprecht, 1984), pp. 58–59.

8. Italo Calvino, introduction to *Italian Folktales*, trans. George Martin (New York: Pantheon Books, 1980), p. xxix.

9. Calvino, *Italian Folktales*, p. 83.

10. Joseph Jacobs, *English Fairy Tales* (London: Bodley Head, 1968), pp. 42, 44, 69.

11. On the false dichotomies set up by that debate, see Jack Zipes, "Don't Bet on the Prince: Feminist Fairy Tales and the Feminist Critique in America," in *Opening Texts: Psychoanalysis and the Culture of the Child*, ed. Joseph H. Smith and William Kerrigan (Baltimore, MD: Johns Hopkins University Press, 1985), pp. 69–99.

12. P. M. Pickard, *I Could a Tale Unfold: Violence, Horror and Sensationalism in Stories for Children* (London: Tavistock, 1961), p. 1.

13. Johnson's remarks are cited by Hester Lynch Piozzi in *Anecdotes of the late Samuel Johnson LL.D., during the last twenty years of his Life* (London: Cambridge University Press, 1925), p. 14. Edgeworth's reply is cited by Gillian Avery in *Nineteenth Century Children: Heroes and Heroines in English Children's Stories, 1780–1900* (London: Hodder and Stoughton, 1965), p. 27.

GENERAL INDEX

INDEX OF TALES

Library of Congress Cataloging-in-Publication Data

TATAR, MARIA M., 1945–
THE HARD FACTS OF THE GRIMMS' FAIRY TALES.
BIBLIOGRAPHY: P.
INCLUDES INDEX.
1. KINDER- UND HAUSMÄRCHEN. 2. GRIMM, WILHELM,
1786–1859—CRITICISM AND INTERPRETATION. 3. GRIMM,
JACOB, 1785–1863—CRITICISM AND INTERPRETATION.
4. FAIRY TALES—GERMANY—HISTORY AND CRITICISM.
I. TITLE.
PT921.T38 1987 398.2'1'0943 87-45541
ISBN 0–691–06722–8
(ALK. PAPER)